To the Instructor

Thank you for your interest in the Townsend Press vocabulary series—the most widely-used vocabulary books on the college market today. Our goal in this series has been to produce nothing less than excellent books at nothing more than reasonable prices.

About the Book

Notice that the introduction to students (page 1) immediately makes clear to them just why vocabulary study is important. Students are motivated to learn by the four compelling kinds of evidence for word study. The back cover as well convinces students that "a solid vocabulary is a source of power."

You may want to look then at the preface, starting on page vii, which describes in detail the nine distinctive features of the book.

You'll see that a second color is used in the text to make the material as inviting as possible. You'll note, too, that while each chapter takes up only four pages, those pages contain a great deal of hands-on practice to help ensure that students master each word. And you'll find that the practice materials themselves are far more carefully done, and more appealing, than the run-of-the-mill items you typically find in a skills text. The quality and interest level of the content will help students truly learn the words, without either boring them or insulting their intelligence.

Supplements to the Book

Adding to the value of *Building Vocabulary Skills*, which has a net price of only $7.90, is the quality of the supplements:

- An *Instructor's Edition*, which you hold in your hand. The Instructor's Edition is identical to the student text except that it includes (in *italic type*) the answers to all of the practices and tests.

- A combined *Instructor's Manual and Test Bank*, free with adoptions of 20 or more copies. This booklet contains a general vocabulary placement test as well as a pretest and a posttest for the book and for each of the five units in the text. It also includes teaching guidelines, suggested syllabi, an answer key, and an additional mastery test for each chapter.

- A comprehensive series of IBM or Macintosh *computer disks*, which provide a general placement test and up to four additional tests for each vocabulary chapter in the book. Free with adoptions of 200 or more copies, the disks contain a number of user- and instructor-friendly features, including brief explanations of answers, a sound option, frequent mention of the user's first name, a running score at the bottom of the screen, and a record-keeping file.

Adopters of the book can obtain any of these supplements by calling our toll-free number, 1-800-772-6410, or by writing or faxing Townsend Press at the numbers shown on page iv.

(Continues on next page)

New Features of the Book

Among the changes in a book that has undergone significant revision are the following:

- Each chapter now begins with a multiple-choice format that gets students interacting immediately with each word.

- To provide more review and reinforcement, most of the words in each chapter are repeated in context in later chapters of the book.

- The print in the book has been enlarged, a pronunciation key now appears on the inside front cover, a crossword puzzle has been added as a unit review, and the introduction to the book has been expanded to include an explanation of the different types of context clues.

- Answer spaces can now be marked either with the word itself or with a number or letter—so that a Scantron machine or answer key can be used for easy grading.

A Comprehensive Vocabulary Program

There are seven books in the Townsend Press vocabulary series:

- *Groundwork for a Better Vocabulary, 2/e* (reading level 5–8)
- *Building Vocabulary Skills, 2/e* (reading level 7–9)
- *Improving Vocabulary Skills, 2/e* (reading level 9–11)
- *Advancing Vocabulary Skills, 2/e* (reading level 11–12)
- *Building Vocabulary Skills, Short Version, 2/e* (reading level 7–9)
- *Improving Vocabulary Skills, Short Version, 2/e* (reading level 9–11)
- *Advancing Vocabulary Skills, Short Version, 2/e* (reading level 11–12)

Note that the short versions of the three books are limited to 200 words, as opposed to the 260 words and 40 word parts in each of the long versions. For some students and classes, the short versions of the book will provide an easier, more manageable approach to vocabulary development.

BUILDING VOCABULARY SKILLS SECOND EDITION

DONALD J. GOODMAN
MUSKEGON COMMUNITY COLLEGE

SHERRIE L. NIST
UNIVERSITY OF GEORGIA

CAROLE MOHR

TOWNSEND PRESS   Marlton, NJ 08053

Books in the Townsend Press Vocabulary Series:

GROUNDWORK FOR A BETTER VOCABULARY, 2/e
BUILDING VOCABULARY SKILLS, 2/e
IMPROVING VOCABULARY SKILLS, 2/e
ADVANCING VOCABULARY SKILLS, 2/e
BUILDING VOCABULARY SKILLS, SHORT VERSION, 2/e
IMPROVING VOCABULARY SKILLS, SHORT VERSION, 2/e
ADVANCING VOCABULARY SKILLS, SHORT VERSION, 2/e

Books in the Townsend Press Reading Series:

GROUNDWORK FOR COLLEGE READING, 2/e
KEYS TO BETTER COLLEGE READING
TEN STEPS TO BUILDING COLLEGE READING SKILLS, FORM A, 2/e
TEN STEPS TO BUILDING COLLEGE READING SKILLS, FORM B, 2/e
TEN STEPS TO IMPROVING COLLEGE READING SKILLS, 2/e
IMPROVING READING COMPREHENSION SKILLS
TEN STEPS TO ADVANCING COLLEGE READING SKILLS, 2/e

Supplements Available for Most Books:

Instructor's Edition
Instructor's Manual, Test Bank, and Computer Guide
Set of Computer Disks (IBM or Macintosh)

Copyright © 1997 by Townsend Press, Inc.
Printed in the United States of America
ISBN 0-944210-31-7
9 8 7 6 5 4 3 2 1

Send book orders to:

**Townsend Press
1038 Industrial Drive
West Berlin, New Jersey 08091**

For even faster service, call us at our toll-free number:

1-800-772-6410

Or FAX your request to:

1-609-753-0649

ISBN 0-944210-31-7

Contents

Note: Twenty-six of the chapters present ten words apiece. The other four chapters each cover ten word parts and are so marked. For ease of reference, the title of the selection that closes each chapter is included.

Preface

The problem is all too familiar: *students just don't know enough words*. Reading, writing, and content teachers agree that many students' vocabularies are inadequate for the demands of courses. Weak vocabularies limit students' understanding of what they read and the clarity and depth of what they write.

The purpose of *Building Vocabulary Skills* and the other books in the Townsend Press vocabulary series is to provide a solid, workable answer to the vocabulary problem. In the course of 30 chapters, *Building Vocabulary Skills* teaches 260 important words and 40 common word parts. Here are the book's distinctive features:

1 **An intensive words-in-context approach.** Studies show that students learn words best by reading them repeatedly in different contexts, not through rote memorization. The book gives students an intensive in-context experience by presenting each word in six different contexts. Each chapter takes students through a productive sequence of steps:

- Students infer the meaning of each word by considering two sentences in which it appears and then choosing from multiple-choice options.
- On the basis of their inferences, students identify each word's meaning in a matching test. They are then in a solid position to deepen their knowledge of a word.
- Finally, they strengthen their understanding of a word by applying it three times: in two sentence practices and in a selection practice.

Each encounter with a word brings it closer to becoming part of the student's permanent word bank.

2 **Abundant practice.** Along with extensive practice in each chapter, there are a crossword puzzle and a set of unit tests at the end of every six-chapter unit. The puzzle and tests reinforce students' knowledge of the words in each chapter. In addition, most chapters reuse several words from earlier chapters (such repeated words are marked with small circles), allowing for more reinforcement. Last, there are supplementary tests in the *Test Bank* and the computer disks that accompany the book. All this practice means that students learn in the surest possible way: by working closely and repeatedly with each word.

3 **Controlled feedback.** The opening activity in each chapter gives students three multiple-choice options to help them decide on the meaning of a given word. The multiple-choice options also help students to complete the matching test that is the second activity of each chapter. A limited answer key at the back of the book then provides answers for the third activity in the chapter. All these features enable students to take an active role in their own learning.

4 **Focus on essential words.** A good deal of time and research went into selecting the 260 words and 40 word parts featured in the book. Word frequency lists were consulted, along with lists in a wide range of vocabulary books. In addition, the authors and editors each prepared their own lists. A computer was used to help in the consolidation of the many word lists. A long process of group discussion then led to final decisions about the words and word parts that would be most helpful for students on a basic reading level.

5 **Appealing content.** Dull practice materials work against learning. On the other hand, meaningful, lively, and at times even funny sentences and selections can spark students' attention and thus enhance their grasp of the material. For this reason, a great deal of effort was put into creating sentences and selections with both widespread appeal and solid context support. We have tried throughout to make the practice materials truly enjoyable for teachers and students alike. Look, for example, at the selection on page 11 that closes the first chapter of this book.

6 **Clear format.** The book has been designed so that its very format contributes to the learning process. Each chapter consists of two two-page spreads. In the first two-page spread (the first such spread is on pages 8–9), students can easily refer to all ten words in context while working on the matching test, which provides a clear meaning for each word. In the second two-page spread, students can refer to a box that shows all ten words while they work through the fill-in activities on these pages.

7 **Supplementary materials.**

a A convenient *Instructor's Edition* is available at no charge to instructors using the book. It is identical to the student book except that it contains answers to all of the activities and tests.

b A combined *Instructor's Manual and Test Bank* is also offered at no charge to instructors who have adopted the book. This booklet contains a general vocabulary placement test as well as a pretest and a posttest for the book and for each of the five units in the text. It also includes teaching guidelines, suggested syllabi, an answer key, and an additional mastery test for each chapter.

c A *comprehensive series of computer disks* also accompanies the book. Free to adopters of 200 or more copies, these disks provide up to four tests for each vocabulary chapter in the book. The disks include a number of user- and instructor-friendly features: brief explanations of answers, a sound option, frequent mention of the user's first name, a running score at the bottom of the screen, a record-keeping file, and (in the case of the Macintosh disks) actual pronunciation of each word.

   Probably in no other area of reading instruction is the computer more useful than in reinforcing vocabulary. This vocabulary program takes full advantage of the computer's unique capabilities and motivational appeal. Here's how the program works:

   • Students are tested on the ten words in a chapter, with each word in a sentence context different from any in the book itself.

   • After students answer each question, they receive immediate feedback: The computer tells if a student is right or wrong and why, frequently using the student's first name and providing a running score.

   • When the test is over, the computer supplies a test score and—this especially is what is unique about this program—a chance to retest on the specific words the student got wrong. For example, if a student misses four items on a test, the retest provides four different sentences that test just those four words. Students then receive a score for this special retest. What is so valuable about this, of course, is that the computer gives students added practice in the words they most need to review.

   • In addition, the computer offers a second, more challenging test in which students must identify the meanings of the chapter words without benefit of context. This test is a final check that students have really learned the words. And, again, there is the option of a retest, tailor-made to recheck only those words missed on the first definition test.

By the end of this program, students' knowledge of each word in the chapter will have been carefully reinforced. And this reinforcement will be the more effective for having occurred in an electronic medium that especially engages today's students.

To obtain a copy of any of the above materials, instructors may write to the Reading Editor, Townsend Press, Pavilions at Greentree—408, Marlton, NJ 08053. Alternatively, instructors may call our toll-free number: 1-800-772-6410.

8 **Realistic pricing.** As with the first edition, the goal has been to offer the highest possible quality at the best possible price. While *Building Vocabulary Skills* is comprehensive enough to serve as a primary text, its modest price also makes it an inexpensive supplement.

9 **One in a sequence of books.** The most basic book in the Townsend Press vocabulary series is *Groundwork for a Better Vocabulary*. It is followed by the three main books in the series: *Building Vocabulary Skills* (also a basic text), *Improving Vocabulary Skills* (an intermediate text), and *Advancing Vocabulary Skills* (a more advanced text). There are also short versions of these three books. Suggested grade levels for the books are included in the *Instructor's Manual*. Together, the books can help create a vocabulary foundation that will make any student a better reader, writer, and thinker.

NOTES ON THE SECOND EDITION

A number of changes have been made to the book.

- Instead of an opening preview, each chapter now begins with a new format that uses a multiple-choice question to get students interacting immediately with each word. Teachers' and students' responses to this change have been extremely favorable.

- For ease of grading, including the use of Scantron machines, answer spaces can now be marked either with the letter or number of the word or with the word itself.

- The print in the book has been enlarged, a pronunciation key now appears on the inside front cover, a crossword puzzle has been added as a unit review, and the introduction to the book has been expanded. In addition, hundreds of changes have been made throughout the book to make each practice item work as clearly and effectively as possible.

- Thanks to feedback from reviewers and users, many of the words in each chapter are now repeated in context in later chapters (and marked with small circles). Such repetition provides students with even more review and reinforcement.

ACKNOWLEDGMENTS

We are grateful for the enthusiastic comments provided by users of the Townsend Press vocabulary books over the life of the first edition. Particular thanks go to the following reviewers for their many helpful suggestions: Barbara Brennan Culhane, Nassau Community College; Carol Dietrick, Miami-Dade Community College; Larry Falxa, Ventura College; Jacquelin Hanselman, Hillsborough Community College; Shiela P. Kerr, Florida Community College at Jacksonville; John M. Kopec, Boston University; Belinda E. Smith, Wake Technical Community College; Daniel Snook, Montcalm Community College; and William Walcott, Montgomery College. We appreciate as well the editing work of Eliza Comodromos and the design, editing, and proofreading skills of the multi-talented Janet M. Goldstein. Finally, we dedicate this book to the memory of our computer programmer, Terry Hutchison.

Donald J. Goodman   *Sherrie L. Nist*   *Carole Mohr*

Introduction

WHY VOCABULARY DEVELOPMENT COUNTS

You have probably often heard it said, "Building vocabulary is important." Maybe you've politely nodded in agreement and then forgotten the matter. But it would be fair for you to ask, "*Why* is vocabulary development important? Provide some evidence." Here are four compelling kinds of evidence.

1 Common sense tells you what many research studies have shown as well: vocabulary is a basic part of reading comprehension. Simply put, if you don't know enough words, you are going to have trouble understanding what you read. An occasional word may not stop you, but if there are too many words you don't know, comprehension will suffer. The content of textbooks is often challenge enough; you don't want to work as well on understanding the words that express that content.

2 Vocabulary is a major part of almost every standardized test, including reading achievement tests, college entrance exams, and armed forces and vocational placement tests. Test developers know that vocabulary is a key measure of both one's learning and one's ability to learn. It is for this reason that they include a separate vocabulary section as well as a reading comprehension section. The more words you know, then, the better you are likely to do on such important tests.

3 Studies have indicated that students with strong vocabularies are more successful in school. And one widely known study found that a good vocabulary, more than any other factor, was common to people enjoying successful careers in life. Words are in fact the tools not just of better reading, but of better writing, speaking, listening, and thinking as well. The more words you have at your command, the more effective your communication can be, and the more influence you can have on the people around you.

4 In today's world, a good vocabulary counts more than ever. Far fewer people work on farms or in factories. Far more are in jobs that provide services or process information. More than ever, words are the tools of our trade: words we use in reading, writing, listening, and speaking. Furthermore, experts say that workers of tomorrow will be called on to change jobs and learn new skills at an ever-increasing pace. The keys to survival and success will be the abilities to communicate skillfully and learn quickly. A solid vocabulary is essential for both of these skills.

Clearly, the evidence is overwhelming that building vocabulary is crucial. The question then becomes, "What is the best way of going about it?"

WORDS IN CONTEXT: THE KEY TO VOCABULARY DEVELOPMENT

Memorizing lists of words is a traditional method of vocabulary development. However, a person is likely to forget such memorized lists quickly. Studies show that to master a word (or a word part), you must see and use it in various contexts. By working actively and repeatedly with a word, you greatly increase the chance of really learning it.

The following activity will make clear how this book is organized and how it uses a words-in-context approach. Answer the questions or fill in the missing words in the spaces provided.

Inside Front Cover and Contents

Turn to the inside front cover.

- The inside front cover provides a _____*pronunciation guide*_____ that will help you pronounce all the vocabulary words in the book.

Now turn to the table of contents on pages v-vi.

- How many chapters are in the book? ___*30*___

- Most chapters present vocabulary words. How many chapters present word parts? ___*4*___

- Three short sections follow the last chapter. The first of these sections provides a limited answer key, the second gives helpful information on using _____*the dictionary*_____, and the third is an index of the 260 words and 40 word parts in the book.

Vocabulary Chapters

Turn to Chapter 1 on pages 8–11. This chapter, like all the others, consists of five parts:

- The ***first part*** of the chapter, on pages 8–9, is titled _____*Ten Words in Context*_____.

  The left-hand column lists the ten words. Under each **boldfaced** word is its _____*pronunciation*_____ (in parentheses). For example, the pronunciation of *acknowledge* is _____ăk-nŏl′ij_____. For a guide to pronunciation, see the inside front cover as well as "Dictionary Use" on page 179.

  Below the pronunciation guide for each word is its part of speech. The part of speech shown for *acknowledge* is ___*verb*___. The vocabulary words in this book are mostly nouns, adjectives, and verbs. **Nouns** are words used to name something—a person, place, thing, or idea. Familiar nouns include *boyfriend, city, hat,* and *truth.* **Adjectives** are words that describe nouns, as in the following word pairs: *former* boyfriend, *large* city, *red* hat, *whole* truth. All of the **verbs** in this book express an action of some sort. They tell what someone or something is doing. Common verbs include *sing, separate, support,* and *imagine.*

  To the right of each word are two sentences that will help you understand its meaning. In each sentence, the **context**—the words surrounding the boldfaced word—provides clues you can use to figure out the definition. There are four common types of context clues—examples, synonyms, antonyms, and the general sense of the sentence. Each is briefly described below.

  1 Examples

  A sentence may include examples that reveal what an unfamiliar word means. For instance, take a look at the following sentence from Chapter 1 for the word *drastic*:

  The company's new president took **drastic** steps, closing two factories and laying off three hundred employees.

The sentence provides two examples of steps that are drastic—the closing of two factories and the laying off of three hundred employees. To figure out what *drastic* means in that sentence, think about those examples. What kind of steps are being described? Look at the answer choices below, and in the answer space provided, write the letter of the one you feel is correct.

   ___ *Drastic* means   a. unimportant.   b. extreme.   c. easy.

Since the steps being described in the sentence are rather severe, or extreme, you probably guessed —correctly—that answer *b* is the right choice.

2 Synonyms

Synonyms are words that mean the same or almost the same as another word. For example, the words *joyful, happy*, and *delighted* are synonyms—they all mean about the same thing. Synonyms serve as context clues by providing the meaning of an unknown word that is nearby. The sentence below from Chapter 1 provides a synonym clue for *appropriate.*

> Although it is **appropriate** for a man to take his hat off in a church, in a synagogue it is proper for a man to cover his head.

Rather than repeat *appropriate* in the second part of the sentence, the author used a synonym. Find that synonym, and then choose the letter of the correct answer from the choices below.

   ___ *Appropriate* means   a. illegal.   b. fun.   c. proper.

In the sentence from Chapter 1, *proper* is used as a synonym for *appropriate.* Both words refer to what is considered correct.

3 Antonyms

Antonyms are words with opposite meanings. For example, *help* and *harm* are antonyms, as are *work* and *rest.* Antonyms serve as context clues by providing the opposite meaning of an unknown word. The sentence below from Chapter 1 for the word *comply* provides an antonym clue.

> If someone with an iron pipe demands your wallet, it is safer to **comply** than to resist.

To make a point, the author used an antonym of *comply.* Find the antonym, and then choose the letter below of the meaning of *comply.*

   ___ *Comply* means   a. to argue.   b. to do as asked.   c. to hear.

The sentence includes two reactions to being asked for your wallet: *to comply* and *to resist.* Since we can guess that *to comply* is probably the opposite of *to resist*, we can conclude that *comply* means "to do as asked."

4 General Sense of the Sentence

Even when there is no example, synonym, or antonym clue in a sentence, you can still figure out the meaning of an unfamiliar word. For example, look at the sentence from Chapter 1 for the word *acknowledge.*

> Even after most of the votes had been counted, Senator Rice refused to **acknowledge** that he had lost.

After studying the context carefully, you should be able to choose the meaning of *acknowledge* from the three options presented. Write the letter of your choice.

   ___ *Acknowledge* means   a. to deny.   b. to admit.   c. to remember.

From the general sense of the sentence above, we can guess that the senator refused "to admit" that he had lost.

By looking closely at the pair of sentences provided for each word, as well as the answer choices, you should be able to decide on the meaning of a word. As you figure out each meaning, you are working actively with the word. You are creating the groundwork you need to understand and to remember the word. *Getting involved with the word and developing a feel for it, based upon its use in context, is the key to word mastery.*

It is with good reason, then, that the directions at the top of page 8 tell you to use the context to figure out each word's _____*meaning*_____. Doing so deepens your sense of the word and prepares you for the next activity.

- The *second part* of the chapter, on page 9, is titled _____*Matching Words with Definitions*_____.

According to research, it is not enough to see a word in context. At a certain point, it is helpful as well to see the meaning of a word. The matching test provides that meaning, but it also makes you look for and think about that meaning. In other words, it continues the active learning that is your surest route to learning and remembering a word.

Note the caution that follows the test. Do not proceed any further until you are sure that you know the correct meaning of each word as used in context.

Keep in mind that a word may have more than one meaning. In fact, some words have quite a few meanings. (If you doubt it, try looking up in a dictionary, for example, the word *make* or *draw*.) In this book, you will focus on one common meaning for each vocabulary word. However, many of the words have additional meanings. For example, in Chapter 1, you will learn that *avert* means "to prevent," as in the sentence "Stop signs avert accidents." If you then look up *avert* in the dictionary, you will discover that it has another meaning—"to turn away," as in "The suspect averted her head to avoid being recognized." After you learn one common meaning of a word, you will find yourself gradually learning its other meanings in the course of your school and personal reading.

- The *third part* of the chapter, on page 10, is titled _____*Sentence Check 1*_____.

Here are ten sentences that give you an opportunity to apply your understanding of the ten words. After inserting the words, check your answers in the limited key at the back of the book. Be sure to use the answer key as a learning tool only. Doing so will help you to master the words and to prepare for the last two activities and the unit tests, for which answers are not provided.

- The *fourth and fifth parts* of the chapter, on pages 10–11, are titled _____*Sentence Check 2*_____ and _____*Final Check*_____.

Each practice tests you on all ten words, giving you two more chances to deepen your mastery. In the fifth part, you have the context of an entire passage in which you can practice applying the words.

At the bottom of the last page of this chapter is a box where you can enter your score for the final two checks. These scores should also be entered into the vocabulary performance chart located on the inside back page of the book. To get your score, take 10% off for each item wrong. For example, 0 wrong = 100%. 1 wrong = 90%, 2 wrong = 80%, 3 wrong = 70%, 4 wrong = 60%, and so on.

Word Parts Chapters

Word parts are building blocks used in many English words. Learning word parts can help you to spell and pronounce words, unlock the meanings of unfamiliar words, and remember new words.

This book covers forty word parts—prefixes, suffixes, and roots. **Prefixes** are word parts that are put at the beginning of words. When written separately, a prefix is followed by a hyphen to show that something follows it. For example, the prefix *ex* is written like this: *ex-*. One common meaning of *ex-* is "out," as in the words *exit* and *exhale*.

Suffixes are word parts that are added to the end of words. To show that something always comes before a suffix, a hyphen is placed at the beginning. For instance, the suffix *ful* is written like this: *-ful*. A common meaning of *-ful* is "full of," as in the words *beautiful* and *fearful*.

Finally, **roots** are word parts that carry the basic meaning of a word. Roots cannot be used alone. To make a complete word, a root must be combined with at least one other word part. Roots are written without hyphens. One common root is *vis*, which means "to see," as in the words *visible* and *vision*.

Each of the four chapters on word parts follows the same sequence as the chapters on vocabulary do. Keep the following guidelines in mind as well. To find the meaning of a word part, you should do two things.

1　First decide on the meaning of each **boldfaced** word in "Ten Word Parts in Context." If you don't know a meaning, use context clues to find it. For example, consider the two sentences and the answer options for the word part *ex-* in Chapter 6. Write the letter of your choice.

"Inhale as you lower your head," called out the exercise instructor, "and **exhale** as you do the sit-up."

My uncle isn't a very good businessman. He once tried to **export** rice to China and vodka to Russia.

＿＿＿ The word part *ex-* means　　a. before.　　b. out.　　c. not.

You can conclude that *exhale* means the opposite of *inhale* ("to breathe in"); thus *exhale* means "to breathe out." You can also determine that *export* means "to send goods out of a country to sell them."

2　Then decide on the meaning each pair of boldfaced words has in common. This will also be the meaning of the word part they share. In the case of the two sentences above, both words include the idea of something going out. Thus *ex* must mean ＿＿＿＿*out*＿＿＿＿.

You now know, in a nutshell, how to proceed with the words in each chapter. Make sure that you do each page very carefully. *Remember that as you work through the activities, you are learning the words.*

How many times in all will you use each word? If you look, you'll see that each chapter gives you the opportunity to work with each word six times. Each "impression" adds to the likelihood that the word will become part of your active vocabulary. You will have further opportunities to use the word in the crossword puzzle and unit tests that end each unit and on the computer disks that are available with the book.

In addition, many of the words are repeated in context in later chapters of the book. Such repeated words are marked with small circles. For example, what words from Chapter 1 are repeated in the Final Check on page 15 of Chapter 2?

＿＿＿*alternative*＿＿＿　　　＿＿＿*anecdote*＿＿＿

A FINAL THOUGHT

The facts are in. A strong vocabulary is a source of power. Words can make you a better reader, writer, speaker, thinker, and learner. They can dramatically increase your chances of success in school and in your job.

But words will not come automatically. They must be learned in a program of regular study. If you commit yourself to learning words, and you work actively and honestly with the chapters in this book, you will not only enrich your vocabulary—you will enrich your life as well.

Unit One

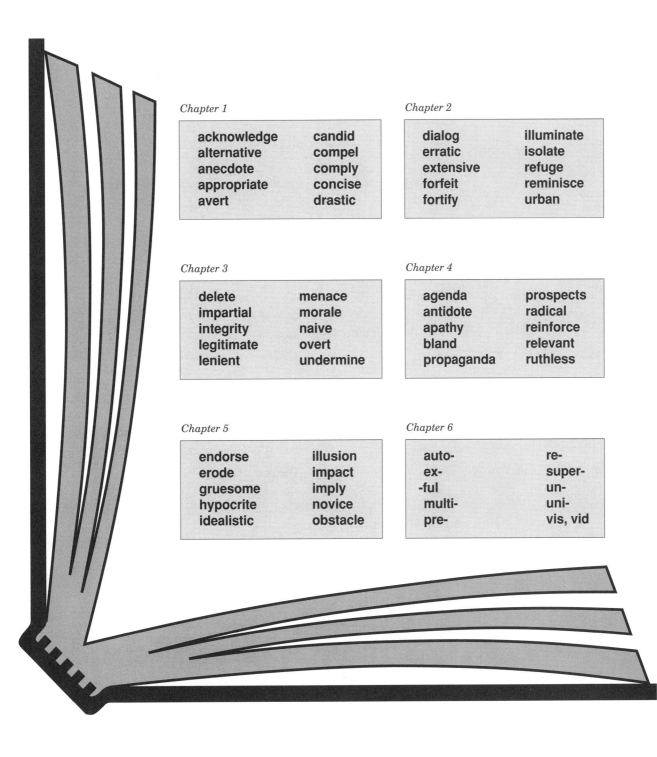

Chapter 1

acknowledge	candid
alternative	compel
anecdote	comply
appropriate	concise
avert	drastic

Chapter 2

dialog	illuminate
erratic	isolate
extensive	refuge
forfeit	reminisce
fortify	urban

Chapter 3

delete	menace
impartial	morale
integrity	naive
legitimate	overt
lenient	undermine

Chapter 4

agenda	prospects
antidote	radical
apathy	reinforce
bland	relevant
propaganda	ruthless

Chapter 5

endorse	illusion
erode	impact
gruesome	imply
hypocrite	novice
idealistic	obstacle

Chapter 6

auto-	re-
ex-	super-
-ful	un-
multi-	uni-
pre-	vis, vid

acknowledge	candid
alternative	compel
anecdote	comply
appropriate	concise
avert	drastic

Ten Words in Context

In the space provided, write the letter of the meaning closest to that of each **boldfaced** word. Use the context of the sentences to help you figure out each word's meaning.

1 acknowledge
(ăk-nŏl′ĭj)
-verb

- Stubborn people often find it difficult to **acknowledge** their errors. They hate to admit they were wrong.
- Even after most of the votes had been counted, Senator Rice refused to **acknowledge** that he had lost.

_b_ *Acknowledge* means   a. to deny.   b. to admit.   c. to remember.

2 alternative
(ôl-tûr′nə-tĭv)
-noun

- The teacher stated the **alternatives** to Tim—retake the test or get a D for the course.
- When her dog began to suffer from cancer, Wanda felt she had no **alternative**. He would have to be put to sleep.

_a_ *Alternative* means   a. a choice.   b. a command.   c. an assignment.

3 anecdote
(ăn′ĭk-dōt′)
-noun

- Dad told the children an **anecdote** about getting his tie caught in a file cabinet at work just as the boss walked in.
- I once heard an **anecdote** about a stagehand's revenge on a bossy actor. The stagehand put wheels on a table used in the play, so when the actor leaped onto the table during the most dramatic scene, he rolled straight off into the wings.

_b_ *Anecdote* means   a. error.   b. short, interesting story.   c. article.

4 appropriate
(ə-prō′prē-ĭt)
-adjective

- Chuck has little sense of what is socially **appropriate**. For example, he went to his sister's wedding in jogging shoes.
- Although it is **appropriate** for a man to take his hat off in church, in a synagogue it is proper for a man to cover his head.

_c_ *Appropriate* means   a. illegal.   b. fun.   c. proper.

5 avert
(ə-vûrt′)
-verb

- Renata **averted** an unpleasant meeting with her ex-boyfriend by leaving the store before he saw her.
- To **avert** an accident, Larry turned his car sharply to the right and ran into a stop sign.

_b_ *Avert* means   a. to begin.   b. to prevent.   c. to report.

6 candid
(kăn′dĭd)
-adjective

- I'll give you my **candid** opinion, but you may not like what you hear.
- A child is a striking combination of boldfaced liar ("I didn't eat the cookie") and painfully **candid** reporter ("Gee, you've gotten really fat").

_a_ *Candid* means   a. honest.   b. friendly.   c. careful.

7 **compel**
(kəm-pĕl′)
-*verb*

- My history teacher would often **compel** us to do useless work, such as memorizing the date each state entered the union.
- If the law did not **compel** people to pay taxes, no one would pay them.

_c_ *Compel* means   a. to help.   b. to forbid.   c. to force.

8 **comply**
(kəm-plī′)
-*verb*

- If someone with an iron pipe demands your wallet, it is safer to **comply** than to resist.
- My husband is so used to being boss at work that he is annoyed when I don't **comply** with his every request at home.

_b_ *Comply* means   a. to argue.   b. to do as asked.   c. to hear.

9 **concise**
(kŏn-sīs′)
-*adjective*

- Because of limited space, most newspaper articles must be **concise**.
- Unlike many politicians, our mayor is **concise**—his speeches are short but say much.

_c_ *Concise* means   a. wordy.   b. correct.   c. clear and brief.

10 **drastic**
(drăs′tĭk)
-*adjective*

- The company's new president took **drastic** steps, closing two factories and laying off three hundred employees.
- "This time I will let you off with just an hour of staying after school," the principal said. "But if it happens again, the punishment will be more **drastic**."

_b_ *Drastic* means   a. unimportant.   b. extreme.   c. easy.

Matching Words with Definitions

Following are definitions of the ten words. Clearly write or print each word next to its definition. The sentences above and on the previous page will help you decide on the meaning of each word.

1. _____comply_____   To do as commanded or asked

2. _____appropriate_____   Proper; suitable to the situation

3. _____alternative_____   A choice

4. _____drastic_____   Extreme; harsh or intense

5. ____acknowledge____   To admit or confess

6. _____compel_____   To force

7. _____candid_____   Very honest

8. _____anecdote_____   An entertaining short story about an event

9. _____concise_____   Saying much in a few clear words

10. _____avert_____   To prevent; to avoid

CAUTION: Do not go any further until you are sure the above answers are correct. Then you can use the definitions to help you in the following practices. Your goal is eventually to know the words well enough so that you don't need to check the definitions at all.

➤ *Sentence Check 1*

Using the answer line provided, complete each item below with the correct word from the box. Use each word once.

a. **acknowledge**	b. **alternative**	c. **anecdote**	d. **appropriate**	e. **avert**
f. **candid**	g. **compel**	h. **comply**	i. **concise**	j. **drastic**

candid   1. Because Frank seems so ___, everyone believes him even when he tells a lie.

anecdote   2. The drummer told interesting ___s about famous rock singers he had played for.

drastic   3. People often take ___ steps in anger, and they later regret their extreme actions.

avert   4. When he saw no way to ___ the plane crash, the pilot parachuted to safety.

concise   5. In a traditional wedding, the clergyman or clergywoman is often wordy, while the bride and groom are very ___, saying just "I do."

comply   6. Any player who does not ___ with the rules will be dropped from the team.

compel   7. A couple of older boys tried to ___ some first-graders to hand over their lunch money.

alternative   8. To earn money for college, Theo felt he had to either join the army or get a job. He didn't like either ___.

acknowledge   9. When the real ax-murderer confessed, the police had to ___ that the wrong man had been jailed.

appropriate   10. In most American schools, it is not ___ for students to call their teachers by their first names.

NOTE: Now check your answers to these questions by turning to page 175. Going over the answers carefully will help you prepare for the next two practices, for which answers are not given.

➤ *Sentence Check 2*

Using the answer lines provided, complete each item below with **two** words from the box. Use each word once.

acknowledge
candid   1–2. "I ___ that you have a perfect right to do whatever you like with your hair," said the teenage girl's mother. "But, to be ___, I don't find green curls attractive."

appropriate
comply   3–4. In colonial America, it was thought ___ for a wife to ___ with all her husband's commands.

alternative
compel   5–6. "The poor economic situation leaves me no ___," said the company president. "It ___s me to lay off some of our workers."

_____anecdote_____   7–8. Our business instructor told an ___ about a company that ___(e)d
_____avert_____   failure by sharing ownership with all its workers.

_____concise_____   9–10. The sale sign was huge but ___. It said only, "___ price cuts."
_____Drastic_____

➤ *Final Check:* Taking Exams

Here is a final opportunity for you to strengthen your knowledge of the ten words. First read the following selection carefully. Then fill in each blank with a word from the box at the top of the previous page. (Context clues will help you figure out which word goes in which blank.) Use each word once.

There are five test-taking methods to consider when faced with exams. The first is to impress your teachers with very clever answers. For example, you might respond to any question beginning with the word "Why" with a simple, (1)_____concise_____ reply: "Why not?" This is not recommended, however, unless you know that an instructor has great respect for humor. A second method is simply to refuse to take an exam. You might try writing something like, "This is a free country, so you can't (2)_____compel_____ me to take this test. Besides, I partied all last night." This method should not be used unless you are in (3)_____drastic_____ need, as it involves a great deal of risk. It is (4)_____appropriate_____ only if you have shown yourself to be very brilliant throughout the course and you are the teacher's pet. Otherwise, you can expect your teacher to fail you. A third way of dealing with a test is to (5)_____candid_____ly admit helplessness. According to one (6)_____anecdote_____, a student openly (7)_____acknowledge_____(e)d ignorance by writing, "Only God knows the answer to this question." Unfortunately, the instructor's response was, "God gets an A. You get an F." So maybe we'd better move on to the fourth method. This is to cheat. Do this only if you are hopeless and your teacher is both deaf and blind. If you truly want to (8)_____avert_____ failure, you have no (9)_____alternative_____—you must (10)_____comply_____ with school rules. The only real method for dealing with college exams, then, is clear: study hard and learn the material.

| *Scores*   Sentence Check 2 _____% | Final Check _____% |

Enter your scores above and in the vocabulary performance chart on the inside back cover of the book.

dialog	illuminate
erratic	isolate
extensive	refuge
forfeit	reminisce
fortify	urban

Ten Words in Context

In the space provided, write the letter of the meaning closest to that of each **boldfaced** word. Use the context of the sentences to help you figure out each word's meaning.

1 **dialog**
(dī′ə-lŏg′)
-*noun*

- The movie was given an R rating because its **dialog** included a good deal of sexual language.
- At the PTA meeting last night, a **dialog** between parents and the faculty helped to clear up some differences between them.

_b_ *Dialog* means   a. a title.   b. a conversation.   c. an action.

2 **erratic**
(ĭ-răt′ĭk)
-*adjective*

- My son's eating habits are **erratic**. One day he'll barely eat, and the next he'll eat enough for three.
- The driver ahead of me was **erratic**—he kept changing his speed and his lane.

_c_ *Erratic* means   a. noisy.   b. healthy.   c. irregular.

3 **extensive**
(ĕk-stĕn′sĭv)
-*adjective*

- Selina did **extensive** research for her paper—it took her several weeks.
- To save the wounded police officer, doctors performed **extensive** surgery that lasted for hours.

_c_ *Extensive* means   a. done quickly.   b. risky.   c. large in amount.

4 **forfeit**
(fôr′fĭt)
-*verb*

- The basketball players were upset when the team bus broke down and they had to **forfeit** an important game.
- If Phil damages his parents' car again, he will **forfeit** the right to drive it any more.

_a_ *Forfeit* means   a. to give up.   b. to win.   c. to ignore.

5 **fortify**
(fôr′tə-fī′)
-*verb*

- The night before running a marathon, Elsa **fortifies** herself by eating a large plate of pasta.
- The builders plan to **fortify** the old tower with steel beams.

_b_ *Fortify* means   a. to relax.   b. to strengthen.   c. to prove.

6 **illuminate**
(ĭ-lōō′mə-nāt′)
-*verb*

- Before electricity, streets were **illuminated** by gaslight.
- On Halloween, we made our trick-or-treat rounds with a flashlight to **illuminate** the way.

_c_ *Illuminate* means   a. to lose.   b. to clean.   c. to light up.

7 **isolate**
(ī′sə-lāt′)
-*verb*

- I thought I would enjoy **isolating** myself at the vacation cabin, but I soon felt lonely.
- Freddy was such a troublemaker that the teacher put his desk in a far corner to **isolate** him from the other students.

_b_ *Isolate* means   a. to protect.   b. to separate.   c. to recognize.

8 **refuge**
(rĕf′yo̅o̅j)
-*noun*

- A motorcycle offers no **refuge** in bad weather.
- My wife and I first met when we took **refuge** in the same doorway during a sudden rain.

_a_ *Refuge* means   a. a shelter.   b. transportation.   c. a reason.

9 **reminisce**
(rĕm′ə-nĭs′)
-*verb*

- On their wedding anniversary, Lenny and Jean **reminisced** about their first date.
- My father showed me his trophy and **reminisced** about his years as a star basketball player.

_a_ *Reminisce* means   a. to remember.   b. to forget.   c. to ask.

10 **urban**
(ûr′bən)
-*adjective*

- Skyscrapers make for tightly packed **urban** populations. For example, some 35,000 people work in the World Trade Center in New York City.
- Gladys likes **urban** living because she grew up in the city, but Emilio, who grew up on a farm, prefers country life.

_b_ *Urban* means   a. country.   b. city.   c. national.

Matching Words with Definitions

Following are definitions of the ten words. Clearly write or print each word next to its definition. The sentences above and on the previous page will help you decide on the meaning of each word.

1. _____*illuminate*_____   To light up

2. _____*forfeit*_____   To lose through some fault; to be forced to give up by way of penalty

3. _____*refuge*_____   Shelter; protection

4. _____*urban*_____   Of or in a city

5. _____*dialog*_____   A conversation; the conversation between characters in a story, novel, or play

6. _____*isolate*_____   To separate from others

7. _____*extensive*_____   Large in space or amount

8. _____*fortify*_____   To strengthen

9. _____*reminisce*_____   To remember and talk about the past

10. _____*erratic*_____   Not consistent

CAUTION: Do not go any further until you are sure the above answers are correct. Then you can use the definitions to help you in the following practices. Your goal is eventually to know the words well enough so that you don't need to check the definitions at all.

➤ *Sentence Check 1*

Using the answer line provided, complete each item below with the correct word from the box. Use each word once.

a. **dialog**	b. **erratic**	c. **extensive**	d. **forfeit**	e. **fortify**
f. **illuminate**	g. **isolate**	h. **refuge**	i. **reminisce**	j. **urban**

_____erratic_____ 1. The skater's ___ performances showed that she was too inconsistent to hire for the ice show.

_____refuge_____ 2. In London during World War II, bomb shelters provided ___ from air attacks.

_____fortify_____ 3. Vitamins and minerals ___ the body against disease.

_____forfeit_____ 4. Politicians who are caught taking bribes ___ their good names.

_____isolate_____ 5. Criminals are put in prison to ___ them from the rest of society.

_____reminisce_____ 6. The night before graduation, my roommate Gary and I ___(e)d about our four years together.

_____illuminate_____ 7. The pioneers used candles to ___ book pages at night.

_____dialog_____ 8. The author's ___ was always sharp and bare: "You love me?" "Uh-huh." "Good."

_____extensive_____ 9. Before his parents visit him, Don gives his apartment a(n) ___ cleaning; he dusts or scrubs every surface.

_____urban_____ 10. There's a big difference between a(n) ___ sky and a country sky. In the country, there are no bright lights to block the starlight.

NOTE: Now check your answers to these questions by turning to page 175. Going over the answers carefully will help you prepare for the next two practices, for which answers are not given.

➤ *Sentence Check 2*

Using the answer lines provided, complete each item below with **two** words from the box. Use each word once.

_____extensive_____
_____refuge_____
1–2. The loud celebrating on the Fourth of July is so ___ in my neighborhood that the only place I find ___ from the noise is my basement.

_____reminisce_____
_____erratic_____
3–4. Curt ___(e)d for hours, revealing that his life had been very ___. At some points in his life, he was very busy, married, and well off. At other times, he lived alone and was out of work.

_____urban_____
_____illuminate_____
5–6. Because criminals work in darkness, one way to reduce ___ crime would be to ___ streets and playgrounds with brighter lights.

_____ *isolate* _____ 7–8. To keep the opposing army from trying to ___ his weaker force from
_____ *fortify* _____ the rest of the unit, the general decided to ___ his defenses.

_____ *dialog* _____ 9–10. In a ___ with our boss, he warned us that we will ___ our bonuses if
_____ *forfeit* _____ we keep coming to work late.

➤ *Final Check:* Nate the Woodsman

Here is a final opportunity for you to strengthen your knowledge of the ten words. First read the following selection carefully. Then fill in each blank with a word from the box at the top of the previous page. (Context clues will help you figure out which word goes in which blank.) Use each word once.

Nate had spent most of his seventy years in the woods. As a young man, he had the alternative° of working in the city with his brother. But he decided that (1)_____ *urban* _____ life was not for him. He preferred to (2)_____ *isolate* _____ himself from others and find (3)_____ *refuge* _____ in nature from the crowds and noise of the city. He was more than willing to (4)_____ *forfeit* _____ such advantages as flush toilets and electric blankets for the joy of watching a sunrise (5)_____ *illuminate* _____ the frozen pines.

Because Nate had lived alone for so long, his behavior was (6)_____ *erratic* _____. For example, one minute he'd be very quiet, and the next he'd (7)_____ *reminisce* _____ at length about his youth. His knowledge of nature was (8)_____ *extensive* _____, and so I learned much from him through the years.

I will tell you an anecdote° that shows how wise he was about the woods and how miserly he could be with words. One evening Nate, my cousin Arthur, and I were crossing a meadow. Arthur's interest in some little white mushrooms that were growing there led to this (9)_____ *dialog* _____:

"These mushrooms look so good," said Arthur. "Did you ever use them, Nate?"

"Yep," said Nate. "My ma used to cook 'em up."

"Great!" said Arthur. Nate's words seemed to (10)_____ *fortify* _____ Arthur's desire for those mushrooms. He gathered about a hundred of them. "How'd she fix them?" he asked Nate.

"Cooked 'em up in sugar water."

"Really? And then you ate them that way?"

"Ate 'em?" Nate was horrified. "You crazy? We used to put 'em in a bowl on the table to kill flies!"

Scores   Sentence Check 2 _____%   Final Check _____%

Enter your scores above and in the vocabulary performance chart on the inside back cover of the book.

delete	menace
impartial	morale
integrity	naive
legitimate	overt
lenient	undermine

Ten Words in Context

In the space provided, write the letter of the meaning closest to that of each **boldfaced** word. Use the context of the sentences to help you figure out each word's meaning.

1 delete
(dĭ-lēt′)
-verb

- When I accidentally **deleted** several paragraphs of my research paper from the computer, it took ten minutes to retype them.
- The invitation list is too long. Unless we **delete** a few names, the party will be too crowded.

_c_ *Delete* means   a. to type.   b. to add.   c. to erase.

2 impartial
(ĭm-pär′shəl)
-adjective

- Too much publicity before a trial makes it difficult for lawyers to find **impartial** jurors, people with no opinion about the case.
- "I'm an **impartial** judge of character," Dolores joked. "I distrust all people equally, without prejudice."

_b_ *Impartial* means   a. not whole.   b. fair.   c. friendly.

3 integrity
(ĭn-tĕg′rə-tē)
-noun

- Our boss trusts Ramon with the key to the cash register because she knows that he has **integrity**.
- I thought our senator had **integrity**, so I was shocked to hear that she had taken a bribe.

_a_ *Integrity* means   a. honesty.   b. talent.   c. a good memory.

4 legitimate
(lĕ-jĭt′ə-mĭt)
-adjective

- "A need to see the final episode in your favorite soap opera," said the teacher, "is not a **legitimate** excuse for missing class."
- Any company that guarantees to make all investors millionaires can't possibly be **legitimate**.

_b_ *Legitimate* means   a. safe.   b. considered proper.   c. healthy.

5 lenient
(lē′nē-ənt)
-adjective

- Ms. Hall is very **lenient** about late papers. If you hand one in even a week late, she doesn't lower your grade.
- Mom wouldn't let us feed our poodle during dinner. But Dad, who was more **lenient**, would look the other way when we slipped the dog something under the table.

_b_ *Lenient* means   a. heartless.   b. easygoing.   c. honest.

6 menace
(mĕn′ĭs)
-noun

- Acid rain is the biggest **menace** to the survival of freshwater fish.
- Ron's impatient attitude and his fast, zigzag driving make him a **menace** on the road.

_c_ *Menace* means   a. a puzzle.   b. something noticeable.   c. a danger.

7 **morale**
(mə-răl′)
-*noun*

- Art class was good for Tyrone's **morale**. Each time the teacher praised his drawings, his confidence and enthusiasm increased.
- The workers' **morale** was so low that they constantly complained about the job. Only going home could cheer them up.

a Morale means   a. spirit.   b. pay.   c. sense of right.

8 **naive**
(nä-ēv′)
-*adjective*

- Though young, Rhoda is not **naive**. Being on her own for so long has made her streetwise.
- Having had little experience with salespeople, my young daughter is so **naive** that she believes everything they tell her.

a Naive means   a. lacking experience.   b. generous.   c. questioning.

9 **overt**
(ō-vûrt′)
-*adjective*

- Sometimes **overt** racism is easier to deal with than the hidden kind. You can better fight what is out in the open.
- Martha's love of reading was **overt**—books spilled over the shelves in every room of her apartment.

a Overt means   a. obvious.   b. fair.   c. harmful.

10 **undermine**
(ŭn′dər-mīn′)
-*verb*

- Leroy tried to **undermine** the coach's authority by making jokes about him behind his back.
- Numerous floods had **undermined** the foundation so greatly that the house was no longer safe.

c Undermine means   a. to reach.   b. to explore.   c. to weaken.

Matching Words with Definitions

Following are definitions of the ten words. Clearly write or print each word next to its definition. The sentences above and on the previous page will help you decide on the meaning of each word.

1. _____*impartial*_____   Fair; not biased; without prejudice

2. _____*menace*_____   A threat

3. _____*legitimate*_____   In accordance with accepted laws, rules, and standards

4. _____*morale*_____   State of mind with respect to confidence and enthusiasm; spirit

5. _____*delete*_____   To cross out or erase

6. _____*undermine*_____   To gradually weaken or damage

7. _____*overt*_____   Obvious; not hidden

8. _____*lenient*_____   Not strict or harsh in disciplining or punishing; merciful

9. _____*naive*_____   Lacking worldly experience; unsuspecting; unsophisticated

10. _____*integrity*_____   Honesty; strong moral sense

CAUTION: Do not go any further until you are sure the above answers are correct. Then you can use the definitions to help you in the following practices. Your goal is eventually to know the words well enough so that you don't need to check the definitions at all.

➤ Sentence Check 1

Using the answer line provided, complete each item below with the correct word from the box. Use each word once.

a. **delete**	b. **impartial**	c. **integrity**	d. **legitimate**	e. **lenient**
f. **menace**	g. **morale**	h. **naive**	i. **overt**	j. **undermine**

_____impartial_____ 1. When my brother and I argued, my mother remained ___. She didn't want to favor either of us.

_____undermine_____ 2. Alison's repeated criticisms ___ her sister's self-confidence.

_____menace_____ 3. Drugs have become a terrible ___ to the well-being of America's children.

_____morale_____ 4. The team's ___ was high—the players were in good spirits and thought they would win the game.

_____legitimate_____ 5. Although advertising by doctors and lawyers was once considered improper, it is now ___.

_____naive_____ 6. My father is so ___ about business deals that he has been tricked by cheaters more than once.

_____delete_____ 7. Computers make it easy to ___ unwanted information from a report without having to type the report all over again.

_____overt_____ 8. Mrs. Dean's dislike for the mayor was ___. She stood right up in front of the crowd and called him a two-faced liar.

_____lenient_____ 9. "The boss is ___ the first time an employee makes a mistake," Sherry's coworker warned, "but he's very strict the second time."

_____integrity_____ 10. Mark Twain once joked that he had even more ___ than George Washington. "Washington could not lie," he said. "I can, but I won't."

NOTE: Now check your answers to these questions by turning to page 175. Going over the answers carefully will help you prepare for the next two practices, for which answers are not given.

➤ Sentence Check 2

Using the answer lines provided, complete each item below with **two** words from the box. Use each word once.

_____overt_____
_____naive_____
1–2. Nick's interest in Janice's money is ___ enough for all her friends to notice. But Janice is so ___ that she has no idea about the real reason for Nick's attention.

_____morale_____
_____legitimate_____
3–4. The employees' ___ quickly fell when they learned that some of the company's earnings were put into a business that was not ___ and that was being investigated by the police.

_____integrity_____
_____delete_____
5–6. To give her essay ___, Isabel ___d some statements that were not entirely true.

_____menace_____   7–8. Donald is a real ___ in the classroom. It's not uncommon for him to
_____undermine_____   ___ classroom order by snapping little spitballs at other students.

_____impartial_____   9–10. My parents should be ___, but they're much more ___ with my sisters
_____lenient_____   than with me. My sisters often get off with a scolding. In contrast, I'm
                            often compelled° to stay home for a night.

➤ _Final Check:_ Who's on Trial?

Here is a final opportunity for you to strengthen your knowledge of the ten words. First read the following selection carefully. Then fill in each blank with a word from the box at the top of the previous page. (Context clues will help you figure out which word goes in which blank.) Use each word once.

"I must be really (1)_____naive_____ about our justice system," Karen said as we

left the courtroom to get lunch. "I truly believed that if I pressed charges against that man for

attacking me, he would have a trial with a jury that would be (2)_____impartial_____ enough

to fairly consider all the evidence, which would be brought out by reasonable questioning. That

man is the criminal, but I felt as if I were the one on trial. I'm ready to give up."

After sitting at the trial all morning, I could easily understand why Karen's

(3)_____morale_____ was so low. The opposing lawyer's attempts to embarrass her and

(4)_____undermine_____ her image before the jury were so (5)_____overt_____ that

nobody in the courtroom could miss them. He seemed to have no (6)_____integrity_____ at

all. His misleading questions about her sex life and her manner of dressing were clearly meant to

give the false impression that it had been her own actions that were not

(7)_____legitimate_____, that Karen had "asked" to be attacked by behaving improperly. Her

lawyer succeeded in having certain remarks (8)_____delete_____d from the record, but

the damage was done. The jury had already heard things like "short skirts" and "sleep with your

boyfriend." They might jump to conclusions instead of considering the extensive° evidence her

own lawyer had presented against the attacker. I just hoped they would comply° with the judge's

instructions to consider all the evidence carefully. I also prayed that the judge would not be

(9)_____lenient_____, but would see what a(n) (10)_____menace_____ to

society this man was and sentence him to many years in prison.

| _Scores_ | Sentence Check 2 _____% | Final Check _____% |

Enter your scores above and in the vocabulary performance chart on the inside back cover of the book.

agenda	prospects
antidote	radical
apathy	reinforce
bland	relevant
propaganda	ruthless

Ten Words in Context

In the space provided, write the letter of the meaning closest to that of each **boldfaced** word. Use the context of the sentences to help you figure out each word's meaning.

1 agenda
(ə-jĕn′də)
-*noun*

- There are two items on the **agenda** for today's office meeting: the company's new product and the Christmas party.
- Items on Ralph's daily **agenda** include driving his granddaughter to school, working at the soup kitchen, and walking his dog after dinner.

_a_ *Agenda* means   a. a schedule.   b. a desk.   c. work.

2 antidote
(ăn′tĭ-dōt′)
-*noun*

- Because there was no **antidote** for the snake's poison, the cat that was bitten died.
- For me, a good **antidote** to feeling low is to bake a batch of brownies.

_c_ *Antidote* means   a. a short story.   b. a cause.   c. a remedy.

3 apathy
(ăp′ə-thē)
-*noun*

- The students' **apathy** turned to intense interest when the psychology teacher discussed Freud's views on sex.
- Voter **apathy** was high, causing a low turnout on election day.

_c_ *Apathy* means   a. pity.   b. understanding.   c. lack of interest.

4 bland
(blănd)
-*adjective*

- The addition of a bright red scarf changed Linda's grey outfit from **bland** to striking.
- Mexicans, accustomed to hot and spicy foods, often find American dishes **bland** by comparison.

_b_ *Bland* means   a. old.   b. dull.   c. bitter.

5 propaganda
(prŏp′ə-găn′də)
-*noun*

- The **propaganda** put out by cigarette companies says that nicotine doesn't harm people's health.
- The political candidates ran TV ads made up largely of **propaganda** directed against their opponents.

_c_ *Propaganda* means   a. research.   b. support.   c. publicity.

6 prospects
(prŏs′pĕkts)
-*noun*

- The movie's **prospects** for doing well at the box office were harmed by several bad reviews in the newspapers and on TV.
- What are my **prospects** of finding a hotel room in this town during Super Bowl weekend?

_b_ *Prospects* means   a. reasons.   b. chances.   c. fears.

7 radical
(răd′ĭ-kəl)
-*adjective*

- I won't vote for the **radical** candidate—his beliefs are too extreme for me.
- Most students tried to change school policy through peaceful compromise, but a **radical** group wanted to take over the president's office by force.

a Radical means   a. extreme.   b. average.   c. young.

8 reinforce
(rē′ĭn-fôrs′)
-*verb*

- Jonathan's wisecrack **reinforced** the teacher's opinion that he was interested only in fooling around.
- Some pantyhose are **reinforced** at the heels and toes with extra layers of material, so they won't rip.

b Reinforce means   a. to ruin.   b. to strengthen.   c. to repeat.

9 relevant
(rĕl′ə-vənt′)
-*adjective*

- History is always **relevant** to our lives because it shows us what results can follow certain actions.
- "The weather is not **relevant** to this conversation," Yvonne's mother said. "Don't change the subject when I bring up your speeding tickets."

b Relevant means   a. known.   b. related.   c. threatening.

10 ruthless
(rōōth′lĭs)
-*adjective*

- My English teacher is a **ruthless** grader of essay exams. He shows no mercy for weak reasoning or faulty grammar.
- Barry is so **ruthless** that he would step on coworkers to advance himself.

c Ruthless means   a. sweet.   b. confusing.   c. without mercy.

Matching Words with Definitions

Following are definitions of the ten words. Clearly write or print each word next to its definition. The sentences above and on the previous page will help you decide on the meaning of each word.

1. _____ *prospects* _____   Chances of success

2. _____ *apathy* _____   Lack of interest and concern

3. _____ *reinforce* _____   To strengthen; to add support to

4. _____ *agenda* _____   A list of things to be done; a schedule

5. _____ *ruthless* _____   Lacking pity; merciless

6. _____ *bland* _____   Dull; not interesting or exciting

7. _____ *relevant* _____   Related to the matter at hand; to the point

8. _____ *radical* _____   Favoring extreme changes, especially in politics and government

9. _____ *antidote* _____   Something that reduces the effects of a poison; anything that relieves a harmful situation

10. _____ *propaganda* _____   Ideas spread to support or oppose a cause

CAUTION: Do not go any further until you are sure the above answers are correct. Then you can use the definitions to help you in the following practices. Your goal is eventually to know the words well enough so that you don't need to check the definitions at all.

➤ *Sentence Check 1*

Using the answer line provided, complete each item below with the correct word from the box. Use each word once.

a. **agenda**	b. **antidote**	c. **apathy**	d. **bland**	e. **propaganda**
f. **prospects**	g. **radical**	h. **reinforce**	i. **relevant**	j. **ruthless**

_____ruthless_____ 1. There are ___ drivers who make no effort to avoid hitting animals on the road.

_____bland_____ 2. Carlos's personality is so ___ and unexciting that people tend not to notice him.

_____relevant_____ 3. Your statement isn't ___; it has nothing to do with our conversation.

_____reinforce_____ 4. Victoria will ___ the plant by tying its thin stem to a strong stick.

_____prospects_____ 5. My sister's ___ of passing Accounting II aren't good. She hasn't studied all term.

_____antidote_____ 6. All medicine cabinets should contain a general ___ for accidental poisoning.

_____agenda_____ 7. Every morning Lin writes out her ___, jotting down what she needs to accomplish that day.

_____radical_____ 8. Because Todd wants to do away with all private ownership of guns, many people consider his views too ___.

_____apathy_____ 9. Sidewalk litter is a sign of ___, showing that people don't care about a clean environment.

_____propaganda_____ 10. Advertisements are an important part of the ___ used by companies to persuade us to buy their products.

NOTE: Now check your answers to these questions by turning to page 175. Going over the answers carefully will help you prepare for the next two practices, for which answers are not given.

➤ *Sentence Check 2*

Using the answer lines provided, complete each item below with **two** words from the box. Use each word once.

_____antidote_____
_____apathy_____
1–2. Working at top speed, the doctors injected the poisoned woman with a powerful ___. Everyone in the emergency room seemed anxious and tense except the woman's husband, so we wondered at his apparent ___.

_____agenda_____
_____ruthless_____
3–4. Gang members are a menace° to our neighborhoods. The only items on their ___ are theft and violence. Their ___ methods—threats, beatings, and even murder—cause terror among local businesspeople.

_____ _bland_ _____ 5–6. Professor Turner's lectures would not seem so ___ to students if he
_____ _relevant_ _____ didn't speak in such a dull tone of voice and if he included information
that seemed ___ to their lives.

_____ _propaganda_ _____ 7–8. The German Nazi Party used ___ in booklets, speeches, and films to
_____ _radical_ _____ spread its lies. Eventually this ___ group took over the German
government.

_____ _prospects_ _____ 9–10. If Henry starts exercising, his ___ for getting into shape will be very
_____ _reinforce_ _____ good. His desire to exercise was ___(e)d by the fact that he gained ten
pounds last year.

➤ _Final Check:_ Students and Politics

Here is a final opportunity for you to strengthen your knowledge of the ten words. First read the following selection carefully. Then fill in each blank with a word from the box at the top of the previous page. (Context clues will help you figure out which word goes in which blank.) Use each word once.

During the 1960s, the country's morale° was weakened by the Vietnam war and social

problems. At that time, many young people were attracted to (1)_____ _radical_ _____

political groups. The groups all had a similar list of things they wanted to accomplish. Their

(2)_____ _agenda_ _____ included ending the war in Vietnam, feeding the hungry, and

doing away with all forms of social prejudice. University students demanded courses more

(3)_____ _relevant_ _____ to the times: women's studies, African American literature,

and world religions. These activists hoped to serve as a(n) (4)_____ _antidote_ _____ to

the "traditional" thinking of the 1950s they considered so harmful. The music and literature of the

day helped spread the movement's antiwar, pro-love and often pro-drug

(5)_____ _propaganda_ _____. Many small newspapers that sprang up helped to

(6)_____ _reinforce_ _____ these messages.

Some who were politically active in the '60s are concerned by the (7)_____ _apathy_ _____

of young people today, who don't seem to care about their world. The middle-aged activitists fear

that today's students are, at best, so lacking in spirit as to be (8)_____ _bland_ _____ and

harmless. At worst, they are so money-hungry and (9)_____ _ruthless_ _____ that they

couldn't care less about people who are poverty-stricken. But others believe that the

(10)_____ _prospects_ _____ for social progress are better than they might seem. Students,

they say, will soon again take the lead in pushing for social change.

Scores Sentence Check 2 _____%	Final Check _____%

Enter your scores above and in the vocabulary performance chart on the inside back cover of the book.

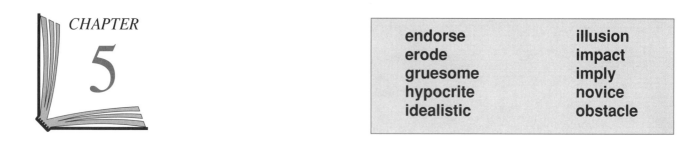

endorse	illusion
erode	impact
gruesome	imply
hypocrite	novice
idealistic	obstacle

Ten Words in Context

In the space provided, write the letter of the meaning closest to that of each **boldfaced** word. Use the context of the sentences to help you figure out each word's meaning.

1 **endorse**
(ĕn-dôrs′)
-verb

- "If you **endorse** the new shopping mall," said the speaker, "you're supporting a large increase in neighborhood traffic."
- Some athletes earn more money **endorsing** such products as cereal and sneakers than they do playing their sport.

_b_ *Endorse* means   a. to buy.   b. to support.   c. to see.

2 **erode**
(ĭ-rōd′)
-verb

- As water **eroded** the topsoil, the tree roots beneath it became more and more visible.
- The nation's confidence in its leader was **eroded** by his increasingly wild accusations against his opponents.

_a_ *Erode* means   a. to wear away.   b. to build up.   c. to escape.

3 **gruesome**
(groo′səm)
-adjective

- The automobile accident was so **gruesome** that I had to look away from the horrible sight.
- The young campers sat around the fire and scared each other with **gruesome** horror stories.

_c_ *Gruesome* means   a. unfair.   b. boring.   c. frightening.

4 **hypocrite**
(hĭp′ə-krĭt′)
-noun

- Dominic is such a **hypocrite**. He cheats his customers yet complains about how hard it is to be an honest, struggling salesman.
- I feel that the worst **hypocrites** are those who preach love and then attack anyone of a different culture or faith.

_a_ *Hypocrite* means   a. an insincere person.   b. a religious person.   c. a loud person.

5 **idealistic**
(ī-dē′ə-lĭs′tĭk)
-adjective

- Very **idealistic** people are drawn to professions like teaching or the ministry, in which they feel they can help make the world a better place.
- My sister is too **idealistic** ever to marry for wealth or fame—she would marry only for love.

_b_ *Idealistic* means   a. full of ideas.   b. emphasizing ideals.   c. young.

6 **illusion**
(ĭ-loo′zhən)
-noun

- Rena's belief that she and Jon had a strong relationship turned out to be an **illusion**. She wasn't aware that he had been dating other women.
- The idea that the sun sets and rises is an **illusion**. It is really the earth that is turning away from and then toward the sun.

_c_ *Illusion* means   a. a fact.   b. a new idea.   c. a false impression.

7 impact
(ĭm′păkt)
-noun

- When birds accidentally fly into windows, the **impact** of hitting the glass often kills them.
- That boxer punches with such power that the **impact** of his uppercut can knock out most opponents.

_a_ *Impact* means   a. a force.   b. a possibility.   c. a sight.

8 imply
(ĭm-plī′)
-verb

- To Sherlock Holmes, the clues **implied** that the murderer was an elderly man who carried a cane.
- When my friend asked me, "Do you feel all right?" she **implied** that I did not look well.

_c_ *Imply* means   a. to hide.   b. to overlook.   c. to suggest.

9 novice
(nŏv′ĭs)
-noun

- Because my father has never played tennis, he will join the class for **novices**.
- "Don't buy an expensive camera for a **novice**," said the saleswoman. "Let your son first get some experience with a cheap camera."

_b_ *Novice* means   a. a child.   b. a beginner.   c. a friend.

10 obstacle
(ŏb′stə-kəl)
-noun

- I'd better clean my apartment soon. There are too many **obstacles** on the floor between my bed and the refrigerator.
- The major **obstacle** to Hal's getting a promotion is his laziness.

_c_ *Obstacle* means   a. something hidden.   b. something helpful.   c. something that gets in the way.

Matching Words with Definitions

Following are definitions of the ten words. Clearly write or print each word next to its definition. The sentences above and on the previous page will help you decide on the meaning of each word.

1. _____imply_____   To express indirectly; suggest

2. _____obstacle_____   Something that gets in the way; a barrier

3. _____hypocrite_____   One who claims to be something he or she is not; an insincere person

4. _____illusion_____   A false impression; a mistaken view of reality

5. _____endorse_____   To support; express approval of; to state in an ad that one supports a product or service, usually for a fee

6. _____gruesome_____   Horrible; shocking; frightful

7. _____novice_____   A beginner; someone new to a field or activity

8. _____impact_____   The force of one thing striking another

9. _____erode_____   To gradually wear (something) away

10. _____idealistic_____   Tending to emphasize ideals and principles over practical concerns

CAUTION: Do not go any further until you are sure the above answers are correct. Then you can use the definitions to help you in the following practices. Your goal is eventually to know the words well enough so that you don't need to check the definitions at all.

➤ *Sentence Check 1*

Using the answer line provided, complete each item below with the correct word from the box. Use each word once.

a. **endorse**	b. **erode**	c. **gruesome**	d. **hypocrite**	e. **idealistic**
f. **illusion**	g. **impact**	h. **imply**	i. **novice**	j. **obstacle**

gruesome   1. The horror movie became too ___ when the monster started eating people.

erode   2. Year after year, the waves continue to ___ the beach, wearing it away by constantly beating against it.

imply   3. Poems often ___ an idea. That is, they hint at the idea rather than state it directly.

novice   4. I was such a(n) ___ at computers that I didn't even know how to insert a disk.

idealistic   5. Karen is the least ___ person I know. She is guided only by a desire to get ahead.

hypocrite   6. Don't be such a(n) ___! If you don't like Arlene, then you shouldn't pretend that you do.

endorse   7. An actress hired to ___ meat products on TV was fired when it was learned she was a vegetarian.

impact   8. Ballet dancers sometimes break their toes when they land with too great a(n) ___ after a leap.

obstacle   9. I can never drive straight into our driveway because there are always ___s there—tricycles, garbage cans, or toys.

illusion   10. When the moon is low in the sky, it looks much larger than when it is overhead. This difference in size, however, is only a(n) ___.

NOTE: Now check your answers to these questions by turning to page 175. Going over the answers carefully will help you prepare for the next two practices, for which answers are not given.

➤ *Sentence Check 2*

Using the answer lines provided, complete each item below with **two** words from the box. Use each word once.

imply
endorse   1–2. "Just because I let them meet in the church basement," said Reverend Lucas, "does not ___ that I ___ everything the group stands for."

illusion
impact   3–4. When the first soldier to fly in an airplane took off in 1908, he had no ___ about the danger, but he never expected to die from the ___ of crashing into a cemetery wall.

_____idealistic_____ 5–6. The first Peace Corps volunteers may have been ___, but they were

_____obstacle_____ tough about their dreams. No ___ would keep them from working for a better world.

_____novice_____ 7–8. Because she was just out of college, Faye was a(n) ___ at interviewing

_____hypocrite_____ job applicants. Nevertheless, she could see that Perry was a(n) ___ who boasted about job skills he didn't have.

_____erode_____ 9–10. Ten years in the soil had ___(e)d the body down to a mere skeleton.

_____gruesome_____ But when a gardener's shovel uncovered the ___ remains of the murder victim, she could still be identified by a gold locket around her neck.

➤ _Final Check:_ Night Nurse

Here is a final opportunity for you to strengthen your knowledge of the ten words. First read the following selection carefully. Then fill in each blank with a word from the box at the top of the previous page. (Context clues will help you figure out which word goes in which blank.) Use each word once.

I'm no (1)_____hypocrite_____, so I'll admit I sometimes wish I'd never taken the job of

nurse on the midnight shift in a hospital emergency room. Not a single person in my family would

(2)_____endorse_____ my career decision, and maybe my family was right. I had no

(3)_____illusion_____s about the difficulty of the work. I knew the emergency room

would be tough, but I wasn't going to let that be a(n) (4)_____obstacle_____. Still, I guess I

did start out more (5)_____idealistic_____ about helping the world than I am now, ten

months later. I don't mean to (6)_____imply_____ that I've given up on nursing,

because I haven't. But when I rushed that first stretcher off the ambulance—as a mere

(7)_____novice_____ at the job—disappointment and regret had not yet started to

(8)_____erode_____ my hopeful outlook.

I work at one of the biggest urban° hospitals in the state. More often than not, each shift

brings a series of bloody, (9)_____gruesome_____ cases. There are ruthless° shootings

and stabbings, and I often see skull fractures resulting from the (10)_____impact_____

of baseball bats on human heads.

The other day, when I went to buy some shoes for work, the clerk asked me, "What kind of

soles would you like?"

Before I could stop myself, I answered, "Some that won't slip in blood."

Scores   Sentence Check 2 _____%   Final Check _____%

Enter your scores above and in the vocabulary performance chart on the inside back cover of the book.

6

auto-	re-
ex-	super-
-ful	un-
multi-	uni-
pre-	vis, vid

Ten Word Parts in Context

Common word parts—also known as *prefixes, suffixes,* and *roots*—are used in forming many words in English. Figure out the meanings of the following ten word parts by looking *closely* and *carefully* at the context in which they appear. Then, in the space provided, write the letter of the meaning closest to that of each word part.

1 **auto-**

- In restaurants called **automats**, you serve yourself by putting coins in slots and removing food from behind small glass doors.
- It is possible to hypnotize yourself through a process called **autohypnosis**.

b The word part *auto-* means   a. see.   b. self.   c. above.

2 **ex-**

- "Inhale as you lower your head," called out the exercise instructor, "and **exhale** as you do the sit-up."
- My uncle isn't a very good businessman. He once tried to **export** rice to China and vodka to Russia.

b The word part *ex-* means   a. before.   b. out.   c. not.

3 **-ful**

- Even though the movie and the meal were pretty bad, I had a **delightful** evening because the company was so good.
- Many children, **fearful** of the dark, feel comforted by a night-light.

b The word part *-ful* means   a. not.   b. full of.   c. again.

4 **multi-**

- Belle is **multilingual**—she speaks English, French, and Chinese.
- Ours is a **multiracial** neighborhood. In fact, the area attracts people who want their children to grow up among many races.

a The word part *multi-* means   a. many.   b. one.   c. out.

5 **pre-**

- People who believe in fate think our lives are mainly **predetermined** and that we therefore can't do much to change things.
- I like to get to the theater in time to see the **previews** of coming movies.

c The word part *pre-* means   a. again.   b. one.   c. before.

6 **re-**

- **Reheated** coffee tastes like mud.
- My aunt bought a house that was in poor condition, fixed it up, and then **resold** it for a profit.

a The word part *re-* means   a. again.   b. above.   c. see.

7 **super-**
- When you're a **superstar** like Oprah Winfrey, it's impossible to have privacy in public.
- The **superintendent** of schools has called a meeting of all the principals to discuss the growing drug problem.

_c_ The word part *super-* means   a. out.   b. see.   c. above.

8 **un-**
- Our history teacher has an **unusual** approach to teaching. He often wears costumes to class and lectures as one of the historical people we're learning about.
- When I am involved in reading a good novel, I am totally **unaware** of the world around me.

_b_ The word part *un-* means   a. before.   b. not.   c. many.

9 **uni-**
- The company combined crayons, paints and paper into one **unit** and sold it as a children's art kit.
- The dancers in the chorus line kicked their legs up and down in perfect **unison**, as if they were one body.

_a_ The word part *uni-* means   a. one.   b. not.   c. before.

10 **vis, vid**
- Our teacher prefers that our oral reports include **visual** aids such as slide shows and illustrated handouts.
- My husband made a **videotape** of our baby's birth.

_c_ The word part *vis* or *vid* means   a. again.   b. before.   c. see.

Matching Word Parts with Definitions

Following are definitions of the ten word parts. Clearly write or print each word part next to its definition. The sentences above and on the previous page will help you decide on the meaning of each word part.

1. _____*multi-*_____   Many

2. _____*un-*_____   Not

3. _____*uni-*_____   One

4. _____*auto-*_____   Self

5. _____*ex-*_____   Out, from

6. _____*re-*_____   Again

7. _____*vis, vid*_____   See

8. _____*pre-*_____   Before

9. _____*super-*_____   Greater, above

10. _____*-ful*_____   Full of

CAUTION: Do not go any further until you are sure the above answers are correct. Then you can use the definitions to help you in the following practices. Your goal is eventually to know the word parts well enough so that you don't need to check the definitions at all.

➤ Sentence Check 1

Using the answer line provided, complete each *italicized* word in the sentences below with the correct word part from the box. Use each word part once.

a. **auto-**	b. **ex-**	c. **-ful**	d. **multi-**	e. **pre-**
f. **re-**	g. **super-**	h. **un-**	i. **uni-**	j. **vis**

rebuilt 1. After the earthquake, the city was (. . . *built*) ___ a few miles away, in a safer location.

visible 2. Bees and butterflies can see certain colors that are not (. . . *ible*) ___ to the human eye.

supermarkets 3. It is difficult for neighborhood food stores to compete with (. . . *markets*) ___.

prejudge 4. Jurors must not (. . . *judge*) ___ a case. They must listen to all the evidence before coming to a conclusion.

restful 5. I find it (*rest* . . .) ___ to vacation at home, where I can relax and catch up on reading and movies.

unicorn 6. The legendary (. . . *corn*) ___, a horselike animal with one horn, is often shown as having a lion's tail and a goat's beard.

extract 7. My grandfather used to (. . . *tract*) ___ my loose baby teeth by tying each to a string and then yanking the string.

autobiography 8. In her (. . . *biography*) ___, *Blackberry Winter*, Margaret Mead writes about her childhood, her three marriages, and her career.

multipurpose 9. My bedroom is really a (. . . *purpose*) ___ room. I read, watch TV, eat snacks, talk on the phone, do push-ups, daydream and sleep there.

unlucky 10. Anyone who bumps into a stonefish is really (. . . *lucky*) ___, for it has thirteen poisonous spines sticking out of its body.

NOTE: Now check your answers to these questions by turning to page 175. Going over the answers carefully will help you prepare for the next two practices, for which answers are not given.

➤ Sentence Check 2

Using the answer lines provided, complete each *italicized* word in the sentences below with the correct word part from the box. Use each word part once.

unfolded
handful 1–2. The magician (. . . *folded*) ___ a small red cloth and held it up so that we could see all of it. Then, in a flash, he had a (*hand* . . .) ___ of flowers.

expelled
automatically 3–4. Students caught drinking anywhere on the school grounds are (. . . *pelled*) ___ from school (. . . *matically*) ___.

_____envision_____ 5–6. Unless we learn to be more accepting of each other, I cannot (*en . . . ion*)
_____unified_____ ___ a time when this family will be peaceful and (. . . *fied*) ___.

_____supervisor_____ 7–8. I painted the company president's office last week, but my (. . . *visor*)
_____repaint_____ ___ said I now have to (. . . *paint*) ___ it in a different color. The
president thinks the gray is too bland°.

_____predicted_____ 9–10. A psychic (. . . *dicted*) ___ an improvement in my financial situation.
_____multiplied_____ She was right: my debts have (. . . *plied*) ___.

➤ *Final Check:* Theo's Perfect Car

Here is a final opportunity for you to strengthen your knowledge of the ten word parts. First read the following selection carefully. Then complete each *italicized* word in the parentheses below with a word from the box at the top of the previous page. (Context clues will help you figure out which word part goes in which blank.) Use each word part once.

My young son Theo wants to be a(n) (. . . *mobile*) (1)_____automobile_____ designer

some day. In the meanwhile, he feels he can (. . . *pare*) (2)_____prepare_____ for that

day by working on his design of a (. . . *ior*) (3)_____superior_____ car.

So far, this great car of his runs on air. Theo says that means future gas stations will need only

air pumps, for both the tank and the tires. In addition, his car has the ability to become (*in . . . ible*)

(4)_____invisible_____. (Theo feels it would be (*help . . .*) (5)_____helpful_____ for a

car to disappear whenever the driver is chased by bad guys.) The car will also have trays for candy

instead of ashes and an (. . . *tended*) (6)_____extended_____ trunk, to hold lots of luggage,

toys, and plastic bags for people who get carsick. The front of the car will have an electric eye to

warn the driver when obstacles° are on the road and a third headlight to help illuminate° very dark

roads and tunnels. The tires will be (. . . *colored*) (7)_____multicolored_____, with circles of

red, yellow, purple, and blue.

I tell Theo that his car is imaginative and (. . . *que*) (8)_____unique_____; surely there

is none other like it in the world. But then I (. . . *mind*) (9)_____remind_____ him that if he

doesn't do his math homework, it's (. . . *likely*) (10)_____unlikely_____ that General

Motors will hire him as a designer.

Scores	Sentence Check 2 _____%	Final Check _____%

Enter your scores above and in the vocabulary performance chart on the inside back cover of the book.

UNIT ONE: Review

The box at the right lists twenty-five words from Unit One. Using the clues at the bottom of the page, fill in these words to complete the puzzle that follows.

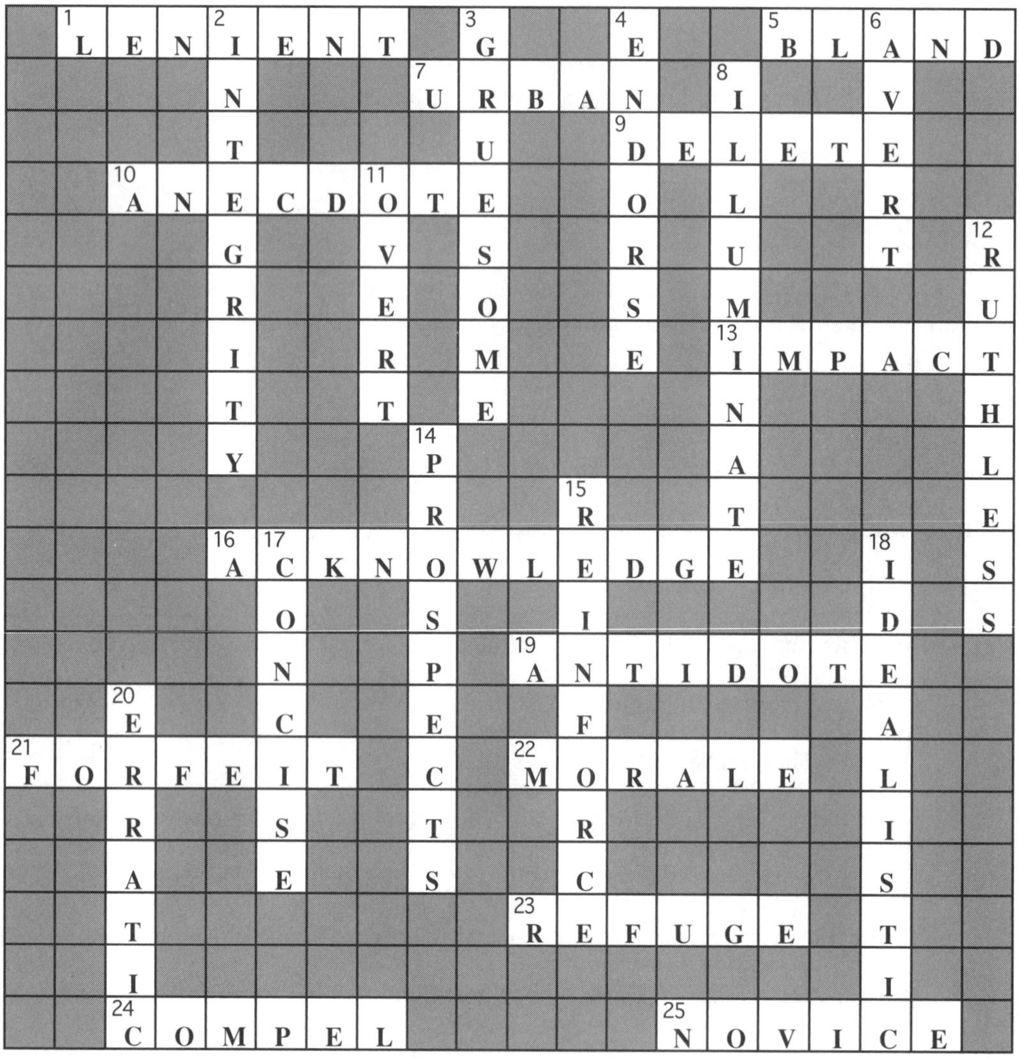

The crossword grid contains the following filled answers:

1 Across: L E N I E N T
5 Across: B L A N D
7 Across: U R B A N
9 Across: D E L E T E
10 Across: A N E C D O T E
13 Across: I M P A C T
16 Across: A C K N O W L E D G E
19 Across: A N T I D O T E
21 Across: F O R F E I T
22 Across: M O R A L E
23 Across: R E F U G E
24 Across: C O M P E L
25 Across: N O V I C E

Word list:

- acknowledge
- anecdote
- antidote
- avert
- bland
- compel
- concise
- delete
- endorse
- erratic
- forfeit
- gruesome
- idealistic
- illuminate
- impact
- integrity
- lenient
- morale
- novice
- overt
- prospects
- refuge
- reinforce
- ruthless
- urban

ACROSS

1. Not strict or harsh in punishing; merciful
5. Dull; not interesting or exciting
7. Of or in a city
9. To cross out or erase
10. An entertaining short story about an event
13. The force of one thing striking another
16. To admit or confess
19. Something that reduces the effects of a poison or relieves a harmful situation
21. To lose through some fault; to be forced to give up by way of penalty
22. State of mind with respect to confidence and enthusiasm; spirit
23. Shelter; protection
24. To force
25. A beginner; someone new to a field or activity

DOWN

2. Honesty; strong moral sense
3. Horrible; shocking; frightful
4. To support; express approval of; to state in an ad that one supports a product or service, usually for a fee
6. To prevent; to avoid
8. To light up
11. Obvious; not hidden
12. Lacking pity; merciless
14. Chances of success
15. To strengthen; add support to
17. Saying much in a few clear words
18. Tending to emphasize ideals and principles over practical concerns
20. Not consistent

UNIT ONE: Test 1

PART A
Choose the word that best completes each item and write it in the space provided.

_____antidote_____ 1. There are hunters who dip their arrows in the poison from a tiny frog—a deadly poison for which there is no ___.

    a. anecdote   b. integrity   c. antidote   d. obstacle

_____undermine_____ 2. Smoking and drinking ___ your health.

    a. fortify   b. undermine   c. reinforce   d. isolate

_____avert_____ 3. To ___ disaster in river rafting, you must steer clear of rocks.

    a. avert   b. erode   c. compel   d. endorse

_____extensive_____ 4. Damage to the old car was so ___ that repairs would have cost more than the car did.

    a. bland   b. extensive   c. impartial   d. concise

_____concise_____ 5. One speaker spoke for over an hour, but Greg was ___, taking only ten minutes to make his points.

    a. drastic   b. erratic   c. naive   d. concise

_____bland_____ 6. A salt-free diet doesn't have to be ___. Throw in a few hot peppers, and your dish will have zing.

    a. bland   b. overt   c. legitimate   d. gruesome

_____endorse_____ 7. The nurses asked our union to ___ their strike by signing a letter of support.

    a. comply   b. undermine   c. endorse   d. isolate

_____alternative_____ 8. After I failed my first two algebra quizzes, I decided that the sensible ___ to flunking was to get some tutoring.

    a. alternative   b. agenda   c. impact   d. morale

_____gruesome_____ 9. Although the movie is titled _Tears of Blood_, it isn't ___; it contains no violence or blood.

    a. erratic   b. candid   c. gruesome   d. relevant

_____novice_____ 10. When Jimmy practiced saying dirty words in first grade, he was only a ___, but by sixth grade he was an expert.

    a. hypocrite   b. novice   c. menace   d. refuge

_____urban_____ 11. One advantage of ___ living is the city's wealth of live entertainment, including plays and concerts.

    a. erratic   b. idealistic   c. ruthless   d. urban

(Continues on next page)

_____candid_____ 12. When my boyfriend agreed with me that my new perm looked terrible, I regretted that he was always so ___.

        a. drastic   b. radical   c. candid   d. lenient

_____agenda_____ 13. The ___ of our Humor Club meetings usually consists of swapping funny stories and then playing a practical joke on some unlucky nonmember.

        a. propaganda   b. dialog   c. agenda   d. apathy

PART B
Write **C** if the italicized word is used **correctly**. Write **I** if the word is used **incorrectly**.

_I_ 14. The tornado *reinforced* the house, ripping off the roof.

_C_ 15. Alaskan wolves are no *menace* to humans—they don't attack people.

_C_ 16. The newly fallen snow was so bright under the moonlight that it *illuminated* the entire street.

_I_ 17. In seventeenth-century Massachusetts, one *lenient* jury hanged a dog accused of being a witch.

_I_ 18. *Impartial* employers often prejudge overweight job applicants as likely to be lazy.

_I_ 19. The candidate was happy to see his support among factory workers start to *erode*.

_C_ 20. Since he wanted to borrow the car that night, Harry decided to *comply* with his mother's request that he clean his room.

_I_ 21. The businessman was well loved for his *ruthless* treatment of his employees and partners.

_C_ 22. The *impact* of the baseball was so great that my hand stung even though I was wearing a mitt.

_C_ 23. The walls around many European cities were built as *obstacles* to attackers.

_I_ 24. To *forfeit* my health, I take plenty of vitamins, eat well, and get enough sleep.

_C_ 25. As I grew older, the *illusion* that my parents were stupid gradually faded.

Score (Number correct) _____ x 4 = _____ %

Enter your score above and in the vocabulary performance chart on the inside back cover of the book.

UNIT ONE: Test 2

PART A
Complete each item with a word from the box. Use each word once.

a. **acknowledge**	b. **delete**	c. **dialog**	d. **drastic**	e. **fortify**
f. **hypocrite**	g. **integrity**	h. **isolate**	i. **morale**	j. **propaganda**
k. **prospects**	l. **refuge**	m. **reminisce**		

_____*fortify*_____ 1. The old wooden beams in the barn were so weak that we had to ___ them with metal rods.

_____*prospects*_____ 2. I'd say Bruno's ___ of getting the job are excellent—his father owns the company.

_____*drastic*_____ 3. In the 1870s one man took ___ action when his wife refused to serve him breakfast: he divorced her.

_____*acknowledge*_____ 4. Americans ___ that they have a great fear of cancer. When surveyed, most report that they fear this disease more than any other.

_____*refuge*_____ 5. There is no hunting in the state park, which serves as a(n) ___ for wildlife.

_____*propaganda*_____ 6. A large part of war is ___: spreading information that makes the enemy look bad.

_____*Morale*_____ 7. ___ is so low in my office that no one even wants to talk about how depressed we all are.

_____*delete*_____ 8. When the R-rated movie was shown on TV, all curse words were ___d. As a result, nearly every sentence had gaps.

_____*isolate*_____ 9. People who work alone in toll booths must often feel their job ___s them too much, especially late at night.

_____*dialog*_____ 10. Westerns are shown throughout the world. Still, it's odd to think of cowboys speaking their ___ in German, French, or Japanese.

_____*integrity*_____ 11. Dominic has ___. When he accidentally backed into a parked car and smashed one of its lights, he was honest enough to leave a note with his name and number.

_____*hypocrite*_____ 12. That woman is a(n) ___. She gives speeches about the evils of alcohol but has been arrested three times for drunk driving.

_____*reminisce*_____ 13. I listened to my grandparents ___ about all the crazy fads they've seen come and go, including T-shirts that gave off a smell of chocolate, garlic, or fish when scratched.

(Continues on next page)

PART B
Write **C** if the italicized word is used **correctly**. Write **I** if the word is used **incorrectly**.

_I_ 14. It is always *appropriate* to drink and drive.

_C_ 15. On most American beaches, it's not *legitimate* for women to go topless.

_I_ 16. Flora is so *idealistic* that she accepted a great sales job even though the store is known to discriminate against women.

_I_ 17. My little sister is *naive* about baseball. She knows the names and records of dozens of players.

_C_ 18. Ray's feelings for Julie are certainly *overt*. He once paid for a billboard on Main Street that read, "Julie, I love you. Ray."

_C_ 19. Our school will soon make a *drastic* change in its dress code. From now on, all students will have to wear uniforms to school.

_I_ 20. Winston Churchill had such a good memory he could *imply* an entire Shakespearean play word for word.

_I_ 21. Our strict parents often *compel* us to eat too much candy, dirty the carpet, and stay up late.

_C_ 22. "What you do in your private life certainly is *relevant* to our team," yelled the coach, "especially if you do it until four in the morning."

_C_ 23. Cesar's moodiness makes his work *erratic*. One week he's a top salesman, and the next week he can't seem to sell a thing.

_I_ 24. When his team won the basketball game, Doug was filled with such *apathy* that he jumped up and down shouting "Yeah!" until he sprained his ankle.

_C_ 25. In fifth-century France and Spain, a doctor was required to leave a cash deposit before caring for a patient. If the patient lived, the doctor got his money back. If the patient died, the doctor *forfeited* the deposit.

Score   (Number correct) _____ x 4 = _____ %

Enter your score above and in the vocabulary performance chart on the inside back cover of the book.

UNIT ONE: Test 3

PART A

Complete each sentence in a way that clearly shows you understand the meaning of the **boldfaced** word. Take a minute to plan your answer before you write.

Example: If you receive a wedding invitation, it is **appropriate** ___*to respond by the date requested*___ .

1. One well-known product **endorsed** by a well-known person is ___*(Answers will vary.)*___

    _____.

2. Two things that can **illuminate** a room are _____

    _____.

3. The driver **averted** a crash by _____

    _____.

4. One **obstacle** to professional success is _____

    _____.

5. A sign of high **morale** on a team is _____

    _____.

6. The judge was so **lenient** that _____

    _____.

7. Being a **novice** as a waiter, Artie _____

    _____.

8. The following remark could **undermine** someone's confidence: " _____

    _____."

9. I know that my father has **integrity** because _____

    _____.

10. When it comes to taxes, Dinah is so **radical** that she believes _____

    _____.

(Continues on next page)

PART B

After each **boldfaced** word are a *synonym* (a word that means the same as the boldfaced word), an *antonym* (a word that means the opposite of the boldfaced word), and a word that is neither. On the answer line, write the letter of the word that is the antonym.

Example: __a__ **delete**   a. restore   b. erase   c. insult

__a__ 11. **isolate**   a. include   b. freeze   c. separate

__b__ 12. **concise**   a. old   b. wordy   c. brief

__b__ 13. **impartial**   a. fair   b. prejudiced   c. small

__c__ 14. **gruesome**   a. horrible   b. powerful   c. lovely

__c__ 15. **apathy**   a. illness   b. unconcern   c. interest

PART C

Use five of the following ten words in sentences. Make it clear that you know the meaning of the word you use. Feel free to use the past tense or plural form of a word.

| a. **agenda** | b. **compel** | c. **drastic** | d. **erode** | e. **erratic** |
| f. **illusion** | g. **legitimate** | h. **menace** | i. **prospects** | j. **urban** |

16. _____ *(Answers will vary.)* _____

_____

17. _____

_____

18. _____

_____

19. _____

_____

20. _____

_____

Score   (Number correct) _____ x 5 = _____ %

Enter your score above and in the vocabulary performance chart on the inside back cover of the book.

UNIT ONE: *Test 4 (Word Parts)*

PART A

Listed in the left-hand column below are ten common word parts, along with words in which the parts are used. In each blank, write in the letter of the correct definition on the right.

Word Parts	Examples	Definitions
_i_ 1. **auto-**	automat, autohypnosis	a. Before
_j_ 2. **ex-**	exhale, export	b. See
_c_ 3. **-ful**	delightful, fearful	c. Full of
_d_ 4. **multi-**	multilingual, multiracial	d. Many
_a_ 5. **pre-**	predetermined, previews	e. One
_h_ 6. **re-**	reheated, resold	f. Not
_g_ 7. **super-**	superstar, superintendent	g. Greater, above
_f_ 8. **un-**	unusual, unaware	h. Again
_e_ 9. **uni-**	unit, unison	i. Self
_b_ 10. **vis, vid**	visual, videotape	j. Out, from

PART B

Using the answer line provided, complete each *italicized* word in the sentences below with the correct word part from the box. Not every word part will be used.

a. **auto-**	b. **ex-**	c. **-ful**	d. **multi-**	e. **pre-**
f. **re-**	g. **super-**	h. **un-**	i. **uni-**	j. **vis**

regrow   11. If the tail of a certain lizard is cut off, the tail will (. . . *grow*) ___ to full size.

vision   12. According to surveys, Americans consider the worst physical handicap to be a loss of (. . . *ion*) ___.

union   13. In some early marriages, the bride and groom "tied the knot" by having their sleeves tied together, as a symbol of their (. . . *on*) ___.

multiplying   14. Bacteria never die—they just keep (. . . *plying*) ___. One splits into two, two split into four, and so on.

expenses   15. My girlfriend says my problem is not that my income is too low but that my (. . . *penses*) ___ are too high.

(Continues on next page)

PART C

Use your knowledge of word parts to determine the meaning of the **boldfaced** words. On the answer line, write the letter of each meaning.

_b_ 16. In our garden, weeds are **plentiful**.

   a. lacking   b. numerous   c. spread out

_a_ 17. Factories are increasingly **automated**.

   a. self-running   b. high-speed   c. complicated

_c_ 18. The teacher thinks Alice writes **superlative** essays.

   a. wordy   b. poor   c. of the highest quality

_c_ 19. I opened the suitcase and found my china clown **unbroken**.

   a. broken in half   b. broken to bits   c. not broken

_a_ 20. My decision to get a job was **premature**.

   a. made before the right time   b. made at exactly the right time   c. made after the right time

---

Score	(Number correct) _____ x 5 = _____%

Enter your score above and in the vocabulary performance chart on the inside back cover of the book.

Unit Two

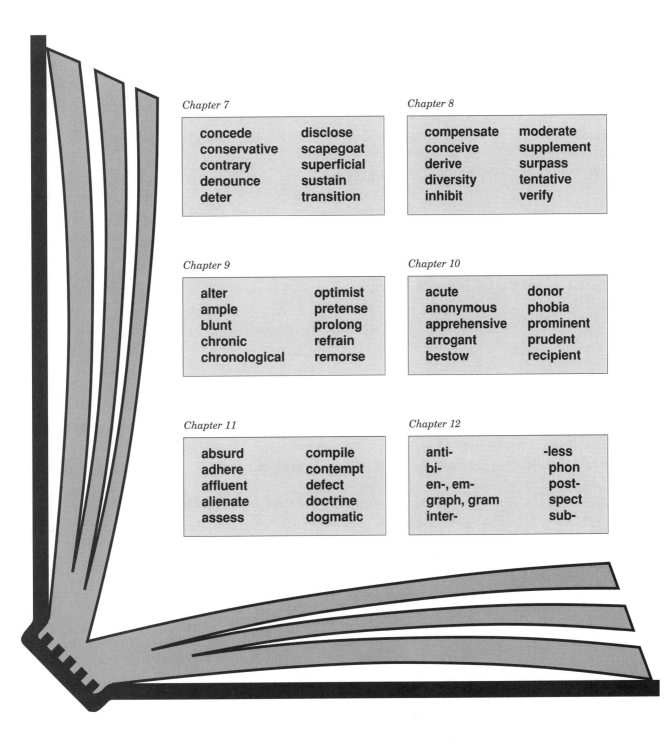

Chapter 7

concede	disclose
conservative	scapegoat
contrary	superficial
denounce	sustain
deter	transition

Chapter 8

compensate	moderate
conceive	supplement
derive	surpass
diversity	tentative
inhibit	verify

Chapter 9

alter	optimist
ample	pretense
blunt	prolong
chronic	refrain
chronological	remorse

Chapter 10

acute	donor
anonymous	phobia
apprehensive	prominent
arrogant	prudent
bestow	recipient

Chapter 11

absurd	compile
adhere	contempt
affluent	defect
alienate	doctrine
assess	dogmatic

Chapter 12

anti-	-less
bi-	phon
en-, em-	post-
graph, gram	spect
inter-	sub-

concede	disclose
conservative	scapegoat
contrary	superficial
denounce	sustain
deter	transition

Ten Words in Context

In the space provided, write the letter of the meaning closest to that of each **boldfaced** word. Use the context of the sentences to help you figure out each word's meaning.

1 **concede**
(kən-sēd′)
-*verb*

- Our aunt hates to admit an error. She will never **concede** that she might be wrong.
- After pretending it was easy learning to use the new computer, Ross had to **concede** that he was struggling and ask for help.

_b_ *Concede* means   a. to forget.   b. to admit.   c. to prove.

2 **conservative**
(kən-sûr′və-tĭv)
-*adjective*

- My **conservative** relatives were shocked when I broke with tradition and wore a rose-colored wedding gown.
- When the mayor suggested a new method of recycling garbage, a **conservative** member of the audience called out, "What we've done in the past is good enough. Why change things?"

_c_ *Conservative* means   a. playful.   b. amused.   c. traditional.

3 **contrary**
(kŏn′trĕr-ē)
-*adjective*

- Claire's father insists that she share his views. He doesn't allow her to express an opinion **contrary** to his.
- Dale and her husband have **contrary** ideas on how to spend a vacation. He wants to sleep on the beach for a week, but she prefers visiting museums.

_a_ *Contrary* means   a. different.   b. favorable.   c. similar.

4 **denounce**
(dĭ-nouns′)
-*verb*

- In Nazi Germany, anyone who publicly **denounced** Hitler as cruel or mad risked imprisonment, torture, and death.
- When Eugene said he saw me steal from another student's locker, I **denounced** him as a liar.

_c_ *Denounce* means   a. to imitate.   b. to defend.   c. to condemn.

5 **deter**
(dĭ-tûr′)
-*verb*

- No one is sure how much the threat of execution **deters** murder.
- Beth's parents disapproved of her dating someone from a different culture, but their prejudice didn't **deter** her—she still dated Po-Yen.

_a_ *Deter* means   a. to discourage.   b. to encourage.   c. to change.

6 **disclose**
(dĭs-klōz′)
-*verb*

- When I applied for financial aid, I had to **disclose** my annual income. But it embarrassed me to reveal this information.
- The police don't **disclose** all the facts of a murder to the newspapers. That way, there will be some information which only the murderer would know.

_a_ *Disclose* means   a. to reveal.   b. to deny.   c. to replace.

7 **scapegoat**
(skāp′gōt′)
-noun

- Several girls put dye into their high school swimming pool. In need of a **scapegoat**, they blamed another student who knew nothing about the prank.
- Because the manager wanted a **scapegoat** for his own mistake, he fired an innocent employee.

_c_ *Scapegoat* means   a. a correction.   b. a punishment.   c. someone to blame.

8 **superficial**
(sōō′pər-fĭsh′əl)
-adjective

- Sal and Anita are interested only in appearances. They are so **superficial** that it's impossible to have a deep friendship with them.
- My teacher said my essay on divorce was too **superficial** because I didn't go into the subject in detail.

_a_ *Superficial* means   a. lacking depth.   b. complicated.   c. satisfactory.

9 **sustain**
(sə-stān′)
-verb

- My diets usually last three days at the most. I can't **sustain** my willpower any longer than that.
- An opera singer can **sustain** a high note for a long period of time.

_c_ *Sustain* means   a. to remember.   b. to delay.   c. to continue.

10 **transition**
(trăn-zĭsh′ən)
-noun

- Mark's parents were amazed at how easily he made the **transition** from full-time student to full-time employee.
- "The **transition** from being childless to being a parent is extreme," said the new father. "Last week, only two quiet people lived at home. Suddenly, we have a third, noisy resident."

_c_ *Transition* means   a. an explanation.   b. a trip.   c. a change.

Matching Words with Definitions

Following are definitions of the ten words. Clearly write or print each word next to its definition. The sentences above and on the previous page will help you decide on the meaning of each word.

1. _____superficial_____   Lacking depth or meaning; shallow

2. _____contrary_____   Totally different; opposite; conflicting

3. _____transition_____   A change from one activity, condition, or location to another

4. _____scapegoat_____   Someone blamed for the mistakes of others

5. _____concede_____   To admit to something

6. _____deter_____   To prevent or discourage

7. _____disclose_____   To reveal; make known

8. _____denounce_____   To openly condemn; express disapproval of

9. _____sustain_____   To keep something going; continue

10. _____conservative_____   Tending to resist change; favoring traditional values and views

CAUTION: Do not go any further until you are sure the above answers are correct. Then you can use the definitions to help you in the following practices. Your goal is eventually to know the words well enough so that you don't need to check the definitions at all.

➤ *Sentence Check 1*

Using the answer line provided, complete each item below with the correct word from the box. Use each word once.

a. **concede**	b. **conservative**	c. **contrary**	d. **denounce**	e. **deter**
f. **disclose**	g. **scapegoat**	h. **superficial**	i. **sustain**	j. **transition**

_____scapegoat_____ 1. The teenagers who smashed the window made an innocent bystander a ___, claiming he had thrown the rock.

_____sustain_____ 2. To ___ a high grade point average throughout college requires much studying.

_____denounce_____ 3. The environmental group ___ (e)d a local chemical company for polluting the river.

_____concede_____ 4. Even after Stuart listed scientific facts that support his theory, the teacher refused to ___ that Stuart might be right.

_____deter_____ 5. A childhood stutter didn't ___ Leon. He overcame his speech handicap and reached his goal of being a radio announcer.

_____superficial_____ 6. I try to judge people by their character, not by something as ___ as physical appearance.

_____disclose_____ 7. Knowing my passion for chocolate, my mother refused to ___ the location of the bite-size Hershey bars, which she was saving for company.

_____transition_____ 8. Making the ___ from her own apartment to a nursing home has been difficult for my grandmother.

_____contrary_____ 9. Though Geena and Tom are happily married, they cast ___ votes in almost every election—she's a Republican and he's a Democrat.

_____conservative_____ 10. When Dawn brought home a boyfriend with purple hair and an earring, her ___ parents, who prefer everything old-fashioned and traditional, nearly fainted.

NOTE: Now check your answers to these questions by turning to page 175. Going over the answers carefully will help you prepare for the next two practices, for which answers are not given.

➤ *Sentence Check 2*

Using the answer lines provided, complete each item below with **two** words from the box. Use each word once.

_____transition_____
_____sustain_____

1–2. Starting with the ___ from home to college, some students neglect high school friendships which they had vowed always to ___.

_____superficial_____
_____deter_____

3–4. Stan is more interested in how much money people have than in who they are. He is a ___ person, and that quality ___s people from becoming his friends.

_____denounce_____   5–6. Amy's parents always ___ her, although she is rarely at fault. She has
_____scapegoat_____   become the ___ for the entire family.

_____conservative_____   7–8. Mayor Jones was ___, preferring traditional solutions. So it was hard
_____concede_____   for him to ___ that some of the radical° ideas of his opponent might
                           work.

_____disclose_____   9–10. Once Sandy ___(e)d her true values in the course of our conversation, I
_____contrary_____   realized they were quite ___ to what I had supposed. She was not the
                           type of person that I had believed her to be.

➤ _Final Check:_ Relating to Parents

Here is a final opportunity for you to strengthen your knowledge of the ten words. First read the following selection carefully. Then fill in each blank with a word from the box at the top of the previous page. (Context clues will help you figure out which word goes in which blank.) Use each word once.

When I was a kid, my parents were everything to me—the smartest, most interesting, most loving people in the world. But when I turned 13, there was a drastic° change—I suddenly gained a very (1)_____contrary_____ view of them. Now they appeared mean and strict. While I had become open to fresh ideas and styles, they seemed unpleasantly (2)_____conservative_____, wanting everything to remain the same and resisting every new thing that entered my life. They hated my hair, my music, my friends. Sometimes it seemed they even hated me.

Now that I'm making the (3)_____transition_____ from my teen years to adulthood, I have to (4)_____concede_____ that my parents aren't so bad. Perhaps, at times, I even made them (5)_____scapegoat_____s for problems I had caused myself. Now I'd like to have really deep talks with them, not just the (6)_____superficial_____ chats we've had lately. But it's hard for us to (7)_____sustain_____ a conversation about anything but unimportant subjects. I'd like to (8)_____disclose_____ my plans and dreams to them, but I'm afraid they'll (9)_____denounce_____ my ideas as foolish or wrong. It's hard not to let my fears (10)_____deter_____ me from seeking a better relationship with my parents, but I think it's worth a try.

| _Scores_   Sentence Check 2 _____% | Final Check _____% |

Enter your scores above and in the vocabulary performance chart on the inside back cover of the book.

compensate	moderate
conceive	supplement
derive	surpass
diversity	tentative
inhibit	verify

Ten Words in Context

In the space provided, write the letter of the meaning closest to that of each **boldfaced** word. Use the context of the sentences to help you figure out each word's meaning.

1 **compensate**
(kŏm′pən-sāt′)
-*verb*

- Some companies still don't **compensate** women for their work as much as they pay men who do the same or similar work.
- When an oil rig explosion killed Sam, the company **compensated** his widow with $100,000. However, nothing could really repay her for his loss.

_b_ *Compensate* means   a. to notice.   b. to pay.   c. to hire.

2 **conceive**
(kən-sēv′)
-*verb*

- When studying Australia in school, I **conceived** an interesting class project—each student could write to an Australian pen pal.
- Most people in the 1800s could not have imagined such things as TV and heart transplants. What will the next century bring that we cannot yet **conceive** of?

_a_ *Conceive* means   a. to think of.   b. to expect.   c. to remember.

3 **derive**
(dĭ-rīv′)
-*verb*

- We **derive** plastics from oil. As a result, when oil prices go up, so do the prices of plastic products.
- Sarah **derived** pleasure from visiting and reading to old people after school. She enjoyed their company and felt she was doing something worthwhile.

_b_ *Derive* means   a. to recognize.   b. to get.   c. to want.

4 **diversity**
(dĭ-vûr′sĭ-tē)
-*noun*

- There's a great **diversity** of breakfast cereals at the supermarket. There are so many different kinds that they take up half an aisle.
- "One thing I'm looking for in a college," Sandra told her counselor, "is **diversity**. I want to meet many different kinds of people."

_c_ *Diversity* means   a. sameness.   b. need.   c. variety.

5 **inhibit**
(ĭn-hĭb′ĭt)
-*verb*

- Steve wanted to drive fast in his new car, but the fact that he had already gotten two speeding tickets **inhibited** him.
- Many people believe exercise makes one eat more, but I find that exercise **inhibits** my urge to snack.

_a_ *Inhibit* means   a. to hold back.   b. to get into the habit.   c. to satisfy.

6 **moderate**
(mŏd′ər-ĭt)
-*adjective*

- The trail was neither flat nor extremely steep—it was **moderate**, suitable for the average hiker.
- The prices at this restaurant aren't dirt cheap, but they are **moderate**. So we should be able to have a nice dinner without spending too much.

_b_ *Moderate* means   a. modern.   b. average.   c. difficult.

7 **supplement**
(sŭp′lə-mənt)
-verb

- Many people **supplement** their diet with vitamins.
- At busy times of the year, the department store **supplements** its sales staff with temporary workers.

_b_ *Supplement* means   a. to replace.   b. to add to.   c. to reduce.

8 **surpass**
(sər-păs′)
-verb

- You can reach and even **surpass** many of your highest goals.
- Denise was disappointed that she had only matched Rhonda's record leap in the high jump—she had hoped to **surpass** it.

_a_ *Surpass* means   a. to go beyond.   b. to avoid.   c. to equal.

9 **tentative**
(tĕn′tə-tĭv)
-adjective

- Our wedding date is **tentative**. Before we finalize the date, we have to be sure Ben's parents can make the trip that weekend.
- Class membership was **tentative** because many students were still dropping and adding courses.

_b_ *Tentative* means   a. clear.   b. not definite.   c. early.

10 **verify**
(vĕr′ə-fī′)
-verb

- Race officials **verified** who the winner was by checking a photo of the horses at the finish line.
- We'd love to come to the party, but I have to check my calender to **verify** that we're free that evening.

_c_ *Verify* means   a. to predict.   b. to deny.   c. to check.

Matching Words with Definitions

Following are definitions of the ten words. Clearly write or print each word next to its definition. The sentences above and on the previous page will help you decide on the meaning of each word.

1. _____*diversity*_____   Variety

2. _____*compensate*_____   To make suitable payment to; pay; repay

3. _____*surpass*_____   To do better than; go beyond in achievement or quality

4. _____*verify*_____   To test or check the truth or accuracy of something; prove

5. _____*supplement*_____   To add to, especially to make up for a lack

6. _____*derive*_____   To receive from a source; get

7. _____*tentative*_____   Not definite; not final

8. _____*moderate*_____   Medium; average; not extreme in quality, degree, or amount

9. _____*conceive*_____   To think of; imagine

10. _____*inhibit*_____   To hold back; prevent

CAUTION: Do not go any further until you are sure the above answers are correct. Then you can use the definitions to help you in the following practices. Your goal is eventually to know the words well enough so that you don't need to check the definitions at all.

➤ *Sentence Check 1*

Using the answer line provided, complete each item below with the correct word from the box. Use each word once.

a. **compensate**	b. **conceive**	c. **derive**	d. **diversity**	e. **inhibit**
f. **moderate**	g. **supplement**	h. **surpass**	i. **tentative**	j. **verify**

derive   1. The Mississippi River ___s its name from Indian words meaning "big river."

verify   2. To ___ that his checkbook balance was correct, Craig added the numbers again.

moderate   3. If you aren't very hungry, then take only a ___ helping of food.

tentative   4. The exact cast of the movie remains ___ until it is known whether or not Tom Cruise is available.

surpass   5. Babe Ruth's record number of home runs in a single baseball season was ___(e)d by Roger Maris.

supplement   6. The Motor Vehicle Bureau now ___s its driver's manual with an attached publication on the new driving laws.

inhibit   7. Even with her relatives, shy Yoko didn't feel free to be herself. Their noisy talk ___(e)d her.

conceive   8. Artists feel frustrated when what they ___ of in their minds fails to appear on the painted canvas.

diversity   9. "Hearing a ___ of opinions is fine," said Lynn. "But it would be nice if everyone in this family could agree once in a while."

compensate   10. When my uncle helped me pay for college, he said I could ___ him by helping someone else pay for college when I can afford to.

NOTE: Now check your answers to these questions by turning to page 175. Going over the answers carefully will help you prepare for the next two practices, for which answers are not given.

➤ *Sentence Check 2*

Using the answer lines provided, complete each item below with **two** words from the box. Use each word once.

conceive
inhibit   1–2. I cannot ___ of being in a relationship with someone who would ___ my personal growth.

tentative
verify   3–4. I have ___ plans to meet Cesar at the Midtown Theatre at eight, but first I have to ___ the show time and call him back.

compensate
surpass   5–6. When our company offered to ___ us well for working on Saturdays, the number of volunteers ___(e)d all expectations.

_____derive_____ 7–8. I ___ great pleasure from having my paintings in an art show, and I can
_____supplement_____   ___ my income by selling some of them.

_____diversity_____ 9–10. City College offers a ___ of courses and majors at a ___ price. Many
_____moderate_____   students don't realize they have an unusually wide choice of courses at
        a lower cost than at many other colleges.

➤ *Final Check:* Job Choices

Here is a final opportunity for you to strengthen your knowledge of the ten words. First read the following selection carefully. Then fill in each blank with a word from the box at the top of the previous page. (Context clues will help you figure out which word goes in which blank.) Use each word once.

After job-hunting for two months, Jessica had to choose between two alternatives° for employment—a fashion magazine and a clothing store. She already had (1)_____tentative_____ job offers from both employers. They planned to make the offers definite after they were able to (2)_____verify_____ the information on her job application.

In the meanwhile, Jessica thought about the good and bad points of the two jobs. Both offered the (3)_____diversity_____ that she liked; she hated doing the same thing every day. Both had good benefits, such as sick leave and vacation time. However, the two companies would not (4)_____compensate_____ her equally. At the clothing store, Jessica would start out at a (5)_____moderate_____ salary. With her many expenses, she might even have to find a part-time job in the evenings to (6)_____supplement_____ this salary. But there were other, better points. Working for the store, Jessica would be free to put her many ideas into practice right away. Her manager said he would not (7)_____inhibit_____ any attempts she might make to move up in the company. In fact, he promised her that if her work was good, he would endorse° a promotion for her himself within a few months. At the fashion magazine, Jessica's starting salary would far (8)_____surpass_____ what she would get paid at the clothing store—she wouldn't have to worry about money at all. But the prospects° of getting promotions and raises were not so definite. Jessica could (9)_____conceive_____ of either job as a learning experience and felt she could (10)_____derive_____ much satisfaction from either one. This would not be an easy decision.

___

Scores   Sentence Check 2 _____%   Final Check _____%

Enter your scores above and in the vocabulary performance chart on the inside back cover of the book.

CHAPTER

9

alter	optimist
ample	pretense
blunt	prolong
chronic	refrain
chronological	remorse

Ten Words in Context

In the space provided, write the letter of the meaning closest to that of each **boldfaced** word. Use the context of the sentences to help you figure out each word's meaning.

1 alter
(ôl′tər)
-verb

- Many inventions have changed the course of history. Television **altered** the world, for example, by making it smaller.
- Fern's dramatic weight loss and new hairstyle so **altered** her appearance that we barely recognized her.

_b_ *Alter* means   a. to surprise.   b. to change.   c. to emphasize.

2 ample
(ăm′pəl)
-adjective

- Surprisingly, my compact car has **ample** space inside. Even Mario, who is six feet tall, never feels cramped in it.
- My parents believe that the most important requirement of any celebration is **ample** food, so that no one will be hungry.

_c_ *Ample* means   a. little.   b. healthy.   c. plenty of.

3 blunt
(blŭnt)
-adjective

- "I'll be **blunt**," Phyllis said, as plainspoken as ever. "You're a jerk."
- My best friend is so **blunt** that he never softens the truth. He always states his opinion in a painfully straightforward way.

_b_ *Blunt* means   a. very smart.   b. honest to the point of rudeness.   c. wordy.

4 chronic
(krŏn′ĭk)
-adjective

- Our boss is a **chronic** complainer—we hear only criticism from him day in and day out.
- Leon has been chain-smoking for so long that he has developed a **chronic** cough, heard daily by everyone in the office.

_a_ *Chronic* means   a. constant.   b. rare.   c. harmless.

5 chronological
(krŏn′ə-lŏj′ĭ-kəl)
-adjective

- I could have followed the movie better if it had presented events in **chronological** order, instead of jumping back and forth in time.
- In your résumé, list your jobs in reverse **chronological** order—begin with the most recent job and go backward.

_c_ *Chronological* means   a. brief.   b. mixed up.   c. arranged as events happened.

6 optimist
(ŏp′tə-mĭst)
-noun

- My sister is a true **optimist**. When her friends get out their umbrellas, she puts on suntan lotion.
- Alonso is such an **optimist** that when he lost his job, he said only, "I bet I'll find a better one now."

_b_ *Optimist* means   a. a friendly person.   b. a hopeful person.   c. a troublemaker.

7 **pretense**
(prē′tĕns)
-*noun*

• The robber entered people's houses under the **pretense** of being a repairman.

• I asked several questions about Dean's illness, with the **pretense** of being concerned. In truth, I've never even liked Dean.

<u>a</u> *Pretense* means   a. a false reason.   b. a true statement.   c. a threat.

8 **prolong**
(prə-lông′)
-*verb*

• Pulling off a bandage always hurts, but pulling it off slowly **prolongs** the pain.

• My registration for fall classes was **prolonged** because I forgot my course card and had to stand in two extra lines.

<u>c</u> *Prolong* means   a. to avoid.   b. to wear away.   c. to make longer.

9 **refrain**
(rĭ-frān′)
-*verb*

• I **refrained** from saying what I really thought about Anne's haircut because I didn't want to hurt her feelings.

• Since she's on a diet, Stella **refrained** from eating a second piece of carrot cake.

<u>a</u> *Refrain* means   a. to stop oneself.   b. to return.   c. to keep going.

10 **remorse**
(rĭ-môrs′)
-*noun*

• Russell's mother was filled with **remorse** after she hit him. She always regrets her outbursts of temper.

• Feeling **remorse** over breaking the Sony Walkman, I apologized to my friend and promised to buy her a new one.

<u>c</u> *Remorse* means   a. excitement.   b. ambition.   c. regret.

Matching Words with Definitions

Following are definitions of the ten words. Clearly write or print each word next to its definition. The sentences above and on the previous page will help you decide on the meaning of each word.

1. _____*chronic*_____   Continuing; lasting a long time; constant

2. _____*pretense*_____   A false show or claim

3. _____*optimist*_____   Someone who expects a good outcome

4. _____*alter*_____   To change

5. _____*refrain*_____   To hold oneself back from doing something

6. _____*ample*_____   More than enough; plenty of

7. _____*remorse*_____   A strong feeling of regret and guilt

8. _____*chronological*_____   In the time order in which events happened

9. _____*blunt*_____   Straightforward and brief, often rudely so

10. _____*prolong*_____   To make something last longer

CAUTION: Do not go any further until you are sure the above answers are correct. Then you can use the definitions to help you in the following practices. Your goal is eventually to know the words well enough so that you don't need to check the definitions at all.

➤ *Sentence Check 1*

Using the answer line provided, complete each item below with the correct word from the box. Use each word once.

a. **alter**	b. **ample**	c. **blunt**	d. **chronic**	e. **chronological**
f. **optimist**	g. **pretense**	h. **prolong**	i. **refrain**	j. **remorse**

_____refrain_____   1. I couldn't ___ from laughing when Laurie bent over to pick up her pencil and split her tight jeans.

_____optimist_____   2. My father always expects the worst, but my mother is a(n) ___.

_____alter_____   3. I used to dislike my neighbor, but learning that he drove meals to elderly shut-ins ___(e)d my opinion of him.

_____prolong_____   4. The record store will ___ its "One Day Only" sale to two days, since a storm kept people away the first day.

_____ample_____   5. Use a deep pan when baking the cake, so there will be ___ room for it to rise.

_____remorse_____   6. Immediately after calling her sister an idiot, Lydia felt ___. So she hugged her sister and said, "I didn't mean that."

_____blunt_____   7. If the teacher had been ___, she would have told Kevin his essay was terrible. Instead, she politely said, "It could use much more work."

_____chronological_____   8. A story in which early events are hidden until the end is often more dramatic than one told in exact ___ order.

_____chronic_____   9. Although Pilar's back pain was ___, having lasted for five years, she refused to undergo surgery.

_____pretense_____   10. With the ___ of being attracted to Paula, Emilio asked her to dance; but his real reason was to make his ex-girlfriend jealous.

NOTE: Now check your answers to these questions by turning to page 176. Going over the answers carefully will help you prepare for the next two practices, for which answers are not given.

➤ *Sentence Check 2*

Using the answer lines provided, complete each item below with **two** words from the box. Use each word once.

_____prolong_____
_____optimist_____   1–2. Although her marriage was unhappy, Nell chose to ___ it. An ___, she kept thinking her relationship with her husband would improve. Eventually, however, she realized their relationship had eroded° too much for the marriage to be sustained°.

_____refrain_____
_____chronic_____   3–4. Sylvester can't ___ from sniffling and blowing his nose because he suffers all summer from ___ hay fever.

_____chronological_____   5–6. The ruthless° murderer told what had happened in simple ___ order,
_____remorse_____   without showing any ___: "First I loaded the gun, and then I drove to
                                     the mall. Next, I started shooting people."

_____Blunt_____   7–8. ___ criticism is rarely the best way to ___ someone's behavior. Gentle
_____alter_____   suggestions tend to bring about more change.

_____pretense_____   9–10. Dressed in shabby clothes, Darren made a(n) ___ of being poor. Few
_____ample_____   people knew he had ___ money to live well.

➤ *Final Check:* No Joking

Here is a final opportunity for you to strengthen your knowledge of the ten words. First read the following selection carefully. Then fill in each blank with a word from the box at the top of the previous page. (Context clues will help you figure out which word goes in which blank.) Use each word once.

My poor mother is the worst joke teller I've ever met. She has a(n) (1)_____chronic_____ inability to remember anecdotes° and punchlines—she's been like that for years. She begins a story in (2)_____chronological_____ order and then interrupts herself to say, "No, wait a minute. That's not the way it goes." In this way, she manages to (3)_____prolong_____ jokes, making them more lengthy than funny. Still, she can't (4)_____refrain_____ from trying to tell them. And she has (5)_____ample_____ opportunity to try when our family gets together. My uncle derives° amusement from seeing her embarrass herself, so he makes a(n) (6)_____pretense_____ of thinking she is funny. My father is more (7)_____blunt_____; he tells Mother outright that she has ruined the joke. After each failure, she is filled with (8)_____remorse_____ and swears she'll never tell another joke. But I don't believe she'll ever (9)_____alter_____ her behavior. A(n) (10)_____optimist_____, she always believes her next joke will be her best.

Scores	Sentence Check 2 _____%	Final Check _____%

Enter your scores above and in the vocabulary performance chart on the inside back cover of the book.

acute	donor
anonymous	phobia
apprehensive	prominent
arrogant	prudent
bestow	recipient

Ten Words in Context

In the space provided, write the letter of the meaning closest to that of each **boldfaced** word. Use the context of the sentences to help you figure out each word's meaning.

1 **acute**
(ə-kyōot′)
-*adjective*

- Gil joked, "This painting looks like something my two-year-old son would do." Then he felt **acute** regret when he learned the artist was standing behind him.
- My headache pains were so **acute** that they felt like needles in my head.

a *Acute* means   a. very great.   b. mild.   c. slow.

2 **anonymous**
(ə-nŏn′ə-məs)
-*adjective*

- Many **anonymous** works are very famous. For example, the author of the Christmas carol "God Rest Ye Merry, Gentlemen" is unknown.
- Laura tore up an **anonymous** note that said her husband was seeing another woman. "If the writer was too ashamed to sign the note," said Laura, "why should I believe it?"

b *Anonymous* means   a. short.   b. having an unknown author.   c. poorly written.

3 **apprehensive**
(ăp′rĭ-hĕn′sĭv)
-*adjective*

- Ginny was **apprehensive** as she approached the cow, not knowing if it would try to bite or kick her.
- It is natural to be **apprehensive** when making a major purchase, such as a computer or a car. Only the very wealthy can afford not to be at all nervous at such times.

a *Apprehensive* means   a. fearful.   b. irritated.   c. confident.

4 **arrogant**
(ăr′ə-gənt)
-*adjective*

- Having been a very spoiled child, Becky turned out to be a very **arrogant** grownup.
- One of the most **arrogant** people I know paid the state extra money to get a custom license plate that reads "IMBEST."

c *Arrogant* means   a. polite.   b. quiet.   c. showing too much self-importance.

5 **bestow**
(bĭ-stō′)
-*verb*

- The Manhattan School of Music **bestowed** an honorary degree on a famous musician who had never gone to college.
- At the science fair, the judges **bestowed the** first prize on Vincent, whose experiment showed that dogs are colorblind.

c *Bestow* means   a. to take.   b. to prepare.   c. to award.

6 **donor**
(dō′nər)
-*noun*

- Our soccer team is seeking **donors** to contribute money for new uniforms.
- The man's twin sister was the **donor** of his new kidney.

b *Donor* means   a. one who receives.   b. one who gives.   c. one who doubts.

7 **phobia**
(fō′bē-ə)
-noun

- My roommate has joined a group that helps people with **phobias** because she wants to overcome her extreme fear of even the smallest spiders.
- Ned's fear of flying is so severe that he won't even step onto an airplane. But he says he's in no rush to cure his **phobia**, since driving is cheaper anyway.

_b_ *Phobia* means   a. illness.   b. extreme fear.   c. bad temper.

8 **prominent**
(prŏm′ə-nənt)
-adjective

- Crystal's long black hair is so **prominent** that it's the first thing you notice about her.
- The Big Bird balloon was the most **prominent** one in the parade because it was so large and such a bright yellow.

_c_ *Prominent* means   a. very colorful.   b. expensive.   c. obvious.

9 **prudent**
(prōōd′ənt)
-adjective

- Sidney has learned the hard way that it's not **prudent** to tease our ill-tempered dog.
- **Prudent** as always, Meg thought carefully before finally deciding which of the used cars would be the best buy.

_c_ *Prudent* means   a. relaxed.   b. courageous.   c. careful and wise.

10 **recipient**
(rĭ-sĭp′ē-ənt)
-noun

- Katherine Hepburn was the **recipient** of an Academy Award for her role in *On Golden Pond* in 1981, almost fifty years after her first Academy Award.
- Doug was the annoyed **recipient** of fourteen pieces of junk mail on the same day.

_b_ *Recipient* means   a. one who gives.   b. one who receives.   c. one with good luck.

Matching Words with Definitions

Following are definitions of the ten words. Clearly write or print each word next to its definition. The sentences above and on the previous page will help you decide on the meaning of each word.

1. _____donor_____   A person who gives or contributes

2. _____apprehensive_____   Frightened; uneasy; anxious

3. _____phobia_____   A continuing, abnormally extreme fear of a particular situation or thing

4. _____prudent_____   Cautious; careful; wise

5. _____acute_____   Severe; sharp

6. _____arrogant_____   Filled with self-importance; overly proud and vain

7. _____prominent_____   Very noticeable; obvious

8. _____recipient_____   A person who receives

9. _____anonymous_____   Created or given by an unknown or unidentified person

10. _____bestow_____   To give, as an honor or a gift; award

CAUTION: Do not go any further until you are sure the above answers are correct. Then you can use the definitions to help you in the following practices. Your goal is eventually to know the words well enough so that you don't need to check the definitions at all.

➤ *Sentence Check 1*

Using the answer line provided, complete each item below with the correct word from the box. Use each word once.

a. **acute**	b. **anonymous**	c. **apprehensive**	d. **arrogant**	e. **bestow**
f. **donor**	g. **phobia**	h. **prominent**	i. **prudent**	j. **recipient**

_____ *phobia* _____ 1. Because of her ___, Martha will walk up twenty floors to avoid taking an elevator.

_____ *anonymous* _____ 2. The unsigned letter to the editor was not published because it was the newspaper's policy never to print ___ letters.

_____ *acute* _____ 3. Since I didn't eat all day, I began to feel ___ hunger pains in my stomach by early evening.

_____ *arrogant* _____ 4. The secretary to the president of the company acts very ___. She thinks she's more important than the other secretaries.

_____ *recipient* _____ 5. Carla was so popular that each year she was the ___ of dozens of Valentines.

_____ *bestow* _____ 6. When he retires, the biology professor will ___ on the school his collection of animal skeletons.

_____ *prudent* _____ 7. "Your decision to wait to marry until after graduation seems ___ to me," Larry's father said, pleased that his son was acting so wisely.

_____ *apprehensive* _____ 8. Cliff became more and more ___ about his driver's test. He was afraid he'd forget to signal, fail to park correctly, or even get into an accident.

_____ *donor* _____ 9. Because the new tax laws limit certain deductions, art museums have fewer ___s.

_____ *prominent* _____ 10. The most ___ plants in Denzel's garden are giant lilies. Some of them are eight feet tall.

NOTE: Now check your answers to these questions by turning to page 176. Going over the answers carefully will help you prepare for the next two practices, for which answers are not given.

➤ *Sentence Check 2*

Using the answer lines provided, complete each item below with **two** words from the box. Use each word once.

_____ *arrogant* _____
_____ *donor* _____ 1–2. The millionaire was so ___ that he refused to be a major ___ to the new town library unless it was named for him.

_____ *prudent* _____
_____ *acute* _____ 3–4. It's ___ to keep medication on hand if anyone in the family is subject to ___ asthma attacks.

_____ *apprehensive* _____
_____ *prominent* _____ 5–6. Joey is very ___ when he has to give a speech in class, and his stutter becomes especially ___. As a result, he refrains° from raising his hand in class.

_____recipient_____   7–8. The famous actress was sometimes the ___ of ___ letters from fans too
_____anonymous_____   shy to sign their names.

_____bestow_____   9–10. Carlotta felt her therapist had ___ed upon her the greatest of gifts:
_____phobia_____   freedom from fear of open spaces. Before her treatment, Carlotta's ___
                             had kept her a prisoner in her own home. It had inhibited° her from
                             even walking into her own front yard.

➤ _Final Check:_ Museum Pet

Here is a final opportunity for you to strengthen your knowledge of the ten words. First read the following
selection carefully. Then fill in each blank with a word from the box at the top of the previous page.
(Context clues will help you figure out which word goes in which blank.) Use each word once.

"I've got great news!" the museum director shouted as he ran into the employees' lunchroom.

"Someone wants to (1)_____bestow_____ five million dollars on the museum."

"Who?" one staff member asked excitedly.

"I don't know. He wishes his gift to remain (2)_____anonymous_____. There's just one
obstacle°," he added.

The employees' optimistic° smiles faded, and they began to look (3)_____apprehensive_____.

"It seems our mystery (4)_____donor_____ has a strange (5)_____phobia_____:
he's terribly afraid of cats."

Everyone turned to look at Willard, who had been the museum pet since he'd wandered in as a
tiny kitten more than five years ago. As usual, the big orange cat was stretched out in a
(6)_____prominent_____ spot near the lunchroom entrance. He continued licking himself,
not aware that he was the (7)_____recipient_____ of everyone's attention.

"I'm afraid Willard will have to go," the director said sadly. "This contributor isn't just a little
afraid of cats; his fear is really (8)_____acute_____. Apparently, he panicked when he
saw Willard the last time he came. We can't risk frightening him again. It just wouldn't be
(9)_____prudent_____. Remember, he might give us more money in the future."

"I think it's pretty (10)_____arrogant_____ of this contributor, whoever he is, to ask us
to give up poor old Willard for him, even if he does want to give us the money," one employee said
angrily.

"I know you'll miss Willard," the director said, "but it would be a shame to forfeit° the money.
And I'll be glad to have him come live at my house. You can all visit him whenever you like." And
so Willard found a new home, where he still lives happily. The museum used the five million
dollars to build a new addition, which was known as the Willard Wing.

Scores Sentence Check 2 _____%	Final Check _____%

Enter your scores above and in the vocabulary performance chart on the inside back cover of the book.

absurd	compile
adhere	contempt
affluent	defect
alienate	doctrine
assess	dogmatic

Ten Words in Context

In the space provided, write the letter of the meaning closest to that of each **boldfaced** word. Use the context of the sentences to help you figure out each word's meaning.

1 **absurd**
(ăb-sûrd′)
-adjective

- When six-foot Randy came to the costume party in only a diaper, he looked so **absurd** that everyone burst into laughter.
- It seemed **absurd** to Helen that she had more cooking experience than the teacher of her cooking class.

_c_ *Absurd* means   a. responsible.   b. challenging.   c. ridiculous.

2 **adhere**
(ăd-hēr′)
-verb

- Beware of sitting on a hot car seat in shorts—your thighs may **adhere** to the plastic.
- Angie used bubble gum to make the poster of Whitney Houston **adhere** to her bedroom wall.

_c_ *Adhere* means   a. to belong.   b. to grow.   c. to stick.

3 **affluent**
(ăf′lōō-ənt)
-adjective

- Some people live an **affluent** lifestyle by overcharging on their credit cards—a bad habit that can lead to a mountain of debts.
- Why should tax regulations benefit **affluent** people more than poor people?

_c_ *Affluent* means   a. careless.   b. friendly.   c. rich.

4 **alienate**
(āl′yən-āt′)
-verb

- The teacher often insulted Maria. His rude behavior began to **alienate** the other students, who had once thought of him as a friend.
- Bill and Joanne thought their marriage could survive while they worked in different cities. But being apart so much eventually **alienated** them from each other.

_a_ *Alienate* means   a. to push away.   b. to frighten.   c. to comfort.

5 **assess**
(ə-sĕs′)
-verb

- It is harder for teachers to **assess** answers to essay questions than to grade multiple-choice items.
- After the fire, insurance representatives came to **assess** the damage.

_a_ *Assess* means   a. to judge.   b. to think of.   c. to avoid.

6 **compile**
(kəm-pīl′)
-verb

- Before writing her essay, Sharon **compiled** a list of the points she wanted to make.
- The teacher asked students to **compile** reports on their family histories by interviewing parents and grandparents.

_c_ *Compile* means   a. to read carefully.   b. to divide.   c. to create by gathering information.

7 **contempt**
(kən-tĕmpt′)
-*noun*

- Vera pitied the beggar, but her boyfriend felt only **contempt**, saying, "He's too lazy to get a job."
- Molly expressed her **contempt** for Art's clumsy dancing by leaving him in the middle of the dance floor.

_a_ *Contempt* means   a. disrespect.   b. acceptance.   c. curiosity.

8 **defect**
(dē′fĕkt′)
-*noun*

- The only **defect** in the actor's good looks was that his ears stuck out. Careful camera angles and a longer haircut hid the problem.
- "Check these peaches for **defects**, Tom," said the grocer to his new employee. "Remove any with dark spots or other imperfections."

_a_ *Defect* means   a. a fault.   b. a strength.   c. a pattern.

9 **doctrine**
(dŏk′trĭn)
-*noun*

- Dr. Martin Luther King, Jr., followed the **doctrine** of fighting for social change without violence.
- Many sincerely practice their faith without understanding all its **doctrines**. The fine points of principle do not interest everyone.

_b_ *Doctrine* means   a. a prediction.   b. a teaching.   c. a schedule.

10 **dogmatic**
(dôg-măt′ĭk)
-*adjective*

- The boss's **dogmatic** style bothered me. He listened to only one person's opinions—his own.
- A **dogmatic** teacher demands that students accept what is taught without question. Rather than insisting on their own views, teachers should encourage students to express opinions.

_c_ *Dogmatic* means   a. wild.   b. very patient.   c. one-sided.

Matching Words with Definitions

Following are definitions of the ten words. Clearly write or print each word next to its definition. The sentences above and on the previous page will help you decide on the meaning of each word.

1. _____contempt_____   Disrespect; a feeling that a person or thing is inferior and undesirable

2. _____assess_____   To evaluate; to decide on the quality or value of

3. _____dogmatic_____   Opinionated; stating an opinion as if it were a fact

4. _____adhere_____   To stick firmly

5. _____defect_____   A fault; imperfection

6. _____alienate_____   To cause to become unfriendly; to separate emotionally

7. _____affluent_____   Wealthy

8. _____absurd_____   Ridiculous; opposed to common sense

9. _____compile_____   To gather together in an organized form, such as a list

10. _____doctrine_____   The strict teachings of a religious, political, or other group

CAUTION: Do not go any further until you are sure the above answers are correct. Then you can use the definitions to help you in the following practices. Your goal is eventually to know the words well enough so that you don't need to check the definitions at all.

➤ *Sentence Check 1*

Using the answer line provided, complete each item below with the correct word from the box. Use each word once.

a. **absurd**	b. **adhere**	c. **affluent**	d. **alienate**	e. **assess**
f. **compile**	g. **contempt**	h. **defect**	i. **doctrine**	j. **dogmatic**

assess   1. You cannot always ___ a student's progress by looking just at his or her grades.

affluent   2. Many of the houses in ___ neighborhoods have burglar alarms.

alienate   3. Margo's parents' constant arguments began to ___ her from them.

contempt   4. When Jerry cheated on the exam and then bragged about it as well, Eva felt ___ for him.

compile   5. To ___ an encyclopedia takes many years.

doctrine   6. If you study the ___s of several religions, you may be surprised by the similarity of some of their teachings.

adhere   7. Something in a spider's thread makes the bugs it catches ___ to the web.

defect   8. Vivian was about to buy a red dress when she noticed a small ___: some threads were loose on the collar.

dogmatic   9. My boss has a(n) ___ way of running things—he wants workers to do exactly what he tells them, without asking any questions.

absurd   10. Dee thought Harry was ___ to do a rain dance on their dry front lawn— until she saw the sky blacken and lightning flash immediately afterward.

NOTE: Now check your answers to these questions by turning to page 176. Going over the answers carefully will help you prepare for the next two practices, for which answers are not given.

➤ *Sentence Check 2*

Using the answer lines provided, complete each item below with **two** words from the box. Use each word once.

assess
compile   1–2. To ___ a patient's health, a doctor must ___ a record that includes all the medical tests that have been given.

contempt
doctrine   3–4. I have ___ for any ___ that teaches hatred of groups having different principles and beliefs.

dogmatic
alienate   5–6. Stubborn, ___ parents who deny their children freedom to make some of their own decisions may eventually ___ those children. Helping children learn to think for themselves contributes to a healthy transition° from childhood to adulthood.

_____ *defect* _____   7–8. My little girl thought the roll of tape that is sticky on both sides had

_____ *adhere* _____   a(n) ___, but the tape is actually meant to ___ on both sides.

_____ *absurd* _____   9–10. It seems ___ that anyone should go hungry in a country as ___ as ours.

_____ *affluent* _____

➤ *Final Check:* Unacceptable Boyfriends

Here is a final opportunity for you to strengthen your knowledge of the ten words. First read the following selection carefully. Then fill in each blank with a word from the box at the top of the previous page. (Context clues will help you figure out which word goes in which blank.) Use each word once.

My conservative° father has never liked any of my boyfriends. He always seems determined to

find some (1)_____ *defect* _____ in them. His complaint against Victor was that "he wears

rhinestone earrings." Could Victor help it if he wasn't (2)_____ *affluent* _____ enough to

afford diamond earrings? My father (3)_____ *assess* _____(e)d Lance just as negatively. He

bluntly° claimed that Lance has the IQ of a tree. Obviously, this is a(n) (4)_____ *absurd* _____

accusation. The truth is that Lance strictly follows the (5)_____ *doctrine* _____ of a little-known

religion. The religion preaches, among other things, that followers must put smiles on the faces of

all people they see. But when Lance tried to make a smiley-face sticker (6)_____ *adhere* _____

to Dad's forehead, Dad definitely wasn't happy. His (7)_____ *contempt* _____ for Lance's

beliefs shows just how (8)_____ *dogmatic* _____ Dad is when it comes to religion—as far as he

is concerned, only his view counts.

Now my father is trying to (9)_____ *alienate* _____ me from my friend Joe Bob—he has

started to (10)_____ *compile* _____ a long list of Joe Bob's "faults." The first thing on my

father's list is Joe Bob's collection of poisonous snakes and insects. I acknowledge° that Joe Bob

is an unusual guy, but I don't think it's fair to hold his love of nature against him.

| *Scores* | Sentence Check 2 _____% | Final Check _____% |

Enter your scores above and in the vocabulary performance chart on the inside back cover of the book.

anti-	-less
bi-	phon
en-, em-	post-
graph, gram	spect
inter-	sub-

Ten Word Parts in Context

Figure out the meanings of the following ten word parts by looking *closely* and *carefully* at the context in which they appear. Then, in the space provided, write the letter of the meaning closest to that of each word part.

1 anti-

- **Antifreeze** prevents the water in a car radiator from freezing.
- Many students who disapproved of the United States' involvement in the Vietnam War took part in **antiwar** marches.

b The word part *anti-* means

a. for.   b. against.   c. two.

2 bi-

- In addition to the expected pair of wheels, a **bicycle** built for two also has two seats.
- "You can have only one wife at a time," Judge Graves told the **bigamist**, "not both at once."

a The word part *bi-* means

a. two.   b. look.   c. speech.

3 en-, em-

- A brief kiss, a quick **embrace**, and she was gone.

c The word part *en-* or *em-* means

- On the boss's door were two signs: "**Enter**" and "Exit."

a. sound.   b. below.   c. in, into.

4 graph, gram

- My little sister practices her handwriting so that if she becomes a famous dancer, her **autograph** will look good.
- The **diagram** in my biology book shows that, strange as it may seem, the earthworm has two hearts.

b The word part *-graph* or *-gram* means

a. under.   b. something written or drawn.   c. three.

5 inter-

- When my brother tries to speak while chewing gum, it's impossible to understand him without an **interpreter**.
- "Driving cross-country along the **interstate** highway was great," said Telly. "I got to eat in about twenty different states!"

b The word part *inter-* means

a. something written.   b. between.   c. under.

6 -less

- The mayor spoke sadly about the **homeless**, but he did nothing to build low-income housing.
- The Smiths' marriage was **loveless**. They stayed together for their children, but their constant fighting may have hurt the children more than a divorce would have.

a The word part *-less* means

a. without.   b. with.   c. look.

7 **phon**
- Alexander Graham Bell invented not only the **telephone** but also a kite that could carry a person.
- Whenever Wayne played the **saxophone**, dogs howled, cats screamed, and lovebirds got divorced.

b The word part *phon* means a. under. b. sound. c. watch.

8 **post-**
- Why are baseball games **postponed** because of a slight rain, but football games not called off even if it rains heavily?
- My playful sister included a **postscript** after her letter that said, "P.S. I don't have anything else to say."

c The word part *post-* means a. half. b. speech. c. after.

9 **spect**
- Detective Blake amazed everyone by **inspecting** the tuna casserole the thief was baking and then fishing the jewels out with a fork.
- **Spectators** at a tennis match tend to watch the ball, not the players.

b The word part *spect* means a. hear. b. look. c. not.

10 **sub-**
- Some people won't ride a **subway** because they fear being trapped underground.
- On the **submarine** ride at Disneyland, passengers can see models of such underwater life as seahorses and sharks.

a The word part *sub-* means a. under. b. new. c. over.

Matching Word Parts with Definitions

Following are definitions of the ten word parts. Clearly write or print each word part next to its definition. The sentences above and on the previous page will help you decide on the meaning of each word part.

1. _____*post-*_____ After

2. _____*-graph, -gram*_____ Something written or drawn

3. _____*anti-*_____ Against, acting against

4. _____*en-, em-*_____ Into, in

5. _____*sub-*_____ Under, below

6. _____*bi-*_____ Two

7. _____*inter-*_____ Between, among

8. _____*spect*_____ Look, watch

9. _____*-less*_____ Without

10. _____*phon*_____ Sound, speech

CAUTION: Do not go any further until you are sure the above answers are correct. Then you can use the definitions to help you in the following practices. Your goal is eventually to know the word parts well enough so that you don't need to check the definitions at all.

➤ *Sentence Check 1*

Using the answer line provided, complete each *italicized* word in the sentences below with the correct word part from the box. Use each word part once.

a. **anti-**	b. **bi-**	c. **en-, em-**	d. **graph, gram**	e. **inter-**
f. **-less**	g. **phon**	h. **post-**	i. **spect**	j. **sub-**

_____ spectacular _____   1. Out on the ocean, sunsets can be (. . . *acular*) ___ displays of color really worth seeing.

_____ phonetics _____   2. The French have trouble with English (. . . *etics*) ___, especially the sound of *er*, as in *murder* and *later.*

_____ interrupt _____   3. "We (. . . *rupt*) ___ this program to bring you a special news bulletin," the announcer said.

_____ enclosing _____   4. You can keep brown sugar moist by (. . . *closing*) ___ it in a container with a piece or two of apple.

_____ autobiography _____   5. In her (*autobio* . . . *y*) ___, *The Story of My Life*, Helen Keller tells how she was able to learn despite her blindness and deafness.

_____ antisocial _____   6. Clark was (. . . *social*) ___ in high school, but he became very outgoing in college.

_____ binoculars _____   7. Bird and animal watchers prefer rubber-coated (. . . *noculars*) ___ because they don't click and bang against trees or equipment.

_____ cordless _____   8. A (*cord* . . .) ___ phone allows a parent to talk to a caller while following a wandering child around the house.

_____ Postnatal _____   9. Prenatal care for birds means sitting on the eggs. (. . . *natal*) ___ care involves almost constant feeding during the day.

_____ submerge _____   10. When we saw what appeared to be a floating log (. . . *merge*) ___ and then slide under the water toward our canoe, we knew two things: one, it was no log; two, it wanted to eat us.

NOTE: Now check your answers to these questions by turning to page 176. Going over the answers carefully will help you prepare for the next two practices, for which answers are not given.

➤ *Sentence Check 2*

Using the answer lines provided, complete each *italicized* word in the sentences below with the correct word part from the box. Use each word part once.

_____ antiperspirant _____
_____ odorless _____   1–2. Because I'm allergic to all kinds of perfumes, my (. . . *perspirant*) ___ must be (*odor* . . .) ___.

_____ employee _____
_____ microphone _____   3–4. At the company luncheon, every new (. . . *ployee*) ___ was invited up to the (*micro* . . .) ___ to say a few introductory words.

_____ telegram _____   5–6. In Nazi Germany, every (*tele . . .*) ___ sent was (*in . . . ed*) ___ by
_____ inspected _____   Hitler's secret police, making it hard to keep secrets.

_____ interfered _____   7–8. No one (*. . . fered*) ___ with the mad scientist's plans because he
_____ subbasement _____   worked in a hidden lab in a(n) (*. . . basement*) ___, under the laundry
                                                 room in his basement.

_____ biweekly _____   9–10. I'm accustomed to being paid every two weeks, but my expected
_____ postdate _____   (*. . . weekly*) ___ check hasn't arrived yet, forcing me to (*. . . date*)
                                                 ___ a check to my landlord. I'm going to increase my savings, so that
                                                 I'll have ample° money to cover my bills the next time I'm paid late.

➤ *Final Check:* Coping with Snow

Here is a final opportunity for you to strengthen your knowledge of the ten word parts. First read the following selection carefully. Then complete each *italicized* word in the parentheses below with a word from the box at the top of the previous page. (Context clues will help you figure out which word part goes in which blank.) Use each word part once.

There are plenty of (*. . . joyable*) (1)_____ enjoyable _____ ways to keep your driveway

free of snow. For example, you might (*. . . vene*) (2)_____ intervene _____ between the

snow and the driveway by simply extending the roof of your house until it covers the entire drive.

Or you could paint the drive with (*. . . freeze*) (3)_____ antifreeze _____, so that snowflakes

will melt as soon as they land. Or, with just one quick (*tele . . . e*) (4)_____ telephone _____ call,

you could order a plowing service to come shovel you out. If there's only moderate° snow out

there, attaching a plow to the front of your (*. . . cycle*) (5)_____ bicycle _____ and pedaling

the snow away is another possibility. This method will provide you with plenty of leg exercise. At

the same time, you will make a(n) (*. . . acle*) (6)_____ spectacle _____ of yourself in front of

the neighborhood children, who can (*photo . . .*) (7)_____ photograph _____ you and keep the

pictures for possible blackmail later. Finally, since snow remains only in (*. . . freezing*)

(8)_____ subfreezing _____ temperatures, you can always (*. . . pone*) (9)_____ postpone _____

your actions until a later time—say, May or June. See? There's no reason to feel (*help . . .*)

(10)_____ helpless _____ just because a blizzard piles a foot of snow on your driveway.

| *Scores* | Sentence Check 2 _____% | Final Check _____% |

Enter your scores above and in the vocabulary performance chart on the inside back cover of the book.

UNIT TWO: Review

The box at the right lists twenty-five words from Unit Two. Using the clues at the bottom of the page, fill in these words to complete the puzzle that follows.

Word box:

absurd
affluent
ample
anonymous
arrogant
assess
chronic
compensate
conservative
contempt
denounce
derive
disclose
doctrine
donor
inhibit
optimist
prolong
prominent
recipient
remorse
superficial
supplement
tentative
transition

ACROSS

2. To add to, especially to make up for a lack
4. To pay or repay
5. To receive from a source; get
7. To evaluate; decide on the quality of or value of
9. To reveal; make known
10. Someone who expects a good outcome
11. Tending to resist change; favoring traditional values
15. Disrespect; a feeling that a person or thing is inferior
17. Very noticeable; obvious
18. To hold back; prevent
19. Ridiculous; opposed to common sense
21. A strong feeling of regret and guilt

DOWN

1. The strict teaching of a religious or political group
2. Lacking depth or meaning
3. Filled with self-importance; overly proud and vain
6. A change from one condition or location to another
7. Wealthy
8. More than enough; plenty of
11. Continuing; lasting a long time; constant
12. A person who receives
13. To openly condemn; express disapproval of
14. Written or given by an unknown person
16. Not definite; not final
17. To make something last longer
20. A person who gives or contributes

66

UNIT TWO: Test 1

PART A
Choose the word that best completes each item and write it in the space provided.

_____phobia_____ 1. My sister's ___ about snakes is so strong she actually faints if she sees one.

    a. phobia   b. doctrine   c. diversity   d. transition

_____defect_____ 2. In 1986, a small ___ in the space shuttle _Challenger_ caused it to explode.

    a. pretense   b. remorse   c. phobia   d. defect

_____absurd_____ 3. After you watch _Sesame Street_ for a while, you forget how ___ the enormous, saucer-eyed Big Bird really is.

    a. dogmatic   b. absurd   c. chronic   d. acute

_____anonymous_____ 4. Ronita does not like receiving ___ love letters. She wants to know who her admirers are.

    a. dogmatic   b. ample   c. moderate   d. anonymous

_____chronic_____ 5. Fred is a(n) ___ complainer—as soon as one problem is solved, he'll come up with another.

    a. affluent   b. prudent   c. moderate   d. chronic

_____surpassed_____ 6. I knew Jackie would do well in the polevault, but her wonderful performance ___ even my expectations.

    a. assessed   b. bestowed   c. surpassed   d. sustained

_____alienate_____ 7. I have to admire Mayor Moss for not being afraid to ___ some voters in order to do what he believes is right.

    a. prolong   b. verify   c. alienate   d. compile

_____prolong_____ 8. We made the difficult decision to let our mother's life end rather than ___ her suffering with artificial life-support systems.

    a. prolong   b. deter   c. verify   d. assess

_____derived_____ 9. We usually don't think about the fact that our books, newspapers, and wooden furniture are all ___ from trees.

    a. adhered   b. derived   c. disclosed   d. denounced

_____altered_____ 10. The new drug was pulled off the market when it was learned that researchers had ___ test results to make it look as if the drug were safe.

    a. altered   b. deterred   c. bestowed   d. prolonged

_____verify_____ 11. Since kids sometimes call in orders to pizza parlors as a joke, some pizza clerks now call back to ___ that each order is genuine.

    a. alter   b. verify   c. prolong   d. bestow

(Continues on next page)

_____transition_____ 12. At Gene's ten-year high-school reunion, he was struck by how many of his classmates seemed to have already made the ___ from a youthful to a middle-aged lifestyle.

     a. recipient   b. doctrine   c. transition   d. supplement

_____inhibit_____ 13. I can't imagine how actors play love scenes in front of the camera. Being watched by a film crew would certainly ___ my romantic feelings.

     a. bestow   b. inhibit   c. prolong   d. disclose

PART B

Write **C** if the italicized word is used **correctly**. Write **I** if the word is used **incorrectly**.

_I_ 14. The choir director arranged the children in *chronological* order, from shortest to tallest.

_C_ 15. After being the *recipient* of seven speeding tickets in one month, Marylee lost her license.

_I_ 16. Owen bragged that when he got rich he would buy his mom the most *moderate* diamond necklace in town. He wanted her to have the best.

_I_ 17. The twins are not only identical in appearance—they are *contrary* in their tastes and opinions as well.

_C_ 18. It's easy to find Dwight's house because of the *prominent* display of pink flamingos on the lawn.

_I_ 19. Goldie will never admit that she's been wrong about anything; she'll *concede* she was right to the bitter end.

_C_ 20. The soprano thrilled her audiences with her ability to *sustain* even the highest notes.

_C_ 21. Once he laid eyes on the mint-condition Corvette, nothing could *deter* Paolo from his goal of owning the car.

_C_ 22. Dad got Jen to the house for her surprise party on the *pretense* that she had left a jacket there.

_I_ 23. Whenever my boss makes a mistake, he blames someone else. He loves being the *scapegoat*.

_I_ 24. I'm a little angry at our neighbor Henry. I told him to take just a few tomatoes from our garden, not to *bestow* all the ripe ones.

_C_ 25. Knowing that the thieves would be back again, Luisa *conceived* a plan to leave a package of gift-wrapped garbage on the seat of her unlocked car.

Score (Number correct) _____ x 4 = _____ %

Enter your score above and in the vocabulary performance chart on the inside back cover of the book.

UNIT TWO: *Test 2*

PART A
Complete each item with a word from the box. Use each word once.

a. **adhere**	b. **affluent**	c. **arrogant**	d. **blunt**	e. **compensate**
f. **conservative**	g. **denounce**	h. **disclose**	i. **diversity**	j. **prudent**
k. **remorse**	l. **supplement**	m. **tentative**		

arrogant	1. I can't stand that ___ movie critic. He always speaks as if his reviews came directly from God.
affluent	2. Our family isn't ___ by American standards, but we're rich compared with people from many other countries.
blunt	3. Tom wouldn't take a hint, so Rebecca finally had to be ___ and say she just didn't want to go out with him.
adhere	4. Because of all the steam in our bathroom, the wallpaper there no longer ___s very well.
denounce	5. Prisoners of war may be tortured until they are willing to publicly ___ their own governments.
compensate	6. I hung my dress outside the dry-cleaning shop when the owner refused to ___ me for ruining it by running the colors together.
disclose	7. After I'd known Patty for years, she ___(e)d to me that the girl known as her little sister was actually her daughter.
prudent	8. After running out of gas on the way to the hospital for an emergency, I decided it was ___ to keep the tank full at all times.
conservative	9. The Monahans are famous in town for their ___ ways. They have gone to the same church, eaten in the same restaurants, and read the same newspaper for three generations.
tentative	10. The mugger's victim made a(n) ___ identification of her attacker from a photo. However, she said she would have to see him in person to be sure.
supplement	11. The young mother was still giving her toddler only milk. The doctor explained that it was time for her to ___ the child's diet with solid food.
diversity	12. I like our women's group because of its ___. Among the black, Hispanic and white members are grandmothers, young mothers, and young single women.
remorse	13. My brother expressed ___ for having stolen my slice of chocolate pie, but I think he was just trying to avoid getting into trouble with Dad.

(Continues on next page)

PART B
Write **C** if the italicized word is used **correctly**. Write **I** if the word is used **incorrectly**.

_I_ 14. When I had *ample* income, I had to watch my expenses very carefully.

_C_ 15. Mother warned us children to *refrain* from calling Uncle Milton "Mr. Pink Nose" to his face.

_C_ 16. Working in a jewelry store, Gail learned how to *assess* the value of a diamond.

_I_ 17. The high school seniors are *donors* of college scholarships, which they received from a generous local business owner.

_C_ 18. When my sister doubled over with sudden, *acute* pain, we suspected that her appendix had become infected.

_C_ 19. A central *doctrine* of Native American religions is respect for all living things.

_I_ 20. The first-grade teacher expressed her *contempt* for the responsible way her students behaved at the circus.

_C_ 21. The defense attorneys *compiled* a great deal of evidence showing that their client was innocent.

_I_ 22. Lucy was *apprehensive* about going to an Indian restaurant. She loved spicy Indian food more than anything.

_C_ 23. Janie is such an *optimist* that I like to be on her volleyball team—she always makes me feel I can win.

_I_ 24. The Chinese students were surprised by the American teachers' *dogmatic* style, which allowed for free discussion and debate with their students.

_I_ 25. Professor Wise gained his *superficial* knowledge of the mating and parenting habits of bedbugs through years of research.

Score   (Number correct) _____ x 4 = _____ %

Enter your score above and in the vocabulary performance chart on the inside back cover of the book.

UNIT TWO: Test 3

PART A
Complete each sentence in a way that clearly shows you understand the meaning of the **boldfaced** word. Take a minute to plan your answer before you write.

Example: I **altered** my appearance for the party by _____ *putting on a blond wig* _____.

1. When Peter gained ten pounds, his **blunt** friend Buddy remarked, " ____ *(Answers will vary.)* ____

   _____."

2. People who write letters to advice columns like to be **anonymous** because _____

   _____.

3. Harold was filled with **contempt** when he saw the big, strong man _____

   _____.

4. Fran decided to **supplement** her income by _____

   _____.

5. Mrs. Carson was the most **dogmatic** teacher in school. For example, she used to tell students, " ____

   _____

   _____."

6. If I suddenly discovered that I had become **affluent**, the first thing I would do is_____

   _____.

7. Pauline is so **arrogant** that when Greg told her she looked pretty, she replied, " _____

   _____."

8. While waiting for my turn for a haircut, I felt **apprehensive** because _____

   _____.

9. My friend Ted was very **prudent** about his money. For instance, _____

   _____.

10. When I served roast goose and a delicious peanut-butter pie for Thanksgiving dinner, my

    conservative brother said, " _____

    _____."

(Continues on next page)

PART B

After each **boldfaced** word are a *synonym* (a word that means the same as the boldfaced word), an *antonym* (a word that means the opposite of the boldfaced word), and a word that is neither. On the answer line, write the letter of the word that is the antonym.

Example: __a__ **endorse**   a. disapprove   b. support   c. compel

__c__ 11. **absurd**   a. lively   b. ridiculous   c. sensible

__c__ 12. **disclose**   a. reveal   b. shut   c. hide

__c__ 13. **arrogant**   a. conceited   b. skillful   c. humble

__b__ 14. **inhibit**   a. analyze   b. encourage   c. prevent

__a__ 15. **chronic**   a. temporary   b. continuing   c. extreme

PART C

Use five of the following ten words in sentences. Make it clear that you know the meaning of the word you use. Feel free to use the past tense or plural form of a word.

a. **adhere**	b. **assess**	c. **bestow**	d. **denounce**	e. **derive**
f. **diversity**	g. **phobia**	h. **pretense**	i. **remorse**	j. **surpass**

16. _____ *(Answers will vary.)* _____

_____

17. _____

_____

18. _____

_____

19. _____

_____

20. _____

_____

Score   (Number correct) _____ x 5 = _____ %

Enter your score above and in the vocabulary performance chart on the inside back cover of the book.

UNIT TWO: Test 4 (Word Parts)

PART A

Listed in the left-hand column below are ten common word parts, along with words in which the parts are used. In each blank, write in the letter of the correct definition on the right.

Word Parts		Examples	Definitions
_a_	1. **anti-**	antifreeze, antiwar	a. Against, acting against
_h_	2. **bi**	bicycle, bigamist	b. Without
_j_	3. **en-, em-**	embrace, enter	c. Look, watch
_d_	4. **graph, gram**	autograph, diagram	d. Something written or drawn
_i_	5. **inter-**	interpreter, interstate	e. Under, below
_b_	6. **-less**	homeless, loveless	f. Sound, speech
_f_	7. **phon**	telephone, saxophone	g. After
_g_	8. **post-**	postpone, postscript	h. Two
_c_	9. **spect**	inspecting, spectator	i. Between, among
_e_	10. **sub-**	subway, submarine	j. Into, in

PART B

Using the answer line provided, complete each *italicized* word in the sentences below with the correct word part from the box. Not every word part will be used.

a. **anti-**	b. **bi-**	c. **en-**	d. **graph**	e. **inter-**
f. **-less**	g. **phon**	h. **post-**	i. **spect**	j. **sub-**

postscript	11. "P. S." at the end of a note or letter stands for (. . . *script*) ___.
inspected	12. Our fifth-grade teacher, who tried to teach us good grooming, (*in . . . ed*) ___ our fingernails every Monday morning.
subway	13. In Moscow, taking a (. . . *way*) ___ is a pleasant experience. The underground stations have marble floors, stained glass, and statues.
wingless	14. The flying squirrel is actually (*wing . . .*) ___. It "flies" by spreading folds of skin as it glides short distances.
interact	15. Zulu tribesmen are not allowed to (. . . *act*) ___ directly with their mothers-in-law but may communicate with them only through another person.

(Continues on next page)

PART C

Use your knowledge of word parts to determine the meaning of the boldfaced words. On the answer line, write the letter of each meaning.

_b_   16. Drugs **enslave** people.

       a. arouse against slavery   b. put into slavery   c. come after slavery

_a_   17. My sister is learning **phonics** in her reading class.

       a. the study of speech sounds   b. the study of letters   c. the study of grammar

_c_   18. While my grandfather was in Europe, he sent my grandmother **aerograms**.

       a. tape-recorded messages   b. air-mail gifts   c. air-mail letters

_b_   19. The army experimented with several **antitank** weapons.

       a. with tanks   b. against tanks   c. in place of tanks

_b_   20. Twenty dollars seems a lot of money for a subscription to a magazine that is published **bimonthly**.

       a. every month   b. every two months   c. every three months

Score   (Number correct) _____ x 5 = _____ %

Enter your score above and in the vocabulary performance chart on the inside back cover of the book.

Unit Three

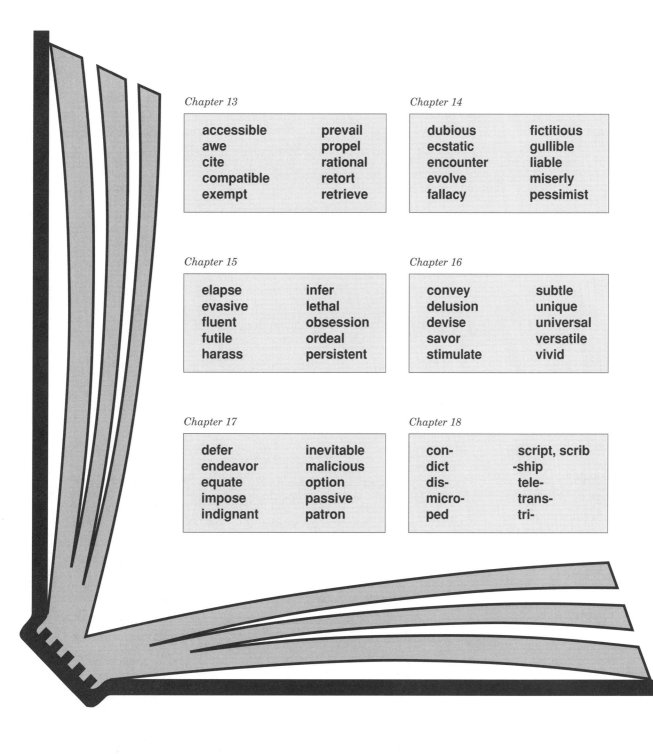

Chapter 13

accessible	prevail
awe	propel
cite	rational
compatible	retort
exempt	retrieve

Chapter 14

dubious	fictitious
ecstatic	gullible
encounter	liable
evolve	miserly
fallacy	pessimist

Chapter 15

elapse	infer
evasive	lethal
fluent	obsession
futile	ordeal
harass	persistent

Chapter 16

convey	subtle
delusion	unique
devise	universal
savor	versatile
stimulate	vivid

Chapter 17

defer	inevitable
endeavor	malicious
equate	option
impose	passive
indignant	patron

Chapter 18

con-	script, scrib
dict	-ship
dis-	tele-
micro-	trans-
ped	tri-

accessible	prevail
awe	propel
cite	rational
compatible	retort
exempt	retrieve

Ten Words in Context

In the space provided, write the letter of the meaning closest to that of each **boldfaced** word. Use the context of the sentences to help you figure out each word's meaning.

1 **accessible**
(ăk-sĕs′ə-bəl)
-*adjective*

- The department store was not **accessible** from her side of the road, so Kristin looked ahead for a U-turn.
- We always hung the candy canes on the Christmas tree's highest branches, where they weren't **accessible** to the younger children.

b *Accessible* means   a. good to look at.   b. within reach.   c. desirable.

2 **awe**
(ô)
-*noun*

- Frank and Donna have different types of idols. Although Frank greatly admires Michael Jordan, Donna is filled with **awe** for Mother Teresa.
- Sid is in **awe** of his gymnastics coach, whom he considers the greatest man he knows.

b *Awe* means   a. anger.   b. respect.   c. hope.

3 **cite**
(sīt)
-*verb*

- Jeff was embarrassed but pleased when the teacher **cited** his essay as an example of good writing.
- Tired of picking up after her sister, Janet **cited** examples of her sloppiness: "stacks of papers, piles of dirty clothes, and unwashed dishes."

b *Cite* means   a. to forget.   b. to mention.   c. to ignore.

4 **compatible**
(kəm-păt′ə-bəl)
-*adjective*

- My girlfriend and I weren't very **compatible**; whenever she wasn't angry with me, I was angry with her.
- Some sweet and salty foods are **compatible**: for example, chocolate-covered pretzels are yummy.

c *Compatible* means   a. well-known.   b. healthy.   c. in agreement.

5 **exempt**
(ĭg-zĕmpt′)
-*adjective*

- Since he had never been spanked, my little brother thought he was **exempt** from punishment — until he wrote on the walls in ink.
- Students with A averages were **exempt** from final exams, so the top three students went to the shore while the rest of us sweated it out on exam day.

a *Exempt* means   a. excused.   b. in fear.   c. hiding.

6 **prevail**
(prĭ-vāl′)
-*verb*

- Most Hollywood movies have a happy ending: good **prevails** over evil.
- Although Kennedy **prevailed** over Nixon in 1960, eight years later Nixon won the presidency.

a *Prevail* means   a. to win.   b. to watch.   c. to lose.

7 **propel**
(prə-pĕl′)
-*verb*

- My brother gave me a shove, which **propelled** me into the lake fully clothed.
- When the wind failed to **propel** the boat, we lowered the sails and turned on the motor.

b *Propel* means   a. to support.   b. to move forward.   c. to raise.

8 **rational**
(răsh′ə-nəl)
-*adjective*

- Mr. Tibbs isn't **rational**; in addition to believing he came from another planet, he does crazy things like shoveling snow in his pajamas.
- The belief that breaking a mirror brings seven years of bad luck isn't **rational**. The only bad luck it could really bring is stepping on a sharp piece of broken glass.

c *Rational* means   a. helpful.   b. kind.   c. reasonable.

9 **retort**
(rĭ-tôrt′)
-*noun*

- Sue, who is slender, boasted, "Thin is in." So Pat, who is heavy, gave this **retort**: "Well, fat is where it's at."
- When Shelley's balding boyfriend made fun of her new perm, her **retort** was, "Jealous?"

b *Retort* means   a. a wish.   b. an answer.   c. a fact.

10 **retrieve**
(rĭ-trēv′)
-*verb*

- My dog Floyd refuses to **retrieve** a thrown Frisbee. Instead of running to bring it back, he only tilts his head and gives me a questioning look.
- I can't **retrieve** my sweater from the library until tomorrow, since the library had closed by the time I realized the sweater was missing.

c *Retrieve* means   a. to remember.   b. to touch.   c. to get back.

Matching Words with Definitions

Following are definitions of the ten words. Clearly write or print each word next to its definition. The sentences above and on the previous page will help you decide on the meaning of each word.

1.	*rational*	Reasonable; logical
2.	*cite*	To mention in support of a point
3.	*retort*	A sharp or clever reply
4.	*propel*	To provide the force that moves something; to move something forward
5.	*accessible*	Easily reached or entered
6.	*retrieve*	To get (something) back
7.	*compatible*	Able to get along well together; combining well
8.	*prevail*	To win out; triumph
9.	*awe*	Great respect mixed with wonder and fear
10.	*exempt*	Free from some unpleasant duty or situation

CAUTION: Do not go any further until you are sure the above answers are correct. Then you can use the definitions to help you in the following practices. Your goal is eventually to know the words well enough so that you don't need to check the definitions at all.

➢ *Sentence Check 1*

Using the answer line provided, complete each item below with the correct word from the box. Use each word once.

a. **accessible**	b. **awe**	c. **cite**	d. **compatible**	e. **exempt**
f. **prevail**	g. **propel**	h. **rational**	i. **retort**	j. **retrieve**

prevail   1. When I go bowling with Joan, she usually wins, but I always ___ in Scrabble.

propel   2. Jet engines ___ a plane forward.

retrieve   3. I ran back to the ladies' room to ___ my purse, but someone had already taken it.

exempt   4. In the 1960s my brother was ___ from the draft because his vision is so poor.

accessible   5. The cabinet above the refrigerator was ___ to Janet but not to her roommate Mieko, who was much shorter.

awe   6. The general's uniform and medals filled Scott with ___. However, Marla, who knew the general personally, felt only disrespect for him.

compatible   7. My husband thinks everything combines well with peanut butter. He even thinks peanut butter and onions are ___ in a sandwich.

cite   8. When Bridget writes up her experiment, she will ___ similar studies by other researchers, to show that her results match theirs.

rational   9. Some people don't think in a(n) ___ way. Their thoughts are governed by emotion, not reason.

retort   10. There are at least two versions of the joke in which a customer complains that a fly is in his soup. The waiter's ___ is either "That's okay—there's no extra charge" or "Don't worry—he won't drink much."

NOTE: Now check your answers to these questions by turning to page 176. Going over the answers carefully will help you prepare for the next two practices, for which answers are not given.

➢ *Sentence Check 2*

Using the answer lines provided, complete each item below with **two** words from the box. Use each word once.

awe *prevail*   1–2. Tony was in ___ of his athletic friend Ben, who seemed to ___ in any contest of strength or speed.

cite *exempt*   3–4. The speaker told his high school audience, "I can ___ dozens of cases of adults who mistakenly thought they were ___ from the harm of cocaine. They all eventually lost their jobs and alienated° their families."

compatible *propel*   5–6. Keith and Sara's matchmaking friends were so sure they'd be ___ that they tried everything to ___ the two into each other's arms.

_____rational_____   7–8. The prudent° and ___ thing to do is to ask Michael to return your
_____retrieve_____   sweater before you sneak into his room to ___ it behind his back.

_____accessible_____ 9–10. When I complained to the landlord that the kitchen shelves were so
_____retort_____   high they were ___ only by ladder, his ___ was, "So get a ladder!"

➤ _Final Check:_ Our Headstrong Baby

Here is a final opportunity for you to strengthen your knowledge of the ten words. First read the following selection carefully. Then fill in each blank with a word from the box at the top of the previous page. (Context clues will help you figure out which word goes in which blank.) Use each word once.

Before our child was born, we truly believed we would be (1)_____exempt_____

from many of the restrictions of our friends who were parents. Being novices° at parenthood, we

were sure a baby and a nicely decorated home could be (2)_____compatible_____. We

thought we could just explain to the baby in a calm, (3)_____rational_____ manner that

certain objects in the house were not to be touched. But now we are parents, and our illusions°

about babies are gone. Now we are in (4)_____awe_____ of a tiny infant's amazing

abilities. We've learned that when an adult and a baby disagree, the baby will almost always

(5)_____prevail_____. We've learned, too, that a child who can't even crawl can

somehow (6)_____propel_____ its little body over to an object that attracts it. It took us

a while to admit defeat—we could (7)_____cite_____ examples of vases broken and

books chewed into pulp. But we finally gave up and realized it was up to us, not the baby, to avert°

daily destruction. We look at our formerly attractive house now and see that every surface which is

(8)_____accessible_____ to the baby has been cleared of everything but toys. So now, when

our childless friends laugh at us as we (9)_____retrieve_____ our belongings from the

uppermost shelves of the house, this is our (10)_____retort_____: "We'll listen to you

when you have a kid of your own."

Scores	Sentence Check 2 _____%	Final Check _____%

Enter your scores above and in the vocabulary performance chart on the inside back cover of the book.

dubious	fictitious
ecstatic	gullible
encounter	liable
evolve	miserly
fallacy	pessimist

Ten Words in Context

Circle the letter of the meaning closest to that of each **boldfaced** word. Use the context of the sentences to help you figure out each word's meaning.

1 dubious
(dōō′bē-əs)
-*adjective*

- Aretha lacked confidence in her math ability. Even after a long tutoring session, she was **dubious** about her ability to pass the geometry exam.
- Matt was **dubious** about graduate school as preparation for a career in clothing design. He felt work experience might be better.

_b_ *Dubious* means   a. certain.   b. unsure.   c. happy.

2 ecstatic
(ĭk-stăt′ĭk)
-*adjective*

- I wouldn't be just glad if I won the five-million-dollar lottery; I'd be absolutely **ecstatic**.
- The smallest thing, like an ice cream cone on a hot day, a train ride, or a ladybug in the grass, can make a child **ecstatic**.

_c_ *Ecstatic* means   a. active.   b. patient.   c. full of joy.

3 encounter
(ĕn-koun′tər)
-*verb*

- Strangely enough, I **encountered** my old boyfriend while I was on my honeymoon.
- I never expected to **encounter** anyone I knew at the crowded concert, but my friend Jeff sat just two rows in front of me.

_b_ *Encounter* means   a. to avoid.   b. to run into.   c. to go with.

4 evolve
(ĭ-vŏlv′)
-*verb*

- The women's club began as an informal get-together and then **evolved** into an educational and support group.
- How did the plan for a block party **evolve** into a citywide celebration?

_a_ *Evolve* means   a. to grow gradually.   b. to fall apart.   c. to shrink.

5 fallacy
(făl′ə-sē)
-*noun*

- It is a **fallacy** for people to think that they can drink and still manage to drive safely.
- To opponents of nuclear energy, the idea that nuclear power plants are safe for humans is a **fallacy**.

_b_ *Fallacy* means   a. a useful idea.   b. an error.   c. a goal.

6 fictitious
(fĭk-tĭsh′əs)
-*adjective*

- The characters in novels are usually totally **fictitious**, but some are based on real people.
- Violence in TV movies may frighten very young children, who have not learned the difference between true and **fictitious** events.

_a_ *Fictitious* means   a. unreal.   b. future.   c. active.

7 **gullible**
   (gŭl′ə-bəl)
   -*adjective*

   • Candace is so **gullible** that she believed me when I told her the White House is really yellow.
   • You might think I'm **gullible** enough to fall for that old line, but you can't fool me that easily.

   _c_ *Gullible* means   a. suspicious.   b. mean.   c. easily fooled.

8 **liable**
   (lī′ə-bəl)
   -*adjective*

   • If you lie to me once, I will think you're **liable** to lie to me again.
   • I'm **liable** to start smoking again if I take even one puff of a cigarette, so I'm careful not to give in even for a moment.

   _a_ *Liable* means   a. likely.   b. unable.   c. unlikely.

9 **miserly**
   (mī′zĕr-lē)
   -*adjective*

   • In *A Christmas Carol*, Scrooge at first hated to spend money, but he later regretted his **miserly** ways.
   • My rich uncle was so **miserly** that he never gave money to charity.

   _b_ *Miserly* means   a. lazy.   b. stingy.   c. bossy.

10 **pessimist**
   (pĕs′ə-mĭst)
   -*noun*

   • A **pessimist** can see a bad side to even the best situation.
   • My family is very balanced: my father sees the best in everything, but my mother is usually a **pessimist**.

   _b_ *Pessimist* means   a. a pest.   b. one who expects the worst.   c. one who is wise.

Matching Words with Definitions

Following are definitions of the ten words. Clearly write or print each word next to its definition. The sentences above and on the previous page will help you decide on the meaning of each word.

1. _fictitious_   Imaginary; made-up

2. _evolve_   To change gradually; develop

3. _encounter_   To meet, especially unexpectedly

4. _ecstatic_   In a state of great joy; overjoyed

5. _liable_   Likely

6. _pessimist_   A person who tends to see the bad side of things

7. _dubious_   Doubtful

8. _miserly_   Stingy and greedy

9. _fallacy_   A mistaken idea

10. _gullible_   Easily fooled

CAUTION: Do not go any further until you are sure the above answers are correct. Then you can use the definitions to help you in the following practices. Your goal is eventually to know the words well enough so that you don't need to check the definitions at all.

➤ *Sentence Check 1*

Using the answer line provided, complete each item below with the correct word from the box. Use each word once.

a. **dubious**	b. **ecstatic**	c. **encounter**	d. **evolve**	e. **fallacy**
f. **fictitious**	g. **gullible**	h. **liable**	i. **miserly**	j. **pessimist**

_____*miserly*_____ 1. Our grandmother is so ___ that all she ever gives us for Christmas is a card.

_____*liable*_____ 2. If you tease the dog too much, you're ___ to get bitten.

_____*fictitious*_____ 3. Many children have ___ friends—people or animals who exist only in their imaginations.

_____*dubious*_____ 4. I am ___ about Andrew's ability to do the job alone, but I am willing to give him a try.

_____*encounter*_____ 5. As I stepped into the garage, I ___(e)d a surprise visitor — a raccoon.

_____*ecstatic*_____ 6. "I'm ___," said Christine on the day of her divorce. "I wasn't this happy even on my wedding day."

_____*pessimist*_____ 7. Don't be such a(n) ___. Just because you did poorly on the midterm doesn't mean you won't pass the course.

_____*fallacy*_____ 8. It is a(n) ___ that reading without good light ruins your sight. Actually, reading in dim light does not harm your vision at all.

_____*gullible*_____ 9. Surprising Allen on his birthday was easy. He's so ___ that we knew he'd believe whatever story we told him.

_____*evolve*_____ 10. Interest in the environment has ___(e)d from a simple love of nature into a troubled awareness that we can destroy our world.

NOTE: Now check your answers to these questions by turning to page 176. Going over the answers carefully will help you prepare for the next two practices, for which answers are not given.

➤ *Sentence Check 2*

Using the answer lines provided, complete each item below with **two** words from the box. Use each word once.

_____*encounter*_____
_____*ecstatic*_____ 1–2. When my sister visited California, she ___(e)d Denzel Washington in a department store. Despite feelings of awe°, she managed to get up enough nerve to get his autograph, and she has been ___ ever since.

_____*gullible*_____
_____*fictitious*_____ 3–4. Angel is so ___ that her friends often tell her totally ___ stories and then tease her about believing them.

_____*miserly*_____
_____*liable*_____ 5–6. A ___ person is ___ to end up with lots of money and few friends.

_____ *pessimist* _____

_____ *fallacy* _____

7–8. An extreme ___ believes that bad luck can't be escaped and that it is a ___ to expect good luck. If such a person were the recipient° of a million dollars, he or she would complain about the taxes.

_____ *dubious* _____

_____ *evolve* _____

9–10. At first I was ___ about the prospects° of our school's basketball team; I did not think that they would win even one game. But as the season progressed, the team surpassed° all my expectations and ___(e)d into championship material.

➤ *Final Check:* Mr. Perfect?

Here is a final opportunity for you to strengthen your knowledge of the ten words. First read the following selection carefully. Then fill in each blank with a word from the box at the top of the previous page. (Context clues will help you figure out which word goes in which blank.) Use each word once.

Kathy was (1)_____ *ecstatic* _____ as she told me that she had (2)_____ *encounter* _____(e)d the "perfect man," as she called him. But I was (3)_____ *dubious* _____ right from the start. Contrary° to Kathy's view, my opinion is that "perfection" is a (4)_____ *fallacy* _____. Nobody I ever met was perfect—especially guys I've met in bars. I must admit that because of some of my experiences in bars over the years, I am (5)_____ *liable* _____ to be more of a (6)_____ *pessimist* _____ than most on this subject. One guy I met was so (7)_____ *miserly* _____ that he never left a tip at a restaurant. Another was addicted to sausages. He ate sausages for breakfast, lunch, and dinner. His strange eating habits alienated° me, and our relationship quickly (8)_____ *evolve* _____(e)d from bad to "wurst." Then there were all of those fellows who sort of forgot to disclose° that they were sort of married until we'd been seeing each other for months. As it turned out, they told me so many (9)_____ *fictitious* _____ details that they should have been novelists. So I am apprehensive° about encouraging Kathy, who is so (10)_____ *gullible* _____ that she believes anything anyone says. I can't wait to meet Mr. Perfect. He's probably either an ax murderer or a married man. And I'm not sure which is worse.

Scores	Sentence Check 2 _____ %	Final Check _____ %

Enter your scores above and in the vocabulary performance chart on the inside back cover of the book.

CHAPTER

15

elapse	infer
evasive	lethal
fluent	obsession
futile	ordeal
harass	persistent

Ten Words in Context

In the space provided, write the letter of the meaning closest to that of each **boldfaced** word. Use the context of the sentences to help you figure out each word's meaning.

1 elapse
(ĭ-lăps′)
-*verb*

- When I'm busy with work I enjoy, the hours seem to **elapse** quickly.
- Although four years had **elapsed** since I last saw Marian, we talked as if we'd never parted.

c Elapse means   a. to develop.   b. to go back.   c. to go by.

2 evasive
(ĭ-vā′sĭv)
-*adjective*

- The Rothmans worried that their son was hiding something when he became **evasive** about where he had been and what he'd been doing.
- We didn't want anyone at school to know our father was in jail, so we were **evasive** about him, saying only, "He has to be away for a while."

b Evasive means   a. truthful.   b. indefinite.   c. detailed.

3 fluent
(flōō′ənt)
-*adjective*

- To work in a foreign country, it helps to be **fluent** in its language.
- Jenna wanted to hear what was wrong with her car in simple, everyday words. She was not **fluent** in the language of auto mechanics.

c Fluent means   a. able to remember.   b. able to teach.   c. able to express oneself.

4 futile
(fyōōt′l)
-*adjective*

- My mother is so stubborn that once she has made a decision, it is **futile** to try to change her mind.
- I'm convinced that washing machines eat socks, so it is **futile** to try and find matching pairs in a load of clean laundry.

a Futile means   a. hopeless.   b. easy.   c. useful.

5 harass
(hə-răs′)
-*verb*

- A few students in the cafeteria like to **harass** everyone else by frequently clinking their silverware and stamping their feet.
- Sometimes it doesn't help to **harass** people about quitting smoking. Bothering them all the time may make them resist quitting.

b Harass means   a. to injure.   b. to annoy.   c. to please.

6 infer
(ĭn-fûr′)
-*verb*

- The fact that the old man left his fortune to strangers led us to **infer** he was not fond of his children.
- Since you went hiking on Super Bowl Sunday, I **inferred** that you were not a football fan.

a Infer means   a. to conclude.   b. to forget.   c. to conceal.

7 **lethal**
(lē′thəl)
-adjective

- My father is not alive today because of a **lethal** combination of driving and drinking.
- Jake is so good at karate that his hands are **lethal** weapons. Because he realizes he could kill somebody, he wouldn't use karate lightly.

b *Lethal* means   a. rare.   b. deadly.   c. hopeful.

8 **obsession**
(əb-sĕsh′ən)
-noun

- Psychologists help people troubled by **obsessions** to gain control over their thinking, so they are not bothered by the same thoughts over and over.
- Going to the racetrack was at first just a hobby. But the track has become such an **obsession** that I can't seem to stop going there.

c *Obsession* means   a. a helpful habit.   b. a possession.   c. a constant thought.

9 **ordeal**
(ôr-dēl′)
-noun

- Even if you are in good physical condition, running cross-country is an **ordeal**.
- Hannah came out of the difficult three-hour test, sighed, and said, "What an **ordeal**. I'm worn out."

c *Ordeal* means   a. a welcome event.   b. a sure success.   c. a difficult challenge.

10 **persistent**
(pər-sĭs′tənt)
-adjective

- At first Tony wouldn't go out with Lola, but she was **persistent** in asking him. Now they're engaged.
- I am a very **persistent** salesman. I work with customers for as long as it takes for them to buy something.

a *Persistent* means   a. stubborn.   b. useless.   c. late.

Matching Words with Definitions

Following are definitions of the ten words. Clearly write or print each word next to its definition. The sentences above and on the previous page will help you decide on the meaning of each word.

1. _____*infer*_____   To draw a conclusion from evidence

2. _____*obsession*_____   An idea or feeling, often unreasonable, which completely fills someone's mind

3. _____*ordeal*_____   A very difficult or painful experience

4. _____*evasive*_____   Deliberately unclear

5. _____*futile*_____   Useless; unable to succeed

6. _____*lethal*_____   Able to cause death; deadly

7. _____*persistent*_____   Refusing to quit; stubbornly continuing

8. _____*elapse*_____   To pass or slip by (usually said of time)

9. _____*fluent*_____   Able to express oneself with skill and ease

10. _____*harass*_____   To constantly irritate or disturb; bother

CAUTION: Do not go any further until you are sure the above answers are correct. Then you can use the definitions to help you in the following practices. Your goal is eventually to know the words well enough so that you don't need to check the definitions at all.

➤ *Sentence Check 1*

Using the answer line provided, complete each item below with the correct word from the box. Use each word once.

a. **elapse**	b. **evasive**	c. **fluent**	d. **futile**	e. **harass**
f. **infer**	g. **lethal**	h. **obsession**	i. **ordeal**	j. **persistent**

fluent 1. Roger knew a few Chinese phrases, but he was not ___ enough in Chinese to carry on a conversation.

harass 2. Photographers ___(e)d the movie star, photographing her even on a private beach.

obsession 3. When I'm on a diet, eating pizza becomes an ___ for me.

evasive 4. Reporters tried to pin the president down on his plan to rescue the hostages, but he always gave a(n) ___ answer.

elapse 5. After ten seconds ___, a bell rings, and the game-show host reads the next question.

lethal 6. Selling drugs can be a(n) ___ occupation—there is almost one drug-related murder a day in Philadelphia alone.

ordeal 7. Going to the veterinarian is a real ___ for our dog, who begins to shiver in fear at the sight of the vet's office.

futile 8. It is ___ to try to have a conversation with Manny when a football game is on television because his eyes are glued to the set.

persistent 9. Carlos had to work full-time to support his family, but he still earned his college degree by being ___ in his studies even when he was busy or tired.

infer 10. It was easy for Professor Anderson to ___ that one of the students had copied the other's paper—both had the same wording in several paragraphs.

NOTE: Now check your answers to these questions by turning to page 176. Going over the answers carefully will help you prepare for the next two practices, for which answers are not given.

➤ *Sentence Check 2*

Using the answer lines provided, complete each item below with **two** words from the box. Use each word once.

obsession
lethal 1–2. Wild mushrooms were an ___ of my aunt, who picked and ate them whenever possible. Unfortunately, her abnormal interest proved ___, for she died after a meal of poisonous creamed mushrooms on toast.

evasive
infer 3–4. The student hesitated and then gave a vague answer. "From your ___ answer," said the teacher, "I ___ that you haven't studied the chapter. In the future, maybe you could put a few minutes of homework on your daily agenda°."

_____elapse_____ 5–6. Five days ___(e)d before the forest fire was put out. It was an especially
_____ordeal_____ difficult ___ for the firefighters, who had to get by on very little sleep.

_____persistent_____ 7–8. You must be ___ in learning a language if you wish to become ___ in
_____fluent_____ it.

_____harass_____ 9–10. Cats on my street have learned they can safely ___ the dog chained in my
_____futile_____ neighbor's yard. And they derive° much pleasure from doing so. The poor
dog, however, hasn't seemed to learn that it is ___ to threaten the cats.

➤ _Final Check:_ A Narrow Escape

Here is a final opportunity for you to strengthen your knowledge of the ten words. First read the following selection carefully. Then fill in each blank with a word from the box at the top of the previous page. (Context clues will help you figure out which word goes in which blank.) Use each word once.

"They're going to hurt us or kill us. They're going to hurt us or kill us." The gruesome° thought had become an (1)_____obsession_____—I could think of nothing else. When Sharon and I hopped into the truck to hitch a ride toward Frankfurt, Germany, we were delighted these two truck drivers were so friendly. Although we were not (2)_____fluent_____ in their language (we couldn't even figure out what language they were speaking!), they knew a little English. So we could (3)_____infer_____ from their words and motions that they would take us to Frankfurt after they delivered a package. But then they drove around for a long time and couldn't seem to make their delivery. Hours (4)_____elapse_____(e)d, and we became annoyed. We began to be dubious° that there really was a delivery, but since we were naive° about such men, it still hadn't occurred to us to be afraid. We asked to be let out so we could get another ride. The men apologized for the delay and were (5)_____persistent_____ in repeating their promise to get us to Frankfurt. But they became more and more (6)_____evasive_____ about exactly when this would occur. Although it was dark and very late, we finally decided it was important just to get out of that truck, so we asked to be dropped off. Instead, they drove to an empty warehouse outside of town. The driver took out a long knife and said, "You sleep here." That's when I knew they would hurt us badly or kill us. I cried, "Oh, no, thank you, we'll get out NOW!" and jumped for the door handle. But my effort was (7)_____futile_____; the men blocked our exit. They began to (8)_____harass_____ us about staying with them. The knife was a(n) (9)_____lethal_____ weapon, but even without it they could easily have killed us. I just sat there shaking and Sharon sobbed and moaned and cried. Suddenly, one of the men threw up his hands and yelled, "OUT." He didn't have to say it twice. We flew out of that truck and back to town. We could hardly believe our (10)_____ordeal_____ was over and that we were still around to tell the tale.

Scores	Sentence Check 2 _____%	Final Check _____%

Enter your scores above and in the vocabulary performance chart on the inside back cover of the book.

CHAPTER

16

convey	subtle
delusion	unique
devise	universal
savor	versatile
stimulate	vivid

Ten Words in Context

In the space provided, write the letter of the meaning closest to that of each **boldfaced** word. Use the context of the sentences to help you figure out each word's meaning.

1 **convey**
(kən-vā′)
-verb

- Using sign language, chimpanzees can **convey** such ideas as "Candy sweet" and "Give me hug."
- On my parents' twenty-fifth wedding anniversary, I sent a telegram to **convey** my congratulations and love.

_c_ *Convey* means   a. to think of.   b. to prevent.   c. to communicate.

2 **delusion**
(dĭ-lo͞o′zhən)
-noun

- Alex clings to the **delusion** of being in total control even when drunk. In reality, he then lacks both judgment and muscle control.
- Quincy holds the **delusion** that money is everything. Sadly, in seeking financial success, he neglects what is truly important, such as family and friends.

_b_ *Delusion* means   a. pleasure.   b. misbelief.   c. action.

3 **devise**
(dĭ-vīz′)
-verb

- In the 1880s an American woman **devised** a machine that sprayed dinnerware with hot, soapy water—the first automatic dishwasher.
- The police had **devised** a plan to catch the thief, but he escaped through the freight elevator.

_a_ *Devise* means   a. to create.   b. to forget.   c. to carry.

4 **savor**
(sā′vər)
-verb

- Katie **savored** the candy bar, eating it bit by bit so that the pleasure would last as long as possible.
- Given a rare chance to enjoy the beach, I **savored** every moment in the warm sun.

_b_ *Savor* means   a. to save for later.   b. to enjoy.   c. to ignore.

5 **stimulate**
(stĭm′yə-lāt′)
-verb

- The teacher hoped to **stimulate** her students' interest in reading by choosing books that related to their own lives.
- I tried to **stimulate** my sick rabbit's appetite by offering him choice bits of carrots and celery.

_a_ *Stimulate* means   a. to make active.   b. to recognize.   c. to discourage.

6 **subtle**
(sŭt′l)
-adjective

- Animal actors are trained to respond to human signals too **subtle** to be noticed by the audience.
- Although Yasmin was born in Alabama, she has lived in New York for many years. As a result, her Southern accent is so **subtle** that some of her friends don't even notice it.

_c_ *Subtle* means   a. obvious.   b. peaceful.   c. slight.

7 **unique**
(yoo-nēk′)
-*adjective*

- Any live musical performance is **unique**—the music will never again be played in exactly the same way.
- My talents are **unique** in my family. For example, I'm the only one who can whistle through my nose.

_c_ *Unique* means   a. active.   b. hardly noticeable.   c. one of a kind.

8 **universal**
(yoo′nə-vûr′səl)
-*adjective*

- The United Nations was founded to advance **universal** freedom and peace.
- The film had **universal** success—it was a hit in all parts of the United States and in other countries as well.

_b_ *Universal* means   a. limited.   b. throughout the world.   c. throughout time.

9 **versatile**
(vûr′sə-təl)
-*adjective*

- My new computer is **versatile**. It can balance my checkbook, do word processing, keep tax records, and play against me in chess.
- Edie is the most **versatile** person I know: she paints, sings, does gymnastics, and is a math whiz.

_a_ *Versatile* means   a. having many abilities.   b. boring.   c. out of control.

10 **vivid**
(vĭv′ĭd)
-*adjective*

- To make the living room bright and dramatic, we decorated it in **vivid** shades of red.
- At funerals, most people wear black or dark gray clothing with little or no **vivid** color.

_b_ *Vivid* means   a. dull.   b. bright.   c. pale.

Matching Words with Definitions

Following are definitions of the ten words. Clearly write or print each word next to its definition. The sentences above and on the previous page will help you decide on the meaning of each word.

1. _____ *unique* _____   Unlike any other; one of a kind

2. _____ *devise* _____   To invent; think up; create

3. _____ *vivid* _____   Bright; brightly colored; striking

4. _____ *subtle* _____   Hardly noticeable; not obvious

5. _____ *convey* _____   To communicate; make known

6. _____ *stimulate* _____   To cause to become active or more active; arouse

7. _____ *universal* _____   Worldwide; widespread

8. _____ *savor* _____   To taste or smell with pleasure; to appreciate fully

9. _____ *delusion* _____   A false opinion or belief

10. _____ *versatile* _____   Able to do many things or serve many purposes well

CAUTION: Do not go any further until you are sure the above answers are correct. Then you can use the definitions to help you in the following practices. Your goal is eventually to know the words well enough so that you don't need to check the definitions at all.

➤ *Sentence Check 1*

Using the answer line provided, complete each item below with the correct word from the box. Use each word once.

a. **convey**	b. **delusion**	c. **devise**	d. **savor**	e. **stimulate**
f. **subtle**	g. **unique**	h. **universal**	i. **versatile**	j. **vivid**

devise   1. The chimp ___(e)d a way of reaching the banana that hung from the ceiling. She piled one box on top of another and climbed up.

universal   2. The "terrible twos" is a ___ stage of childhood. In every culture, children start demanding independence at about this age.

savor   3. Breathing deeply, I ___(e)d my favorite summer smell—freshly-cut grass.

subtle   4. Pam's eyes blinked a ___ message that only her husband saw: "I think we should get ready to leave before it gets any later."

vivid   5. The painting, with its bright stripes of shocking pink, green, and yellow, was so ___ that it glowed even in dim light.

stimulate   6. Even if Mr. Pierce sang his lecture while dancing on his desk, he couldn't ___ my interest in geology. To me, it's the most boring of subjects.

convey   7. When Edward saw the Grand Canyon, he made no attempt to describe it on a postcard. He felt that the glories of this natural wonder were too amazing to ___ in words.

delusion   8. "I thought she loved me, but it was just a ___," said Lawrence. "She was just a good friend."

unique   9. This Egyptian bracelet is ___ since no other bracelet in the world is made with the same combination of gems and precious metals.

versatile   10. From a child's point of view, a simple brown box is very ___. It can be a dollhouse, a bucket, a desk, or even a funny hat.

NOTE: Now check your answers to these questions by turning to page 176. Going over the answers carefully will help you prepare for the next two practices, for which answers are not given.

➤ *Sentence Check 2*

Using the answer lines provided, complete each item below with **two** words from the box. Use each word once.

convey
versatile   1–2. When Jill applies for a job, it will be to her advantage to ___ to interviewers just how ___ she is. Employers will welcome her many different skills.

savor
unique   3–4. I ___ the time I have alone with my brother, who is unlike anyone else. He has a ___ way of looking at things.

_____devise_____   5–6. I wish someone would ___ a way to ___ my children's appetites so
_____stimulate_____   they will feel hungry for something besides pizza and peanut butter.

_____vivid_____   7–8. Rosa enjoys wearing ___ colors, like red and purple, but I prefer more
_____subtle_____   ___ shades, such as pale pinks and blues.

_____universal_____   9–10. Denny truly believes that ___ peace will occur during his lifetime. Being
_____delusion_____   a pessimist°, I think that the possibility of world harmony is a ___.

➤ _Final Check:_ The Power of Advertising

Here is a final opportunity for you to strengthen your knowledge of the ten words. First read the following selection carefully. Then fill in each blank with a word from the box at the top of the previous page. (Context clues will help you figure out which word goes in which blank.) Use each word once.

I am convinced that good advertising agencies could sell people last week's garbage. Being masters of propaganda°, they make everything sound good. Using evasive° language, advertisers make such vague but impressive statements as "Professionals recommend our skin creams." (The careful consumer will ask, "Professionals in what field?") The agencies are also skilled at using richly appealing images. For example, newspaper ads never sell "brightly colored towels." Instead they sell "petal-soft bath sheets in a variety of (1)_____vivid_____ rainbow colors." Perfumes in ads don't make you "smell good"; they "invite you to please that special man in your life with this (2)_____subtle_____ yet unmistakable odor of tea roses." Food ads (3)_____stimulate_____ your appetite by offering "a sauce carefully blended to produce an unforgettable taste that you and your guests will (4)_____savor_____." Clothing ads (5)_____convey_____ the idea that if you wear a particular suit or dress, you will be classier than the next person. Other ads, such as those for computers, tell you how (6)_____versatile_____ their products will make you, suggesting that they will give you more skills than others have. Advertisements must have (7)_____universal_____ appeal to attract millions of people. Yet they must also persuade all those people to accept the (8)_____delusion_____ that they will be (9)_____unique_____ if they buy a particular product. Yes, I bet an advertising agency _could_ sell last week's garbage to gullible° people. The agency would simply (10)_____devise_____ an ad saying, "Nowhere else can you find a gift with so powerful an aroma that it overflows with bittersweet memories of yesterday, yet hints that it will grow stronger with each passing day."

Scores	Sentence Check 2 _____%	Final Check _____%

Enter your scores above and in the vocabulary performance chart on the inside back cover of the book.

defer	inevitable
endeavor	malicious
equate	option
impose	passive
indignant	patron

Ten Words in Context

In the space provided, write the letter of the meaning closest to that of each **boldfaced** word. Use the context of the sentences to help you figure out each word's meaning.

1 **defer**
(dĭ-fûr')
-verb

- The children showed great respect for their grandmother and **deferred** to her every wish.
- When it comes to fixing cars, I **defer** to my son's judgment. He knows much more about auto mechanics than I do.

b *Defer* means   a. to object.   b. to give in.   c. to avoid.

2 **endeavor**
(ĕn-dĕv'ər)
-verb

- Becky **endeavored** to raise money for Christmas presents by selling candy and cookies door to door.
- Your company would be wise to hire Jesse. He will **endeavor** to do his best at whatever jobs you give him.

a *Endeavor* means   a. to try.   b. to pretend.   c. to step aside.

3 **equate**
(ĭ-kwāt')
-verb

- It would be a mistake to **equate** the two teams just because they both have perfect records. One team has played much stronger opponents.
- Don't **equate** all homework assignments with busywork. Homework can increase one's understanding of a subject.

b *Equate* means   a. to exchange.   b. to consider to be the same.   c. to enjoy.

4 **impose**
(ĭm-pōz')
-verb

- I'd rather rent a car for the trip than **impose** on my girlfriend by borrowing her car.
- Roy is always asking favors, yet people never seem to notice how much he **imposes** on them.

a *Impose* means   a. to selfishly bother.   b. to improve.   c. to spy.

5 **indignant**
(ĭn-dĭg'nənt)
-adjective

- My mother becomes **indignant** when she sees parents treat their children with disrespect.
- When she was falsely accused of stealing the gold chain, the student became very **indignant**.

a *Indignant* means   a. angry.   b. patient.   c. amused.

6 **inevitable**
(ĭn-ĕv'ĭ-tə-bəl)
-adjective

- I am such a chocoholic that if you put a brownie in front of me, it is **inevitable** that I will eat it.
- We try so hard to look and stay young, but aging is **inevitable**.

c *Inevitable* means   a. unlikely.   b. surprising.   c. certain.

7 **malicious**
(mă-lĭsh′əs)
-adjective

- Bullies are **malicious**—they take pleasure in hurting others.
- Rachel loves **malicious** gossip. The more spiteful it is, the more she likes it, and the more likely she is to repeat it.

a Malicious means
a. mean.
b. ambitious.
c. common.

8 **option**
(ŏp′shən)
-noun

- When the mugger said to me, "Give me your wallet or I'll kill you," I didn't like either **option**.
- Harry thinks a multiple-choice test allows him to choose more than one **option**.

c Option means
a. opinion.
b. advantage.
c. choice.

9 **passive**
(păs′ĭv)
-adjective

- Taylor is very **passive**. He waits for things to happen instead of making them happen.
- Students learn more when they take part in class discussions instead of simply being **passive** listeners.

b Passive means
a. insincere.
b. inactive.
c. flexible.

10 **patron**
(pā′trən)
-noun

- The punk-rock star was a good **patron** of the beauty shop. She came in at least once a week to change her hair color.
- Many of the diner's **patrons** were stagehands who worked at the theater across the street.

c Patron means
a. an advertiser.
b. an owner.
c. a customer.

Matching Words with Definitions

Following are definitions of the ten words. Clearly write or print each word next to its definition. The sentences above and on the previous page will help you decide on the meaning of each word.

1. _____ option _____   A choice

2. _____ impose _____   To take unfair advantage of

3. _____ passive _____   Being acted upon without acting in return

4. _____ inevitable _____   Sure to happen; unavoidable

5. _____ equate _____   To consider to be equal, the same, or similar

6. _____ endeavor _____   To make a serious effort; to attempt

7. _____ indignant _____   Angry because of some insult or injustice

8. _____ patron _____   A customer, especially a steady one

9. _____ malicious _____   Showing great ill will; mean; deliberately harmful

10. _____ defer _____   To give in to someone else's wishes or judgment; yield out of respect

CAUTION: Do not go any further until you are sure the above answers are correct. Then you can use the definitions to help you in the following practices. Your goal is eventually to know the words well enough so that you don't need to check the definitions at all.

➤ *Sentence Check 1*

Using the answer line provided, complete each item below with the correct word from the box. Use each word once.

| a. **defer** | b. **endeavor** | c. **equate** | d. **impose** | e. **indignant** |
| f. **inevitable** | g. **malicious** | h. **option** | i. **passive** | j. **patron** |

_____*inevitable*_____ 1. When rats are crowded together, it's ___ they will fight with each other.

_____*option*_____ 2. I have only two ___s at work: I can do what my boss asks, or I can be fired.

_____*equate*_____ 3. In our society, we too often ___ happiness with money.

_____*passive*_____ 4. Mort isn't a(n) ___ football fan. He actively participates by jumping out of his seat and yelling until he's hoarse.

_____*patron*_____ 5. I was the store's most loyal ___ until new management raised the prices, and then I started shopping elsewhere.

_____*malicious*_____ 6. Heidi is so ___ that she makes up lies to ruin other people's reputations.

_____*impose*_____ 7. "I don't want to ___ on you," Scott said, "but if you're going to the post office, would you get me some stamps?"

_____*indignant*_____ 8. When his wife accused him of never helping around the house, Mac was ___. Hadn't he just built a deck off the kitchen?

_____*defer*_____ 9. Our instructor doesn't expect us to ___ to his opinions just because he's the teacher; he wants us to think for ourselves.

_____*endeavor*_____ 10. Many climbers who have ___(e)d to reach the top of Mount Everest have died on the way.

NOTE: Now check your answers to these questions by turning to page 176. Going over the answers carefully will help you prepare for the next two practices, for which answers are not given.

➤ *Sentence Check 2*

Using the answer lines provided, complete each item below with **two** words from the box. Use each word once.

_____*Indignant*_____
_____*equate*_____ 1–2. ___ that the boys had thrown rocks at the monkeys and yelled at them, the zookeeper said, "Don't ___ being an animal with having no feelings." Feeling remorse°, the boys later wrote a note of apology.

_____*patron*_____
_____*endeavor*_____ 3–4. Rita, a(n) ___ of Angelo's restaurant for several years, has ___(e)d without success to copy Angelo's delicious spaghetti sauce. Now she has given up. "I've learned it is futile° even to try," she says.

_____*passive*_____
_____*impose*_____ 5–6. "If you remain so ___ that you don't object when Jean takes advantage of you, she'll just ___ on you more and more," my friend warned.

_____ _inevitable_ _____ 7–8. Since Sam's family is so poor, it seems ___ he'll work full-time as soon
_____ _option_ _____ as he finishes high school. He won't have the ___ of going to college
right away. However, he plans to be prudent° in handling the money
he'll earn and then enroll in college in a couple of years.

_____ _malicious_ _____ 9–10. Jerome is so ___ that he goes out of his way to hurt anyone who won't
_____ _defer_ _____ ___ to his wishes. I have great contempt° for people who are that mean
and self-centered.

➤ _Final Check:_ Waiter

Here is a final opportunity for you to strengthen your knowledge of the ten words. First read the following selection carefully. Then fill in each blank with a word from the box at the top of the previous page. (Context clues will help you figure out which word goes in which blank.) Use each word once.

The loud voice of the young man at the next table startled me. He was (1)_____ _indignant_ _____ about some undeserved criticism the waiter had received. He said to the waiter, "Why did you just stand there and let that woman denounce° you like that without sticking up for yourself? You were like a(n) (2)_____ _passive_ _____ little child."

"I beg your pardon, sir," the waiter answered. "That woman is a(n) (3)_____ _patron_ _____ of this restaurant. I (4)_____ _endeavor_ _____ to treat our customers with respect."

"Even those who (5)_____ _impose_ _____ on you by being as demanding as that woman was? Even those who think they're better than you because you're waiting on them?"

"You seem to (6)_____ _equate_ _____ my polite manner with weakness," the waiter answered. "I don't like rude customers, but they're part of a waiter's territory. Standing up publicly to the woman may seem like a smart move to you, but it would have made two things (7)_____ _inevitable_ _____: an ugly scene and the loss of my job."

"But you have no (8)_____ _option_ _____," the customer insisted. "You can't let people step on you, ever—especially when they're being (9)_____ _malicious_ _____, giving you a hard time for no good reason."

"You're giving me just as hard a time as that woman did," was the waiter's retort°. "Why should I (10) _____ _defer_ _____ to your opinion and not hers?"

Scores   Sentence Check 2 _____ %   Final Check _____ %

Enter your scores above and in the vocabulary performance chart on the inside back cover of the book.

con-	script, scrib
dict	-ship
dis-	tele-
micro-	trans-
ped	tri-

Ten Word Parts in Context

Figure out the meanings of the following ten word parts by looking *closely* and *carefully* at the context in which they appear. Then, in the space provided, write the letter of the meaning closest to that of each word part.

1 con-
- Members of the **congregation** screamed when the minister fell down in the middle of his sermon.
- "You know," Mr. Warner told his band, "the trombones are supposed to play *with* the **conductor**, not against him."

b The word part *con-* means   a. write.   b. together.   c. foot.

2 dict
- "The job of our country's **dictator** is to speak," said the general. "He does not have to listen."
- If I say no, Mac says yes. He loves to **contradict** me.

a The word part *dict* means   a. speak.   b. with.   c. foot.

3 dis-
- It **displeases** Tai to hear his girlfriend say bad things about herself all the time.
- Before they **disappeared** from the Earth, dinosaurs were around for 140 million years.

c The word part *dis-* means   a. write.   b. by hand.   c. opposite of.

4 micro-
- In World War II, spies took **microphotographs** and then made them even smaller, the size of a printed period.
- **Microbiology** is the study of life forms so tiny they cannot be seen by the naked eye.

b The word part *micro-* means   a. quality.   b. small.   c. far.

5 ped
- Humans and apes aren't the only **bipeds**. Birds also walk on two feet.
- I like to give myself a **pedicure** in the summer so my toes look neat and polished in open-toed shoes.

c The word part *ped* means   a. over.   b. not.   c. foot.

6 script, scrib
- The author of the play didn't like it when actors spoke words that were not in the **script**.
- The author uses rich, revealing language to **describe** his characters and their surroundings.

b The word part *script* or *scrib* means   a. time.   b. write.   c. remember.

7 -ship

- Does good **citizenship** require following all the rules all the time?
- The two elderly sisters live together to provide each other with help and **companionship**.

_a_ The word part *-ship* means   a. quality.   b. across.   c. the opposite of.

8 tele-

- Through the **telephoto** lens, the distant eagle came clearly into view.
- Before the **telephone** was invented, people could not speak to faraway loved ones.

_c_ The word part *tele-* means   a. before.   b. three.   c. far.

9 trans-

- I had to **transfer** a large package from my right hand to my left in order to reach for my keys and open the door.
- It's hard to **translate** Zulu sounds into written English because the Zulu language includes clicks, ticks, and pops.

_b_ The word part *trans-* means   a. heat.   b. change.   c. again.

10 tri-

- Stan bought three rattles, three little blankets, and three knitted caps. He's the proud grandfather of **triplets**.
- Mara, Tod, and I have formed a guitar **trio**. Now all we need are three guitars.

_b_ The word part *tri-* means   a. beyond.   b. three.   c. good.

Matching Word Parts with Definitions

Following are definitions of the ten word parts. Clearly write or print each word part next to its definition. The sentences above and on the previous page will help you decide on the meaning of each word part.

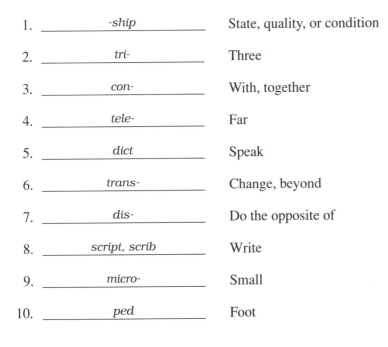

1. _____-ship_____   State, quality, or condition

2. _____tri-_____   Three

3. _____con-_____   With, together

4. _____tele-_____   Far

5. _____dict_____   Speak

6. _____trans-_____   Change, beyond

7. _____dis-_____   Do the opposite of

8. _____script, scrib_____   Write

9. _____micro-_____   Small

10. _____ped_____   Foot

CAUTION: Do not go any further until you are sure the above answers are correct. Then you can use the definitions to help you in the following practices. Your goal is eventually to know the word parts well enough so that you don't need to check the definitions at all.

➤ *Sentence Check 1*

Using the answer line provided, complete each *italicized* word in the sentences below with the correct word part from the box. Use each word part once.

a. **con-**	b. **dict**	c. **dis-**	d. **micro-**	e. **ped**
f. **script, scrib**	g. **-ship**	h. **tele-**	i. **trans-**	j. **tri-**

predicted   1. The weather forecaster (*pre . . . ed*) ___ rain, but we got the opposite of what he'd said: a lovely sunny day.

pedals   2. Only one foot is required to operate the piano (*. . . als*) ___.

tripod   3. To hold her camera still, the photographer put it on a (*. . . pod*) ___, a three-legged support.

transplant   4. The organ (*. . . plant*) ___ involved replacing the child's damaged kidney with a kidney from his father.

partnership   5. In (*partner . . .*) ___ with local businesses, the mayor fought graffiti.

conform   6. "Teenagers don't like to be different. They want to (*. . . form*) ___," said Mr. Gilbert, "but with their friends, who look like Martians, not with their parents."

disagree   7. Asha and Henry get along very well even though they strongly (*. . . agree*) ___ on politics.

microfilm   8. Libraries can store huge amounts of printed material in small spaces by photographing the material on (*. . . film*) ___.

Scriptures   9. My grandfather is not very religious, but he reads the (*. . . ures*) ___ every morning.

televised   10. Because the presentation of Academy Awards is (*. . . vised*) ___ live, even people thousands of miles away can see it as it happens.

NOTE: Now check your answers to these questions by turning to page 176. Going over the answers carefully will help you prepare for the next two practices, for which answers are not given.

➤ *Sentence Check 2*

Using the answer lines provided, complete each *italicized* word in the sentences below with the correct word part from the box. Use each word part once.

disapprove
television   1–2. We (*. . . approve*) ___ of our children's watching more than a couple of hours of (*. . . vision*) ___ each day. Watching TV is passive°, and we feel children should be active.

transformed
manuscript   3–4. The text of a play is often greatly (*. . . formed*) ___ between the time the (*manu . . .*) ___ is first written and the first live performance is given. When an author actually hears the dialog° spoken, he or she is liable° to see many ways to improve the lines.

_____ *pedals* _____   5–6. No matter how hard my little nephew (. . . *als*) ___ his (. . . *cycle*) ___,
_____ *tricycle* _____   he can't keep up with his sister on a two-wheeler. But that doesn't
                             deter° him from trying.

_____ *malediction* _____   7–8. The word (*male . . . ion*) "___" means "curse." It (. . . *nects*) ___ two
_____ *connects* _____   word parts meaning "badly" and "speak."

_____ *scholarship* _____   9–10. "The secret to (*scholar . . .*) ___ in biology," Professor Kant told Don,
_____ *microscope* _____   "is to spend your time looking at cells through a (. . . *scope*) ___, not
                                    staring at all the females in the class!"

➤ *Final Check:* Black Widow Spiders

Here is a final opportunity for you to strengthen your knowledge of the ten word parts. First read the
following selection carefully. Then complete each *italicized* word in the parentheses below with a word
from the box at the top of the previous page. (Context clues will help you figure out which word part goes
in which blank.) Use each word part once.

If you stopped the average (. . . *estrian*) (1)_____ *pedestrian* _____ walking down the street

and asked, "What creature do you fear most?" you might get this answer: "The black widow

spider." However, it's a fallacy° that the black widow is very dangerous. Bees kill 120 times as

many Americans as black widows do. In addition, there is an antidote° to the spider's poison.

People can tolerate bees, but they can't (. . . *cend*) (2)_____ *transcend* _____ their fear of black

widows. Perhaps that fear is fed by the knowledge of how the spiders got their name: the female,

who has an hourglass-shaped red mark on her belly, sometimes eats the male.

My nephew, who lives in California, has repeatedly told me over the (. . . *phone*)

(3)_____ *telephone* _____ of his war with black widows. And nearly every letter he sends

(. . . *tains*) (4)_____ *contains* _____ the (*post . . .*) (5)_____ *postscript* _____ "P. S.

House still has black widows." When he finds the black spider with the double red (. . . *angles*)

(6)_____ *triangles* _____ on her belly, the (*ver . . .*) (7)_____ *verdict* _____ is always

"Guilty." With a can of insect spray, he blasts the almost (. . . *scopic*) (8)_____ *microscopic* _____

little lady in her web. And when he has finished (. . . *honoring*) (9)_____ *dishonoring* _____ the

defenseless spider in this way, he throws away any remaining chance of gaining her (*friend . . .*)

(10)_____ *friendship* _____ by pounding her to death with a rolled-up magazine.

"Fine," I told him. "Fine. But how would you feel if spiders gave us honey?"

| *Scores* | Sentence Check 2 _____% | Final Check _____% |

Enter your scores above and in the vocabulary performance chart on the inside back cover of the book.

UNIT THREE: Review

The box at the right lists twenty-five words from Unit Three. Using the clues at the bottom of the page, fill in these words to complete the puzzle that follows.

accessible
cite
defer
delusion
ecstatic
elapse
equate
evolve
exempt
fictitious
fluent
harass
indignant
lethal
liable
malicious
ordeal
passive
pessimist
propel
retort
savor
subtle
universal
vivid

ACROSS

1. A false opinion or belief
4. To give in to someone else's wishes or judgment
6. Showing great ill will; mean; deliberately harmful
8. A person who tends to see the bad side of things
11. Angry because of some insult or injustice
15. Easily reached or entered
18. A sharp or clever reply
19. To pass or slip by (usually said of time)
21. Likely

23. To consider to be equal, the same, or similar
24. A very difficult or painful experience
25. Imaginary; made-up

DOWN

2. To taste or smell with pleasure; to appreciate fully
3. Being acted upon without acting in return
5. In a state of great joy
7. Hardly noticeable; not obvious
9. Worldwide; widespread

10. Able to express oneself with skill and ease
12. To provide the force that moves something; to move something forward
13. Able to cause death; deadly
14. Bright; brightly colored; striking
16. To mention in support of a point
17. Free from some unpleasant duty or situation
20. To constantly irritate or disturb; bother
22. To change gradually; develop

UNIT THREE: Test 1

PART A
Choose the word that best completes each item and write it in the space provided.

propelled   1. The air escaping from the balloon ___ it across the table and into the punch bowl.

     a. propelled   b. devised   c. inferred   d. imposed

retrieve   2. I used a fishing pole to ___ my hat from the duck pond.

     a. savor   b. retrieve   c. infer   d. stimulate

passive   3. When the usually peppy dog became ___ and wouldn't play, Marta knew he must be ill.

     a. ecstatic   b. passive   c. unique   d. futile

accessible   4. Lisa, who is unusually short, had her kitchen built with cabinets low enough to be ___ to her.

     a. subtle   b. indignant   c. accessible   d. vivid

subtle   5. Separately, the seasonings I put in my pizza sauce are ___. Combined, however, they have a strong flavor.

     a. versatile   b. fluent   c. subtle   d. lethal

ordeal   6. Rita turned her ___ of being lost in the desert into good fortune by selling the story to a movie studio.

     a. ordeal   b. pessimist   c. retort   d. patron

elapse   7. After denting my parents' car, I let several months ___ before I asked to borrow the car again.

     a. evolve   b. prevail   c. devise   d. elapse

convey   8. Using only gestures, Tina managed to ___ to Jerry the message that she would meet him at the Student Center at two o'clock.

     a. impose   b. savor   c. cite   d. convey

dubious   9. I didn't tell my brother about the surprise party because I'm ___ about his ability to keep a secret.

     a. dubious   b. persistent   c. malicious   d. fluent

inevitable   10. Hal was foolish to believe he could seriously date two women at once. It was ___ they would find out about each other.

     a. evasive   b. fictitious   c. compatible   d. inevitable

(Continues on next page)

_____vivid_____ 11. The Broadway dancer dyed her hair a ___ red so she would stand out among all the blondes and brunettes in the chorus line.

      a. vivid   b. versatile   c. futile   d. universal

_____miserly_____ 12. My ___ uncle refuses to give money to charity, claiming that charity begins and ends at home.

      a. exempt   b. miserly   c. liable   d. rational

_____unique_____ 13. Marjorie wanted her prom dress to be ___, and it was—no one else wore a yellow-and-black gown that looked like an overripe banana.

      a. gullible   b. unique   c. dubious   d. lethal

PART B

Write **C** if the italicized word is used **correctly**. Write **I** if the word is used **incorrectly**.

_C_ 14. Pearl and I went to the same party, but it was so crowded that we never *encountered* each other.

_I_ 15. I think of myself as a *pessimist* because I can find something good in even the worst situation.

_C_ 16. Although the movie seemed true to life, the writer swore it was entirely *fictitious*.

_C_ 17. Gina and Steve are *patrons* of the local Japanese restaurant. They eat there every Friday night.

_I_ 18. Efforts to teach chimpanzees to learn words have been *futile*. Some chimps know as many as two hundred words.

_C_ 19. During my history teacher's lecture, I was soon able to *infer* her opinion about the United States' involvement in Vietnam.

_I_ 20. Tony was disappointed when he *prevailed* in the student council election. Maybe he'll do better next year.

_I_ 21. I get tired of Pat's guitar playing. He's so *versatile* that he just plays the same three chords over and over.

_C_ 22. After searching for months for a valuable bracelet, I was *ecstatic* to find it in the sleeve of an old sweater.

_C_ 23. Marie always thinks handsome men are nice. She seems to *equate* good looks with good character.

_C_ 24. It's dangerous to invite my brother to help himself in your kitchen. He's *liable* to eat a week's worth of groceries.

_I_ 25. After Judy's wonderful performance in the play, friends rushed backstage to *harass* her with flowers and praise.

> *Score*   (Number correct) _____ x 4 = _____ %

Enter your score above and in the vocabulary performance chart on the inside back cover of the book.

UNIT THREE: *Test 2*

PART A

Complete each item with a word from the box. Use each word once.

a. **awe**	b. **cite**	c. **delusion**	d. **evolve**	e. **gullible**
f. **impose**	g. **indignant**	h. **lethal**	i. **option**	j. **rational**
k. **retort**	l. **savor**	m. **universal**		

_____indignant_____ 1. After recently lending Trisha money to help her pay her rent, I was ___ when I learned she had been using the money to buy herself expensive jewelry.

_____awe_____ 2. It's thrilling to watch Michael Jordan play basketball. His athletic ability fills me with ___.

_____option_____ 3. We considered several ___s for dinner: cooking, going out, or having a pizza delivered.

_____delusion_____ 4. Our belief that the company was loyal to us workers proved to be a ___. It laid everyone off and moved the plant to a state with cheaper labor.

_____gullible_____ 5. Dad was embarrassed to admit he'd been ___ enough to buy a "genuine diamond wristwatch" from a stranger on the street.

_____evolve_____ 6. As Gwen got to know Peter better, her feelings for him ___(e)d from interest to affection to love.

_____lethal_____ 7. It's dangerous to mix chlorine bleach and other household cleaners. The combination can produce ___ fumes.

_____impose_____ 8. My sister ___s on her husband's good nature by having him run errands for her all the time.

_____savor_____ 9. Knowing the ice cream would be his last before beginning his diet, Jon took time to ___ every rich spoonful.

_____universal_____ 10. The German and American children didn't mind that they couldn't speak the same language. They all knew the ___ language of play.

_____rational_____ 11. Rosa is overly ___ about her love life. She lists a guy's good and bad qualities before deciding if she'll date him again.

_____retort_____ 12. When Paul complained, "Women and computers are both impossible to understand," his wife gave this ___: "No, you just don't know how to turn either of them on."

_____cite_____ 13. To make my point that college can be as stressful as a full-time job, I ___(e)d the pressures of being a student.

(Continues on next page)

PART B
Write **C** if the italicized word is used **correctly**. Write **I** if the word is used **incorrectly**.

_I_   14. If a friend suffers a *fallacy*, it is proper to send a note of sympathy.

_C_   15. Although our teacher is *fluent* in French and Italian, her Russian is shaky.

_C_   16. At some health clinics, people with little income are *exempt* from all fees.

_I_   17. Bob *endeavored* to save the diseased tree, saying, "Let's just chop it down for firewood."

_C_   18. I felt like having pizza, but because it was my girlfriend's birthday, I *deferred* to her desire for Chinese food.

_I_   19. The couple next door often yell and throw things at each other. Clearly, they're *compatible*.

_I_   20. After my sister turned down Gabe's first request for a date, he was so *persistent* that he gave up.

_C_   21. Lynn has repeatedly asked Brian exactly what he does for a living, but she always gets an *evasive* answer like "I work downtown."

_C_   22. The interracial couple were the victims of *malicious* acts. Their windows were smashed, and a cross was burned on their lawn.

_I_   23. Phil has such an *obsession* with how he looks that he sometimes wears socks that don't match or forgets to comb his hair.

_I_   24. My overactive young nephew takes medicine to *stimulate* his tendency to race around the house and throw things.

_C_   25. Someone has *devised* sunglasses that serve as "eyes in the back of your head." Put them on and you see what's behind you.

Score (Number correct) _____ x 4 = _____ %

Enter your score above and in the vocabulary performance chart on the inside back cover of the book.

UNIT THREE: Test 3

PART A

Complete each sentence in a way that clearly shows you understand the meaning of the **boldfaced** word. Take a minute to plan your answer before you write.

Example: Two ways a boat can be **propelled** are by _____*motor and wind*_____.

1. A **unique** color combination for a car would be _____*(Answers will vary.)*_____

   _____.

2. My sister is so **versatile** that _____

   _____.

3. Lonnie needs to get from New York to Florida. One of his **options** is to _____

   _____.

4. Because of her **obsession** with clothes, Sheila _____

   _____.

5. Here's an **evasive** answer to "What did you do on your vacation?": "_____

   _____."

6. Glen is so **miserly** that _____

   _____.

7. A man who believes he and his date are **compatible** might say at the end of an evening, " _____

   _____."

8. Wild teenagers on the street **harassed** passing cars by _____

   _____.

9. An animal-lover would become **indignant** if _____

   _____.

10. An obviously **fictitious** detail about my past is that I _____

    _____.

(Continues on next page)

PART B

After each **boldfaced** word are a *synonym* (a word that means the same as the boldfaced word), an *antonym* (a word that means the opposite of the boldfaced word), and a word that is neither. On the answer line, write the letter of the word that is the antonym.

Example: <u>b</u> **malicious**   a. eager   b. kindly   c. spiteful

<u>a</u> 11. **prevail**   a. lose   b. triumph   c. disguise

<u>a</u> 12. **dubious**   a. certain   b. foolish   c. doubtful

<u>c</u> 13. **vivid**   a. bright   b. angry   c. colorless

<u>c</u> 14. **futile**   a. evil   b. useless   c. effective

<u>b</u> 15. **awe**   a. wisdom   b. contempt   c. respect

PART C

Use five of the following ten words in sentences. Make it clear that you know the meaning of the word you use. Feel free to use the past tense or plural form of a word.

a. **accessible**	b. **delusion**	c. **elapse**	d. **encounter**	e. **impose**
f. **inevitable**	g. **liable**	h. **ordeal**	i. **retrieve**	j. **savor**

16. _____ *(Answers will vary.)* _____

_____

17. _____

_____

18. _____

_____

19. _____

_____

20. _____

_____

Score   (Number correct) _____ x 5 = _____ %

Enter your score above and in the vocabulary performance chart on the inside back cover of the book.

UNIT THREE: Test 4 (Word Parts)

PART A
Listed in the left-hand column below are ten common word parts, along with words in which the parts are used. In each blank, write in the letter of the correct definition on the right.

Word Parts		Examples	Definitions
_j_	1. **con-**	congregation, conductor	a. State, quality, or condition
_c_	2. **dict**	dictator, contradict	b. Write
_i_	3. **dis-**	displease, disappear	c. Speak
_g_	4. **micro-**	microphotograph, microbiology	d. Foot
_d_	5. **ped**	biped, pedicure	e. Three
_b_	6. **script, scrib**	script, describe	f. Far
_a_	7. **-ship**	citizenship, companionship	g. Small
_f_	8. **tele-**	telephoto, telephone	h. Change, beyond
_h_	9. **trans-**	transfer, translate	i. Do the opposite of
_e_	10. **tri-**	triplets, trio	j. With, together

PART B
Using the answer line provided, complete each *italicized* word in the sentences below with the correct word part from the box. Not every word part will be used.

a. **con-**	b. **dict**	c. **dis-**	d. **micro-**	e. **ped**
f. **script**	g. **-ship**	h. **tele-**	i. **trans-**	j. **tri-**

_____contact_____ 11. The easiest way to catch a cold is through skin (. . . *tact*) ___.

_____tricycle_____ 12. Other kids fall from bicycles, but I was so clumsy as a child that I lost my balance even on a (. . . *cycle*) ___.

_____courtship_____ 13. Lamar often brought Tina flowers during their (*court . . .*) ___. After they got married, he planted a garden for her.

_____transformation_____ 14. Is there anything more amazing than the (. . . *formation*) ___ of a creepy caterpillar into a gorgeous butterfly?

_____prescription_____ 15. Allergy medicine bought with a doctor's (*pre . . . ion*) ___ is likely to cost much more than allergy medicines on the drugstore shelf.

(Continues on next page)

PART C
Use your knowledge of word parts to determine the meaning of the **boldfaced** words. On the answer line, write the letter of each meaning.

_c_   16. I'd like to own a **microcomputer**.

    a. a large computer   b. a computer with a sound system   c. a small computer

_a_   17. The office worker was asked if he had ever used a **dictaphone**.

    a. a machine that records spoken words
    b. a machine that has the ability to make copies
    c. a machine that is operated by foot

_c_   18. Wreaths had been placed around the **pedestal** of the statue.

    a. top   b. middle   c. foot

_a_   19. While trying to fix Martha's car, Phil **disabled** it.

    a. made it unable to run   b. improved its ability   c. wrote about its ability

_a_   20. In 1608, the **telescope** was invented by accident when the inventor happened to look through two lenses at once.

    a. an instrument which makes it easier to see distant things
    b. an instrument which makes it easier to see very small things
    c. an instrument which makes it easier to see writing

Score   (Number correct) _____ x 5 = _____ %

Enter your score above and in the vocabulary performance chart on the inside back cover of the book.

Unit Four

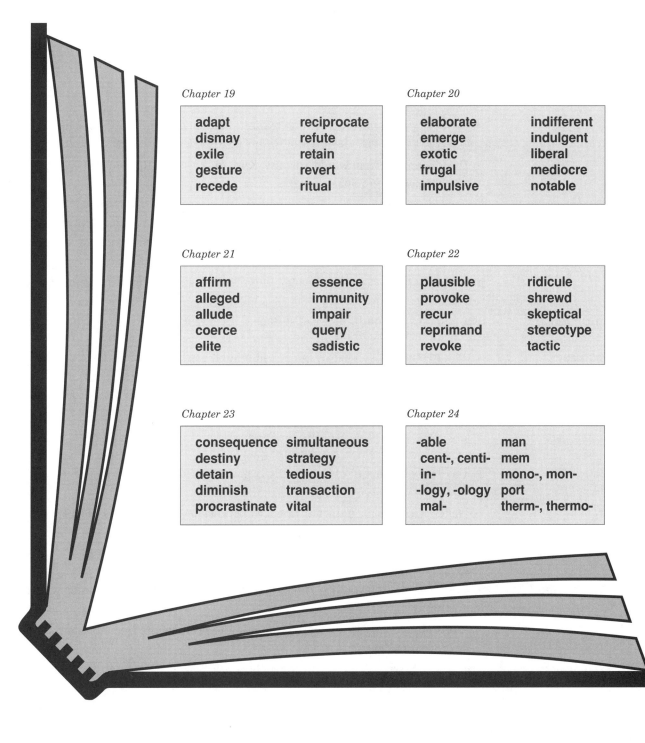

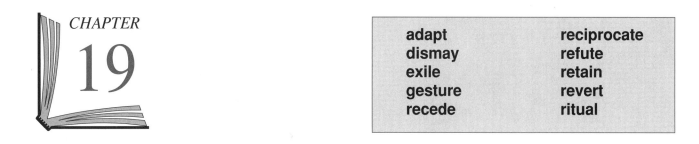

adapt	reciprocate
dismay	refute
exile	retain
gesture	revert
recede	ritual

Ten Words in Context

In the space provided, write the letter of the meaning closest to that of each **boldfaced** word. Use the context of the sentences to help you figure out each word's meaning.

1 **adapt**
(ə-dăpt′)
-*verb*

- After many years of being only a student, I found it hard to **adapt** to the schedule of a full-time job.
- Gina **adapted** well to California. She had no trouble adjusting to living so far from her family and friends.

_b_ *Adapt* means   a. to return.   b. to become accustomed.   c. to travel.

2 **dismay**
(dĭs-mā′)
-*verb*

- Carmen was **dismayed** when he realized that he wouldn't have enough money to buy a special birthday present for his girlfriend.
- The doctor knew it would **dismay** Karl to learn that his injured leg would never regain its previous strength.

_a_ *Dismay* means   a. to discourage.   b. to relieve.   c. to delay.

3 **exile**
(ĕg′zīl)
-*noun*

- The political rebel decided to end his five-year **exile** and return to his native land to oppose the government.
- Fernando fled his native country thirty years ago and has lived in **exile** ever since.

_c_ *Exile* means   a. a long vacation.   b. a bad attitude.   c. a separation from one's homeland.

4 **gesture**
(jĕs′chər)
-*noun*

- As a **gesture** of sympathy, the neighborhood association sent flowers to Milly when her husband died.
- The other workers' **gestures** of friendship made Vic feel at home on the first day of his new job.

_a_ *Gesture* means   a. a sign.   b. a request.   c. a report.

5 **recede**
(rĭ-sēd′)
-*verb*

- The heavy blanket of clouds finally began to **recede**, allowing the sun to warm the crowd at the football game.
- Walter had to wait until the flood water **receded** before he could get to his house to see the damage.

_b_ *Recede* means   a. to grow.   b. to pull back.   c. to return.

6 **reciprocate**
(rĭ-cĭp′rə-kāt′)
-*verb*

- I've done many favors for Anne, but she never **reciprocates** by doing a favor in return.
- Alonso treated me to dinner, so I'm going to **reciprocate** by taking him to my favorite restaurant.

_b_ *Reciprocate* means   a. to celebrate.   b. to pay back.   c. to disappoint.

7 **refute**
(rĭ-fyōot′)
-verb

- The lawyer was able to **refute** the defendant's claim that she was home the night of the murder. He had found a witness who saw her in a town bar that night.
- Some science-fiction fans were disappointed when photos of Mars **refuted** the idea that intelligent life exists there.

c *Refute* means
    a. to support.   b. to repeat.   c. to show to be wrong.

8 **retain**
(rĭ-tān′)
-verb

- Plastic storage containers often **retain** the odors of foods. I have one that still smells like spaghetti sauce after ten washings.
- "I can usually **retain** my sense of humor," Janice said. "But I lose it totally when I'm laid off and break up with my boyfriend in the same week."

a *Retain* means
    a. to hold on to.   b. to adjust to.   c. to lose.

9 **revert**
(rĭ-vûrt′)
-verb

- After his release from jail, Sam **reverted** to his old habit of stealing and ended up in jail again.
- Helene gave up smoking while she was pregnant, but she **reverted** to a pack a day after her daughter was born.

a *Revert* means
    a. to go back.   b. to refer.   c. to say no.

10 **ritual**
(rĭch′ōo-əl)
-noun

- **Rituals**—set practices that are repeated regularly—are important in most religious traditions.
- Each time Mary Ann must fly, she writes a check to a charity, brings it with her on the plane, and mails it at her destination. She believes this **ritual** guarantees a safe flight.

b *Ritual* means
    a. a lesson.   b. a ceremony.   c. a prayer.

Matching Words with Definitions

Following are definitions of the ten words. Clearly write or print each word next to its definition. The sentences above and on the previous page will help you decide on the meaning of each word.

1. _____*revert*_____   To return to a previous habit or condition
2. _____*gesture*_____   Something said or done to show intention or attitude
3. _____*reciprocate*_____   To do in return; pay back
4. _____*exile*_____   Separation from one's native country through force or choice
5. _____*ritual*_____   A ceremony; any actions done regularly in a set manner
6. _____*refute*_____   To prove wrong or false
7. _____*adapt*_____   To adjust to a situation
8. _____*recede*_____   To move back or away from a particular point or limit
9. _____*retain*_____   To keep
10. _____*dismay*_____   To discourage; make fearful or uneasy

CAUTION: Do not go any further until you are sure the above answers are correct. Then you can use the definitions to help you in the following practices. Your goal is eventually to know the words well enough so that you don't need to check the definitions at all.

➤ *Sentence Check 1*

Using the answer line provided, complete each item below with the correct word from the box. Use each word once.

a. **adapt**	b. **dismay**	c. **exile**	d. **gesture**	e. **recede**
f. **reciprocate**	g. **refute**	h. **retain**	i. **revert**	j. **ritual**

_____*dismay*_____ 1. Getting a D on the first math test of the semester ___(e)d Sean. He was sure he'd done well.

_____*recede*_____ 2. If the shoreline continues to ___, there soon won't be any sandy beach at all.

_____*refute*_____ 3. Antonio tried to ___ my argument, but I was able to prove I was right.

_____*gesture*_____ 4. In a(n) ___ of cooperation, the manager and the head of the union shook hands.

_____*retain*_____ 5. To ___ her strength and energy, Mrs. Green does push-ups, sit-ups, and leg-lifts three times a week.

_____*revert*_____ 6. My brother vowed to eat only one Oreo a day, but I'm afraid he'll ___ to his old habit of eating the entire bag of cookies at a sitting.

_____*adapt*_____ 7. As the Ice Age ended, some animals were able to ___ to the new climate. Those who could not adjust failed to survive.

_____*exile*_____ 8. The country's new dictator feared having certain political enemies in the country, so he sent them into ___.

_____*reciprocate*_____ 9. I always send Karim a birthday card, but he doesn't bother to ___ with a card or phone call on my birthday.

_____*ritual*_____ 10. Homer always goes through the same baseball ___ before he bats: he twirls his bat three times, stretches his arms, and says, "Okay, okay, this one will be good."

NOTE: Now check your answers to these questions by turning to page 176. Going over the answers carefully will help you prepare for the next two practices, for which answers are not given.

➤ *Sentence Check 2*

Using the answer lines provided, complete each item below with **two** words from the box. Use each word once.

_____*dismay*_____
_____*refute*_____ 1–2. "I don't want to ___ you," Jack's lawyer told him. "And I will certainly endeavor° to do my best, but it's going to be difficult to ___ the testimony against you."

_____*reciprocate*_____
_____*gesture*_____ 3–4. The Reillys have been so kind to me that I want to ___ in some way. I don't have much money, so I hope they'll understand that a small gift is meant as a(n) ___ of great appreciation.

_____recede_____   5–6. My husband is afraid his hairline will ___, causing him to ___ to the

_____revert_____   bald head he was born with. I tell him to watch out that this obsession° of his doesn't undermine° his self-confidence. He's the same great guy with or without hair.

_____ritual_____   7–8. Any customary ___, such as the Roman Catholic Mass, helps a church

_____retain_____   to ___ a sense of tradition.

_____adapt_____   9–10. The Howards had ___(e)d well to other cultures, but they were still

_____exile_____   pleased to retire from the Foreign Service and return to America after their long ___ in Europe and Asia. Now they love to reminisce° with their friends about their interesting worldwide adventures.

➤ _Final Check:_ Adjusting to a New Culture

Here is a final opportunity for you to strengthen your knowledge of the ten words. First read the following selection carefully. Then fill in each blank with a word from the box at the top of the previous page. (Context clues will help you figure out which word goes in which blank.) Use each word once.

When En-Mei first came to the United States from China, any little problem was enough to

(1)_____dismay_____ her. As a lonely student, she felt as if she were in forced

(2)_____exile_____ from her native country. She didn't like American food and tried to

limit her diet to Chinese dishes. Otherwise, however, she worked hard to (3)_____adapt_____

to an unfamiliar country. Finding it difficult to express herself in English, En Mei at first isolated°

herself from others. But she kept working on her English and eventually became quite fluent° in it.

This helped her to overcome her shyness and learn to (4)_____reciprocate_____ other students'

(5)_____gesture_____s of friendship. When she was with her new friends, homesickness

would (6)_____recede_____ into the background.

But En-Mei didn't try to become "all-American"; she wanted to (7)_____retain_____

her Chinese identity. She taught her new friends about modern China and tried to

(8)_____refute_____ mistaken ideas they had about her country. She even found a group of

friends willing to learn tai chi, an ancient Chinese exercise (9)_____ritual_____ that benefits

body and spirit. It involves a set series of movements which the group performs together.

Of course living in America wasn't always easy. Sometimes En-Mei would miss her family so

badly that she would (10)_____revert_____ to her former unhappiness. But such times

were increasingly rare. By the end of her first year here, En-Mei even found she had become a

devoted fan of pizza and apple pie.

Scores Sentence Check 2 _____%	Final Check _____%

Enter your scores above and in the vocabulary performance chart on the inside back cover of the book.

elaborate	indifferent
emerge	indulgent
exotic	liberal
frugal	mediocre
impulsive	notable

Ten Words in Context

In the space provided, write the letter of the meaning closest to that of each **boldfaced** word. Use the context of the sentences to help you figure out each word's meaning.

1 **elaborate**
(ĭ-lăb′ər-ĭt)
-*adjective*

- The dinner required **elaborate** preparation. Each course included a complicated favorite dish of one of the guests.
- Irma's quilt was very **elaborate**. She used tiny stitches to sew on the very detailed pattern.

b *Elaborate* means   a. easy and simple to do.   b. detailed.   c. ordinary.

2 **emerge**
(ĭ-mûrj′)
-*verb*

- Anna **emerged** from the dressing room, looking beautiful in a blue prom gown.
- When the chick **emerged** from its egg, it was tired and wet, but a day later it was a fluffy yellow ball of energy.

a *Emerge* means   a. to come out.   b. to trip.   c. to call out.

3 **exotic**
(ĭg-zŏt′ĭk)
-*adjective*

- Orchids are grown in the United States, not just in foreign countries. So Americans really should not consider these flowers **exotic**.
- The kiwi fruit, grown in New Zealand, is one of several **exotic** fruits now commonly sold in supermarkets.

b *Exotic* means   a. local.   b. foreign.   c. rare.

4 **frugal**
(frōō′gəl)
-*adjective*

- You can stretch your dollars by being **frugal**. For example, using store coupons and waiting for expensive items to be on sale can save a lot of money.
- Diane buys designer jeans, but because I need to be more **frugal**, I buy store-brand jeans, which are much cheaper.

c *Frugal* means   a. hardworking.   b. lucky.   c. thrifty.

5 **impulsive**
(ĭm-pŭl′sĭv)
-*adjective*

- Ved is too **impulsive** to make plans. He always prefers to act on the spur of the moment.
- Kids are usually more **impulsive** than adults. Children will follow such sudden urges as the desire to climb a tree even if they are wearing their best clothes.

c *Impulsive* means   a. fearful.   b. careful.   c. acting without planning.

6 **indifferent**
(ĭn-dĭf′ər-ənt)
-*adjective*

- Does our society have no interest in homeless children? Are we **indifferent** to the many families who can no longer afford to pay rent?
- Because her husband was **indifferent** to how the apartment would be decorated, Kathy felt free to do the job any way she wanted.

b *Indifferent to* means   a. interested in.   b. unconcerned with.   c. insulted by.

7 **indulgent**
(ĭn-dŭl′jənt)
-adjective

- Monica's grandparents are too **indulgent** with her. They don't scold her even when she splatters the walls with baby food.
- I'm surprised at Robin's self-**indulgent** attitude. It never occurs to her not to give in to every little desire she has.

_b_ *Indulgent* means   a. strict.   b. giving.   c. not caring.

8 **liberal**
(lĭb′ər-əl)
-adjective

- Being a chocolate lover, Amos puts **liberal** amounts of chocolate chips in his tollhouse cookies.
- Norma left the waiter a **liberal** tip because he had been especially friendly and helpful.

_c_ *Liberal* means   a. average.   b. frequent.   c. generous.

9 **mediocre**
(mē-dē-ō′kər)
-adjective

- The mystery movie was neither terrible nor great; it was **mediocre**.
- Although Hank can be quite funny, his jokes are only **mediocre** compared with those of the best comedians.

_a_ *Mediocre* means   a. ordinary.   b. awful.   c. short.

10 **notable**
(nō′tə-bəl)
-adjective

- Winning the Nobel Prize can make a little-known scientist into a **notable** world figure.
- Abraham Lincoln's "Gettysburg Address" is surely his most **notable** speech, especially among the many Americans who memorized it in school.

_b_ *Notable* means   a. ineffective.   b. well-known.   c. generous.

Matching Words with Definitions

Following are definitions of the ten words. Clearly write or print each word next to its definition. The sentences above and on the previous page will help you decide on the meaning of each word.

1. _____emerge_____   To rise up or come forth

2. _____notable_____   Famous; widely known

3. _____indifferent_____   Having no real interest; unconcerned

4. _____liberal_____   Large in amount or quantity; generous

5. _____elaborate_____   Done with great attention to details; complicated

6. _____mediocre_____   Average; ordinary; neither very bad nor very good

7. _____impulsive_____   Tending to act on sudden urges; not in the habit of planning ahead

8. _____exotic_____   Foreign; from a different part of the world; strange or different in an appealing way

9. _____frugal_____   Thrifty; avoiding unnecessary expenses

10. _____indulgent_____   Giving in to someone's desires, often too much so

CAUTION: Do not go any further until you are sure the above answers are correct. Then you can use the definitions to help you in the following practices. Your goal is eventually to know the words well enough so that you don't need to check the definitions at all.

➤ *Sentence Check 1*

Using the answer line provided, complete each item below with the correct word from the box. Use each word once.

a. **elaborate**	b. **emerge**	c. **exotic**	d. **frugal**	e. **impulsive**
f. **indifferent**	g. **indulgent**	h. **liberal**	i. **mediocre**	j. **notable**

_____mediocre_____ 1. Although my father didn't do badly in school, he wasn't a great student. So he's proof it's possible to have a successful career despite ___ grades.

_____indulgent_____ 2. Overly ___ parents, who let young children do whatever they please, will end up with problem teenagers.

_____emerge_____ 3. The puppy ___(e)d from her bath much cleaner than when she entered it, but we doubted that she'd stay clean for long.

_____notable_____ 4. Greg is such a skilled public speaker that we all expect him to become a ___ politician one day.

_____liberal_____ 5. My boss gave each of us such a(n) ___ bonus that I was able to buy a new sofa with the money.

_____elaborate_____ 6. Ella embroidered a(n) ___ design on the back of her sweatshirt. She used four colors in a complicated pattern of swirls and flowers.

_____indifferent_____ 7. People walked past the bleeding, moaning man without even pausing; they were ___ to his need for help.

_____frugal_____ 8. "Gowns are so expensive," Mimi said, "that I've decided to be ___ and rent a wedding dress instead of buying one."

_____impulsive_____ 9. Bruce, as ___ as ever, suddenly changed his mind about going to a restaurant and announced, "Let's have a picnic."

_____exotic_____ 10. A Native American rain dance may seem ___ to many people in the United States, but it is actually more native to this country than square-dancing.

NOTE: Now check your answers to these questions by turning to page 176. Going over the answers carefully will help you prepare for the next two practices, for which answers are not given.

➤ *Sentence Check 2*

Using the answer lines provided, complete each item below with **two** words from the box. Use each word once.

_____notable_____
_____mediocre_____
1–2. The actress, ___ for her great performance, deserved her Academy Award. Compared with her, all of the others appeared ___. Overjoyed, she said, "Thank you, thank you, thank you. This is my first Oscar, and I am too ecstatic° to think of anything else to say."

_____emerge_____
_____frugal_____
3–4. Every time Sylvia shops, she manages to ___ from the store without a single unnecessary purchase. I wish I could be such a(n) ___ shopper.

exotic	5–6. The ___ meal, full of strange but delicious foods, involved ___ preparation that took up most of the afternoon.
elaborate	
indifferent	7–8. When it comes to the suffering of others, Americans are idealistic°. When a disaster strikes, they find it difficult to be ___ to the victims, so they send ___ donations to the Red Cross.
liberal	
impulsive	9–10. Rafael is so ___ that he often decides he wants to go out for dinner or to a movie at the last minute. Overly ___, his wife agrees every time. She even defers° to his wish to eat out after she has already cooked dinner.
indulgent	

➤ _Final Check:_ A Dream About Wealth

Here is a final opportunity for you to strengthen your knowledge of the ten words. First read the following selection carefully. Then fill in each blank with a word from the box at the top of the previous page. (Context clues will help you figure out which word goes in which blank.) Use each word once.

In my student days, when I was very poor, I sometimes daydreamed about being rich and having an amazingly affluent° lifestyle. I imagined being such a(n) (1)_____ _notable_ _____ member of society that my name would turn up in the newspaper columns every time I remarried. I pictured myself traveling to (2)_____ _exotic_ _____ places in faraway lands and being a patron° of the finest restaurants. I would forget no detail when planning (3)_____ _elaborate_ _____ parties for five hundred of my closest friends. There would be nothing (4)_____ _mediocre_ _____ in my life, not even an ordinary, average toaster. No, I would have the finest toasters, the biggest houses, the most glamorous wardrobe—the best. And I would own a unique° art collection—no prints for me, only one-of-a-kind masterpieces by famous artists. Of course, I would be quite (5)_____ _impulsive_ _____: whenever I had the urge, I would buy diamond jewelry or go swimming nude in my Olympic-size pool. But I promised myself that I wouldn't be totally self-(6)_____ _indulgent_ _____. I'd also give (7)_____ _liberal_ _____ amounts of money to help the poor and underprivileged. I would not be (8)_____ _indifferent_ _____ to their needs. And being modest as well as generous, I'd always be an anonymous° donor°.

After graduating, I began saving money, and I stopped daydreaming about being rich. Having some earnings to spend, I had finally (9)_____ _emerge_ _____(e)d from a life of endless budgeting, a life in which I was forced to be extremely (10)_____ _frugal_ _____. Of course, I am still thrifty because I don't want to waste my hard-earned money. But now that I have enough money to be comfortable, I no longer daydream about being super-rich.

Scores	Sentence Check 2 _____%	Final Check _____%	

Enter your scores above and in the vocabulary performance chart on the inside back cover of the book.

affirm	essence
alleged	immunity
allude	impair
coerce	query
elite	sadistic

Ten Words in Context

In the space provided, write the letter of the meaning closest to that of each **boldfaced** word. Use the context of the sentences to help you figure out each word's meaning.

1 affirm
(ə-fûrm')
-verb

- The witness **affirmed** in court that he had seen the defendant commit the robbery.
- Lana did **affirm** during the wedding ceremony that she would love and honor Joseph, but she did not state that she would obey him.

_b_ *Affirm* means   a. to fear.   b. to state.   c. to write.

2 alleged
(ə-lĕjd')
-adjective

- The **alleged** killer was never proven guilty in court, but many people believe he committed the murder.
- Nan, who believed Luther was innocent of starting the fire, reminded her friends that his guilt was only **alleged**.

_a_ *Alleged* means   a. assumed.   b. admired.   c. harmless.

3 allude
(ə-lōōd')
-verb

- Although the mayor won't name her opponent, she plans to **allude** to him by mentioning the scandal he's involved in.
- Regina **alluded** to Sal's weight gain by calling him "Santa."

_b_ *Allude to* means   a. to clearly mention.   b. to hint at.   c. to keep.

4 coerce
(kō-ûrs')
-verb

- To **coerce** the general into giving up, the rebels kidnapped his daughter.
- Our gym teacher used to **coerce** us into doing fifty sit-ups by refusing to let anyone leave before we all had finished.

_c_ *Coerce* means   a. to talk.   b. to join.   c. to force.

5 elite
(ĭ-lēt')
-adjective

- The 57th was the **elite** military unit. Its members were the toughest and the smartest and had trained the longest.
- The **elite** neighborhood in town is surrounded by a high fence and has a guard at its gates.

_b_ *Elite* means   a. worst.   b. best.   c. least important.

6 essence
(ĕs'əns)
-noun

- Trust is the **essence** of a good relationship; without it, the relationship won't last.
- Boiled down to its **essence**, the lecture can be stated in one short sentence: Much important work gets done in America by volunteers.

_a_ *Essence* means   a. the main part.   b. the opposite.   c. the sad part.

7 **immunity**
(ĭ-myōō′nĭ-tē)
-*noun*

• Foreign ambassadors often park in no-parking zones because they have **immunity** from parking fines.

• When the actor punched a police officer, even his wealth and fame didn't get him **immunity** from jail.

_b_ *Immunity* means   a. recognition.   b. freedom.   c. income.

8 **impair**
(ĭm-pâr′)
-*verb*

• Listening to loud music **impairs** hearing by damaging the inner ear.

• The rifle shot didn't kill the deer, but it **impaired** her running ability, leaving her with a limp.

_c_ *Impair* means   a. to involve.   b. to repair.   c. to harm.

9 **query**
(kwēr′ē)
-*verb*

• If no printed schedule is available, please **query** the person at the information booth to learn the time of your train's arrival or departure.

• Reporters repeatedly **queried** the president about taxes, but his only reply was "No comment."

_a_ *Query* means   a. to ask.   b. to quote.   c. to answer.

10 **sadistic**
(sə-dĭs′tĭk)
-*adjective*

• Instead of killing his victims quickly, the **sadistic** murderer first made them suffer.

• Our **sadistic** science teacher had a strange way of teaching about electrical currents. First, he had us hold hands in a circle. Then he put one student's hand on a wire with a slight electrical charge.

_b_ *Sadistic* means   a. sad.   b. cruel.   c. rude.

Matching Words with Definitions

Following are definitions of the ten words. Clearly write or print each word next to its definition. The sentences above and on the previous page will help you decide on the meaning of each word.

1. _____impair_____   To damage; weaken

2. _____allude_____   To refer indirectly

3. _____sadistic_____   Taking pleasure from being cruel

4. _____essence_____   A fundamental characteristic or the most important quality of something; the heart of a matter

5. _____immunity_____   Freedom from something unpleasant or something required of others

6. _____affirm_____   To indicate to be true; state with certainty

7. _____elite_____   Being or intended for the best or most privileged; superior

8. _____coerce_____   To force; compel°

9. _____alleged_____   Supposed to be true or real, but not proved; assumed

10. _____query_____   To question; ask

CAUTION: Do not go any further until you are sure the above answers are correct. Then you can use the definitions to help you in the following practices. Your goal is eventually to know the words well enough so that you don't need to check the definitions at all.

➤ *Sentence Check 1*

Using the answer line provided, complete each item below with the correct word from the box. Use each word once.

a. **affirm**	b. **alleged**	c. **allude**	d. **coerce**	e. **elite**
f. **essence**	g. **immunity**	h. **impair**	i. **query**	j. **sadistic**

_____coerce_____   1. The Puritan colonists ___(e)d Native Americans into slavery by capturing and selling them to buyers in the West Indies.

_____sadistic_____   2. The ___ war criminal had laughed while he tortured his victims.

_____impair_____   3. Drugs and alcohol ___ a person's ability to drive.

_____essence_____   4. The ___ of a paragraph is stated in its topic sentence.

_____immunity_____   5. As a child, I didn't enjoy total ___ from punishment, but my parents rarely spanked me.

_____affirm_____   6. During the spelling bee, the judge would ___ that a spelling was correct by nodding silently.

_____alleged_____   7. The ___ car thief could not possibly be guilty. Not only was he out of town on the day of the theft, but he cannot drive.

_____elite_____   8. A(n) ___ group of doctors, including the country's top brain surgeons, met to discuss a new operation.

_____query_____   9. When two people are arrested for the same crime, the police ___ them separately to see if they give the same answers.

_____allude_____   10. My brother and I used secret names to ___ to certain relatives. For example, if we wished to speak about Aunt Dotty, we instead spoke about "an old Chevy."

NOTE: Now check your answers to these questions by turning to page 177. Going over the answers carefully will help you prepare for the next two practices, for which answers are not given.

➤ *Sentence Check 2*

Using the answer lines provided, complete each item below with **two** words from the box. Use each word once.

_____affirm_____
_____elite_____   1–2. The senator would neither deny nor ___ that the ___, expensive country club he belonged to allowed no minority members. Nevertheless, to avoid any appearance of a problem, he decided it would be appropriate° to resign from the club.

_____query_____
_____essence_____   3–4. I need to ___ my professor more closely about the chemistry theory. Although I've grasped the ___, I don't understand all the details yet.

_____coerce_____   5–6. When my roommate wants to ___ me into doing her some favor, all she
_____allude_____   has to do is ___ to certain dark secrets of mine. The hint that she might
                         tell them leaves me no option° but to help her out.

_____sadistic_____ 7–8. One terrible beating by her ___ husband was enough to ___ the
_____impair_____   woman's sight for life. That's when she decided to get help, before one
                         of his attacks became lethal°.

_____alleged_____   9–10. Nobody is sure if the ___ bribery really took place. The person who
_____immunity_____   would have been the chief suspect was given ___ from arrest by a
                          powerful political figure.

➤ _Final Check:_ Children and Drugs

Here is a final opportunity for you to strengthen your knowledge of the ten words. First read the following
selection carefully. Then fill in each blank with a word from the box at the top of the previous page.
(Context clues will help you figure out which word goes in which blank.) Use each word once.

One of the disturbing things about the selling of illegal drugs is the involvement of children.

Police regularly pick up preteens who are used as lookouts and delivery boys. When the police

(1)_____query_____ them, the children often say the drug dealers (2)_____coerce_____

them into doing these jobs. Fearful of betraying the dealers, the kids only (3)_____allude_____

generally to what has happened to others who have not cooperated.

However, some poor kids don't need to be forced. They are naturally attracted by the money

offered, and they speak of the dealers with awe°. With their fancy cars and rolls of money, the

dealers seem to these children to be members of a(n) (4)_____elite_____ club. According

to the mother of a(n) (5)_____alleged_____ drug delivery boy (the police could never

prove he really was a drug runner), the dealers serve as "role models" to her son and his friends.

Dealers like using kids because their age gives them (6)_____immunity_____ from serious

criminal charges. The police (7)_____affirm_____ that arresting the children doesn't

(8)_____impair_____ the dealers' business much. Also, it doesn't inhibit° other kids from

going to work for the dealers.

To some of the children, serving as lookouts and drug runners is almost a game. They don't

realize what harm could come to them if they got involved with a really (9)_____sadistic_____

dealer, someone who enjoys violence. They don't know just how common such malicious° people

are in the drug world. The use of these children shows that the (10)_____essence_____ of drug

dealing is abuse of people.

| _Scores_   Sentence Check 2 _____% | Final Check _____% |

Enter your scores above and in the vocabulary performance chart on the inside back cover of the book.

plausible	ridicule
provoke	shrewd
recur	skeptical
reprimand	stereotype
revoke	tactic

Ten Words in Context

In the space provided, write the letter of the meaning closest to that of each **boldfaced** word. Use the context of the sentences to help you figure out each word's meaning.

1 **plausible**
(plô′zə-bəl)
-adjective

- Was Buck's excuse for being late **plausible**? Or did he tell you some unbelievable story?
- "Some TV shows are just not **plausible**," said the producer. "Who ever heard of a flying nun or a teenage doctor?"

_b_ *Plausible* means   a. nice.   b. believable.   c. long enough.

2 **provoke**
(prə-vōk′)
-verb

- "Mr. Jackson **provoked** me by saying nasty things about my mother, so I hit him," Terry told the judge.
- My father is slow to anger, but this morning my sister's wisecracks began to **provoke** him.

_c_ *Provoke* means   a. to delay.   b. to confuse.   c. to anger.

3 **recur**
(rĭ-kûr′)
-verb

- Five-year-old Arnie's nightmare of ghosts chasing him tends to **recur** at least once a week.
- "The labor pains are **recurring** every minute," I told the nurse. "Do you think it's about time to go to the delivery room?"

_c_ *Recur* means   a. to disappear.   b. to improve.   c. to happen again.

4 **reprimand**
(rĕp′rə-mănd′)
-noun

- If a boss wants to criticize a worker, the union requires that the **reprimand** be written.
- As a child, when I misbehaved, my father gave me verbal **reprimands**, but my mother would not hesitate to give me a slap on the rear end.

_b_ *Reprimand* means   a. praise.   b. a scolding.   c. an answer.

5 **revoke**
(rĭ-vōk′)
-verb

- Mrs. Byers said she would **revoke** Ken's privileges at the computer lab if he ever again squirted glue between the computer keys.
- To avoid having his driver's license **revoked**, Art paid the $467 he owed for all of his speeding tickets.

_a_ *Revoke* means   a. to cancel.   b. to make longer.   c. to recognize.

6 **ridicule**
(rĭd′ĭ-kyōōl′)
-verb

- Ignorant people often **ridicule** my brother because he is so overweight, as if they themselves have perfect bodies.
- Eugene knew his friends would **ridicule** him for wearing a shirt and shorts with two different plaids, but he had no other clean clothes to wear.

_c_ *Ridicule* means   a. to praise.   b. to notice.   c. to make fun of.

7 **shrewd**
(shrо̄о̄d)
-adjective

- Eddie is a fine musician, but he's no good with money. So he hired a friend with a **shrewd** business sense to handle his financial affairs.
- Sherry is a **shrewd** chess player. She always surprises her opponents with clever winning moves.

<u>c</u> *Shrewd* means   a. lucky.   b. loud.   c. smart.

8 **skeptical**
(skĕp′tĭ-kəl)
-adjective

- Jessica's family is so rich that she is **skeptical** about any man who asks her out. She wonders if he's interested in her or in her money.
- I am **skeptical** about the articles on movie stars and space aliens in supermarket newspapers. My brother, however, believes every word he reads in those papers.

<u>b</u> *Skeptical* means   a. economical.   b. doubtful.   c. believing.

9 **stereotype**
(stĕr′ē-ə-tīp′)
-noun

- Bev still accepts the **stereotype** of all athletes as dumb even though the school's star quarterback is her math tutor.
- Because not all members of a group are alike, **stereotypes** lead to inaccurate judgments of people.

<u>a</u> *Stereotype* means   a. oversimplified image.   b. desired image.   c. true image.

10 **tactic**
(tăk′tĭc)
-noun

- The teacher finally caught on to Greg's sneaky **tactic** for getting his homework done—having his sister do it.
- The best **tactic** for keeping young children from fighting is to separate them.

<u>a</u> *Tactic* means   a. method.   b. result.   c. reason.

Matching Words with Definitions

Following are definitions of the ten words. Clearly write or print each word next to its definition. The sentences above and on the previous page will help you decide on the meaning of each word.

1. _____ *skeptical* _____   Doubting; questioning

2. _____ *shrewd* _____   Clever; tricky

3. _____ *plausible* _____   Believable; appearing truthful or reasonable

4. _____ *provoke* _____   To stir up anger or resentment

5. _____ *revoke* _____   To take away or cancel

6. _____ *tactic* _____   A means to reach a goal; method

7. _____ *reprimand* _____   A formal criticism; a harsh scolding

8. _____ *ridicule* _____   To make fun of; mock

9. _____ *recur* _____   To occur again; happen repeatedly

10. _____ *stereotype* _____   A commonly accepted image that is oversimplified, with no individuality taken into account

CAUTION: Do not go any further until you are sure the above answers are correct. Then you can use the definitions to help you in the following practices. Your goal is eventually to know the words well enough so that you don't need to check the definitions at all.

➤ *Sentence Check 1*

Using the answer line provided, complete each item below with the correct word from the box. Use each word once.

a. **plausible**	b. **provoke**	c. **recur**	d. **reprimand**	e. **revoke**
f. **ridicule**	g. **shrewd**	h. **skeptical**	i. **stereotype**	j. **tactic**

_____ridicule_____ 1. At first the other students ___(e)d Sofi for speaking with an accent, but they stopped teasing her once they got to know her better.

_____stereotype_____ 2. Italian-Americans are rightly bothered by the ___ of all Italians as members of the Mafia.

_____plausible_____ 3. It takes great skill to make a science fiction film seem ___ to the audience.

_____shrewd_____ 4. It was ___ of Connie to move to California last year. Now she can pay in-state fees when she takes courses at San Bernardino Valley College.

_____recur_____ 5. Jordan has headaches that ___ as often as once a day.

_____tactic_____ 6. Some divorced parents who want to see more of their children use an illegal ___: kidnapping.

_____skeptical_____ 7. The roofer's estimate was so low that we became ___ about the quality of his work.

_____reprimand_____ 8. The principal wrote our gym teacher a note of ___ for not having his class leave the gym right after the fire alarm rang.

_____provoke_____ 9. Angelo usually doesn't let his older sister's teasing ___ him, but he gets angry whenever she calls him "baby."

_____revoke_____ 10. Eleanor's parents said she could not attend the prom because of her bad grades, but later they felt sorry for her and ___(e)d the punishment.

NOTE: Now check your answers to these questions by turning to page 177. Going over the answers carefully will help you prepare for the next two practices, for which answers are not given.

➤ *Sentence Check 2*

Using the answer lines provided, complete each item below with **two** words from the box. Use each word once.

_____shrewd_____
_____tactic_____ 1–2. When it comes to preventing cheating, our science teacher is ___. His ___s include checking our hands before a test and having us sit in alternate seats during a test. And he puts students he's suspicious of in prominent° seats near the front of the room.

_____stereotype_____
_____recur_____ 3–4. Some ___s may get their start when certain behavior patterns ___ among members of a particular group.

skeptical

plausible

5–6. "Of course I'm ___ about your excuse," Mel's boss said. "You have to give me a more ___ reason for not compiling° the sales figures than that you couldn't find a pen or pencil."

reprimand

revoke

7–8. "It is both illegal and absurd° to park your hot-dog cart in a McDonald's driveway," said the judge to the owner of the cart. "This time you're getting only a ___. Next time your license may be ___(e)d."

ridicule

provoke

9–10. When some boys teased and ___(e)d a retarded student for being "dumb," the principal was greatly ___(e)d. So she kept the boys after school and compelled° them to write "I am not as smart as I think" five hundred times.

➤ _Final Check:_ Party House

Here is a final opportunity for you to strengthen your knowledge of the ten words. First read the following selection carefully. Then fill in each blank with a word from the box at the top of the previous page. (Context clues will help you figure out which word goes in which blank.) Use each word once.

The loud parties at the Phi Gamma fraternity house had (1)_____provoke_____(e)d its neighbors all year. The neighbors complained to the college, but the Phi Gammas were (2)_____shrewd_____ enough to come up with a (3)_____plausible_____ explanation each time. Each explanation, of course, was an elaborate° lie. For example, they once claimed that one of their members tended to have nightmares which would (4)_____recur_____ throughout finals week, making him cry out loudly throughout the night. This, they said, woke up all of the other members, who had gone to bed early that evening. Again and again, the Phi Gammas were let off by the lenient° college dean with only a (5)_____reprimand_____. But members of the other fraternities were (6)_____skeptical_____ about Phi Gamma's excuses. They also disliked the way the group contributed to a negative (7)_____stereotype_____ of fraternities. So they decided on a (8)_____tactic_____ to get back at Phi Gamma. They secretly tape-recorded one of the Phi Gamma meetings. During that meeting, the Phi Gamma members (9)_____ridicule_____(e)d the dean by mocking the way he always believed their excuses. And, still indifferent° to the comfort of their neighbors, they also made plans for more loud parties. When the dean heard the recording, he (10)_____revoke_____(e)d Phi Gamma's campus license.

| _Scores_ | Sentence Check 2 _____% | Final Check _____% |

Enter your scores above and in the vocabulary performance chart on the inside back cover of the book.

consequence	simultaneous
destiny	strategy
detain	tedious
diminish	transaction
procrastinate	vital

Ten Words in Context

In the space provided, write the letter of the meaning closest to that of each **boldfaced** word. Use the context of the sentences to help you figure out each word's meaning.

1 consequence
(kŏn′sĭ-kwĕns)
-noun

- As a **consequence** of her heavy spending at the mall, Lily was short of cash until her next paycheck.
- Small children reach for hot things and sharp objects because they don't know the **consequences** of such actions.

_a_ *Consequence* means   a. an effect.   b. a cause.   c. a rule.

2 destiny
(dĕs′tə-nē)
-noun

- Believing in fate, the soldier wondered if his **destiny** was to die in the coming battle.
- Marc believes that he and Debbie were born for each other and that it was their **destiny** to meet.

_b_ *Destiny* means   a. habit.   b. fate.   c. hope.

3 detain
(dĭ-tān′)
-verb

- Paul's history teacher **detained** him after class to speak privately about his surprisingly low grade on the test.
- **Detained** at home by a friend in urgent need of advice, Gloria was late for work.

_a_ *Detain* means   a. to delay.   b. to leave.   c. to avoid.

4 diminish
(dĭ-mĭn′ĭsh)
-verb

- After Mother yelled, "Turn that thing down!" the sound from the stereo **diminished** from a roar to a soft hum.
- I waited for my anger to **diminish** before discussing the problem with my boss.

_c_ *Diminish* means   a. to grow.   b. to remain.   c. to become less.

5 procrastinate
(prō-krăs′tə-nāt′)
-verb

- Morgan **procrastinated** so long that when she finally returned the dress to the store, it was too late for a refund.
- I can't **procrastinate** any longer. I must study tonight because the final exam is tomorrow morning.

_c_ *Procrastinate* means   a. to do something efficiently.   b. to remember something.   c. to put off doing something.

6 simultaneous
(sī′məl-tā′nē-əs)
-adjective

- In a fair race, all starts must be **simultaneous**.
- Lightning and thunder don't seem to be **simultaneous**—we see the lightning before we hear the thunder.

_b_ *Simultaneous* means   a. similar.   b. happening at the same time.   c. delayed.

7 strategy
(străt′ə-jē)
-noun

- The best **strategy** for teaching your children manners is to use good manners yourself.
- The general's **strategy** was to surround the enemy troops during the night.

_c_ *Strategy* means   a. reason.   b. place.   c. plan.

8 tedious
(tē′dē-əs)
-adjective

- **Tedious** chores, like washing dishes, are less boring if you do them while listening to the radio or talking with a friend.
- John found the homework assignment very **tedious**; the questions were dull and repetitious.

_a_ *Tedious* means   a. uninteresting.   b. serious.   c. unnecessary.

9 transaction
(trăn-săk′shən)
-noun

- **Transactions** at flea markets often involve bargaining.
- Among some business people, a **transaction** is concluded with a handshake. These business deals are never put in writing.

_b_ *Transaction* means   a. a mood.   b. a business interaction.   c. an instruction.

10 vital
(vīt′l)
-adjective

- Water is **vital** to the survival of all living things. For example, people who stop drinking liquids will die in just a few days.
- For Teresa to pass her math course, it is **vital** that she pass the final exam.

_b_ *Vital* means   a. unimportant.   b. essential.   c. not harmful.

Matching Words with Definitions

Following are definitions of the ten words. Clearly write or print each word next to its definition. The sentences above and on the previous page will help you decide on the meaning of each word.

1. _____simultaneous_____   Happening or done at the same time

2. _____diminish_____   To lessen; decrease

3. _____strategy_____   A method; overall plan

4. _____consequence_____   A result

5. _____transaction_____   A business deal or action; exchange of money, goods, or services

6. _____vital_____   Necessary; extremely important

7. _____tedious_____   Boring; uninteresting because of great length, slowness, or repetition

8. _____detain_____   To delay; keep from continuing

9. _____procrastinate_____   To put off doing something until later

10. _____destiny_____   Something bound to happen to someone; fate

CAUTION: Do not go any further until you are sure the above answers are correct. Then you can use the definitions to help you in the following practices. Your goal is eventually to know the words well enough so that you don't need to check the definitions at all.

➤ *Sentence Check 1*

Using the answer line provided, complete each item below with the correct word from the box. Use each word once.

a. **consequence**	b. **destiny**	c. **detain**	d. **diminish**	e. **procrastinate**
f. **simultaneous**	g. **strategy**	h. **tedious**	i. **transaction**	j. **vital**

transaction 1. The ___ at the checkout counter was delayed by an incorrect price label.

diminish 2. The afternoon sunshine caused the snowman's height to ___ from six feet to three.

procrastinate 3. To ___ is to follow the old saying "Never do today what you can put off until tomorrow."

consequence 4. As a ___ of his staying out too late, Wilson wasn't allowed out for a week.

simultaneous 5. The dancers' movements were meant to be ___. But when the ballerina leaped, her partner failed to move in time to catch her.

strategy 6. Helen's chess ___ is to make her moves so quickly that her opponent believes she's an expert.

destiny 7. Ryan felt it was his wife's ___ to die in the fire. He refused to believe her death was meaningless.

vital 8. The secret agent paid for information he thought was ___ to our national safety, but he had been tricked into buying useless knowledge.

detain 9. "If my science teacher didn't ___ us past the bell every day, I wouldn't be late for my next class," explained George.

tedious 10. To make raking autumn leaves less ___, my sister and I took turns jumping into the newly created piles.

NOTE: Now check your answers to these questions by turning to page 177. Going over the answers carefully will help you prepare for the next two practices, for which answers are not given.

➤ *Sentence Check 2*

Using the answer lines provided, complete each item below with **two** words from the box. Use each word once.

strategy
simultaneous 1–2. Before the tug-of-war started, the blue team decided on a ___: each time the captain shouted "Go!" all team members would give hard ___ pulls.

detain
transaction 3–4. "I'm sorry to ___ you," the salesman said, "but a ___ involving payment with a personal check takes longer than a cash purchase."

consequence
vital 5–6. The ___ of poor nutrition is illness. In addition to enough exercise and ample° sleep, a balanced diet is ___ for health.

procrastinate   7–8. Unfortunately, it doesn't help to ___ in paying your bills—putting them
diminish   off doesn't make them ___ or disappear. In fact, chronic° late payers
not only impair° their credit ratings; they end up paying more because
of late charges and interest payments.

tedious   9–10. "This job is so ___ that I'm afraid I'll die of boredom," said the file
destiny   clerk. "Is it my ___ to put things in alphabetical order for the rest of my
life?"

➤ _Final Check:_ Procrastinator

Here is a final opportunity for you to strengthen your knowledge of the ten words. First read the following
selection carefully. Then fill in each blank with a word from the box at the top of the previous page.
(Context clues will help you figure out which word goes in which blank.) Use each word once.

One of these days there is going to be a "new me": I will no longer (1)_____procrastinate_____.

I'm making this my New Year's resolution. Well, yes, I concede° that it's March and I still haven't

acted. I was going to make this resolution in January, but all that Christmas shopping and cookie

baking (2)_____detain_____(e)d me. In February I figured out a (3)_____strategy_____

to help me stop putting things off, and I'll get around to it soon because I know it's

(4)_____vital_____ for me to change my ways. My problem is that some jobs are

so (5)_____tedious_____ that just thinking of them makes me want to yawn. But I

know that the (6)_____consequence_____ of putting things off is that nothing actually gets

done. And once I get started on my New Year's resolution, a new me will emerge°. My tendency

to delay things will surely gradually (7)_____diminish_____. I'll finish every household

project and financial (8)_____transaction_____ that I start. A good tactic° would be to

make a list of activities that can be done (9)_____simultaneous_____ly, such as sewing while

watching TV, or cleaning my junk drawer and talking to my mother on the phone at the same time.

I'd make a list now if I could just find a pen. I was going to buy pens yesterday, but I figured I'd be

at the mall on Friday, so why make a special trip? I'll make the list later. Oh well, maybe it's just

my (10)_____destiny_____ to put things off. If it's inevitable°, why fight it?

| _Scores_   Sentence Check 2 _____% | Final Check _____% |

Enter your scores above and in the vocabulary performance chart on the inside back cover of the book.

-able	man
cent-, centi-	mem
in-	mono-, mon-
-logy, -ology	port
mal-	therm-, thermo-

Ten Word Parts in Context

Figure out the meanings of the following ten word parts by looking *closely* and *carefully* at the context in which they appear. Then, in the space provided, write the letter of the meaning closest to that of each word part.

1 -able

- The couch was too hard to be a **comfortable** bed.
- Come on, now. Can you really say a movie like *Slaughter in the Subway* is **enjoyable**?

_b_ The word part *-able* means   a. hand.   b. able to.   c. theory.

2 cent-, centi-

- The nineteenth **century** didn't start in 1900. It started in 1801 and ran through 1900.
- The **centipede** doesn't really have a hundred feet; it just has so many that it seems there are a hundred of them.

_b_ The word part *cent-* or *centi-* means   a. two.   b. hundred.   c. remember.

3 in-

- The glass on the door was so clean that it was **invisible**, which explains why I walked into the door instead of opening it.
- "Only an **inexperienced** burglar leaves fingerprints," said the detective.

_a_ The word part *in-* means   a. not.   b. science.   c. heat.

4 -logy, -ology

- "I'd probably major in **biology**," Cybil explained, "if I didn't have to kill those little frogs."
- To help them find petroleum, oil companies hire people who have studied **geology**.

_c_ The word part *-logy* or *-ology* means   a. good.   b. carry.   c. science of.

5 mal-

- What should we do about the many children suffering from neglect and **maltreatment**?
- When the doctor gave his patient a medicine with harmful side effects, the patient sued for **malpractice**.

_b_ The word part *mal-* means   a. in.   b. bad.   c. carry.

6 man

- Mark Twain may have been the first author ever to give a publisher an entire **manuscript** that was typed, rather than handwritten.
- The worker's rough hands show he's done much **manual** labor.

_c_ The word part *man* means   a. against.   b. badly.   c. hand.

7 mem

- I wrote a **memo** to remind me what to do today, but I forgot where I put it.
- In the small cemetery, every flower left in **memory** of a loved one shows up brightly.

_c_ The word part *mem* means

a. carry.   b. heat.   c. remember.

8 mono-, mon-

- When Pastor Brook preached in a **monotone**, he found his congregation snoring in stereo.
- **Monogamy** is not the only type of marriage relationship. In many societies, a person may have more than one mate.

_a_ The word part *mono-* or *mon-* means

a. one.   b. theory.   c. heat.

9 port

- We had so many suitcases that we had a **porter** take them from the airport to our car.
- "My daughter is overly tender toward others," said Salvador. "She feeds the hungry and **supports** both the weak and her husband."

_c_ The word part *port* means

a. write.   b. badly.   c. carry.

10 therm-, thermo-

- In the fall, a **thermos** full of hot soup is a great addition to any hiking gear.
- An electronic **thermometer** beeps when the body heat has been fully measured.

_c_ The word part *therm-* or *thermo-* means

a. new.   b. science.   c. heat.

Matching Word Parts with Definitions

Following are definitions of the ten word parts. Clearly write or print each word part next to its definition. The sentences above and on the previous page will help you decide on the meaning of each word part.

1. _____in-_____   Not, lack of

2. _____-logy, -ology_____   Study of, science of

3. _____cent-, centi-_____   Hundred

4. _____therm-, thermo-_____   Heat

5. _____man_____   Hand

6. _____mono-, mon-_____   One

7. _____mal-_____   Bad, badly

8. _____port_____   Carry

9. _____mem_____   Remember

10. _____-able_____   Able to, able to be

CAUTION: Do not go any further until you are sure the above answers are correct. Then you can use the definitions to help you in the following practices. Your goal is eventually to know the word parts well enough so that you don't need to check the definitions at all.

➤ *Sentence Check 1*

Using the answer line provided, complete each *italicized* word in the sentences below with the correct word part from the box. Use each word part once.

| a. **-able** | b. **cent-, centi-** | c. **in-** | d. **-logy, -ology** | e. **mal-** |
| f. **man** | g. **mem** | h. **mono-, mon-** | i. **port** | j. **therm-, thermo-** |

malnutrition   1. The dogs had been fed so poorly that they suffered from (. . . *nutrition*) ___.

centimeters   2. Five (. . . *meters*) ___ means 5/100 of a meter—the length of an eyebrow.

Criminology   3. (*Crimin* . . .) ___ now includes the study of computer crime.

monorail   4. I always feel unsafe on a(n) (. . . *rail*) ___. I think a train is more safe running on two rails than on one.

memorize   5. To (. . . *orize*) the names of the five Great Lakes, remember "HOMES," which is made up of the lakes' initials: Huron, Ontario, Michigan, Erie, and Superior.

manufactured   6. Before there were machines, everything had to be (. . . *ufactured*) ___ by hand.

inactivity   7. Young children can take only small doses of (. . . *activity*) ___, and then they need to move around.

laughable   8. The union representative objected, saying, "Asking the workers to take a 20 percent pay cut would be (*laugh* . . .) ___ if it weren't so awful."

thermal   9. When I visit my relatives in Alaska during the winter, I pack several pairs of (. . . *al*) ___ underwear.

imported   10. In 1856, the U.S. Cavalry (*im* . . . *ed*) thirty-three camels from Egypt to use as mounts for its soldiers.

NOTE: Now check your answers to these questions by turning to page 177. Going over the answers carefully will help you prepare for the next two practices, for which answers are not given.

➤ *Sentence Check 2*

Using the answer lines provided, complete each *italicized* word in the sentences below with the correct word part from the box. Use each word part once.

monarch
transportation   1–2. "There is room for only one (. . . *arch*) ___ in this country," announced the king. "Anyone who disagrees with me will get free sea (*trans* . . . *ation*) ___—without a boat."

centennial
memorial   3–4. In 1963, during the (. . . *ennial*) ___ of the Civil War (1861–1865), we visited a (. . . *orial*) ___ to some of the soldiers who had died. It's hard to conceive° of the extreme loss of life in that war—at least half a million died in battle!

_____ climatology _____   5–6. While others study (*climat . . .*) ___, I ignore the weather and simply

_____ thermostat _____   leave my (*. . . ostat*) ___ set at a constant, comfortable sixty-eight

degrees.

_____ manicure _____   7–8. I (*. . . icure*) ___ my nails the (*. . . expensive*) ___ way—by biting

_____ inexpensive _____   them.

_____ debatable _____   9–10. It was (*debat . . .*) ___ whether the cake looked so weird because the

_____ malfunctioned _____   oven (*. . . functioned*) ___ or because I forgot an ingredient. To be

candid°, I think it's my fault.

➤ *Final Check:* King of Cats

Here is a final opportunity for you to strengthen your knowledge of the ten word parts. First read the following selection carefully. Then complete each *italicized* word in the parentheses below with a word from the box at the top of the previous page. (Context clues will help you figure out which word part goes in which blank.) Use each word part once.

They called him King of Cats. He was young, impulsive°, and so hotheaded that he had an

(*. . . ability*) (1)_____ inability _____ to keep his temper. He lived in an Italian city baked by

(*. . . al*) (2)_____ thermal _____ winds in the summer. Life in that hot city was never

(*. . . tonous*) (3)_____ monotonous _____ when his street gang encountered° a rival gang.

(*Re . . . s*) (4)_____ Reports _____ of bloodshed often followed such meetings. He was

raised to fight for his family, including his beautiful cousin. He was willing to do anything to keep

her safe from insult or (*. . . treatment*) (5)_____ maltreatment _____.

This girl fell in love with the leader of a rival gang. Perhaps today (*psych . . .*)

(6)_____ psychology _____ could explain why. At the time, it seemed she was simply

(*. . . ipulated*) (7)_____ manipulated _____ by fate to fall in love with someone who would

be (*unaccept . . .*) (8)_____ unacceptable _____ to her relatives. One (*. . . orable*)

(9)_____ memorable _____ afternoon of that sad year in the sixteenth (*. . . ury*)

(10)_____ century _____, blades flashed. The King of Cats stabbed a member of that

rival gang. His cousin's lover reciprocated° by stabbing him back—to his death.

The King of Cats' name was Tybalt Capulet. His cousin was called Juliet; her lover was

Romeo.

Scores   Sentence Check 2 _____%   Final Check _____%

Enter your scores above and in the vocabulary performance chart on the inside back cover of the book.

UNIT FOUR: *Review*

The box at the right lists twenty-five words from Unit Four. Using the clues at the bottom of the page, fill in these words to complete the puzzle that follows.

Word box:
adapt
affirm
allude
consequence
destiny
diminish
elite
emerge
exile
frugal
impair
indifferent
liberal
notable
query
recede
recur
refute
reprimand
revert
ridicule
shrewd
skeptical
tedious
vital

ACROSS

3. Being or intended for the best or most privileged; superior
5. To rise up or come forth
6. To occur again; happen repeatedly
7. Famous; widely known
9. Something bound to happen to someone; fate
12. To refer indirectly
13. Clever; tricky
15. A result
18. To damage; weaken
19. Having no real interest; unconcerned
22. To adjust to a situation
23. Necessary; extremely important
24. A formal criticism; a harsh scolding

DOWN

1. To question; ask
2. To prove wrong or false
4. Separation from one's native country through force or choice
8. To indicate to be true; state with certainty
10. Boring; uninteresting because of great length, slowness, or repetition
11. Large in amount or quantity; generous
13. Doubting; questioning
14. To move back or away from a particular point or limit
16. To lessen; decrease
17. To make fun of; mock
20. Thrifty; avoiding unnecessary expenses
21. To return to a previous habit or condition

UNIT FOUR: Test 1

PART A
Choose the word that best completes each item and write it in the space provided.

plausible   1. It may not seem ___, but it's true—some people need only fifteen minutes of sleep a day.

      a. frugal   b. tedious   c. elaborate   d. plausible

simultaneous   2. In ___ translation, words are translated as they are spoken. The translator has to be able to listen and talk at the same time.

      a. simultaneous   b. liberal   c. mediocre   d. frugal

provoke   3. A bee will usually not sting unless you first ___ it—for example, by swatting at it.

      a. adapt   b. retain   c. provoke   d. allude

reprimands   4. In kindergarten, an afternoon nap was required. Yet in English class, my napping has earned me ___ from the instructor.

      a. strategies   b. reprimands   c. destinies   d. rituals

frugal   5. Many ___ shoppers buy soy-based foods because they are inexpensive sources of protein.

      a. tedious   b. impulsive   c. frugal   d. sadistic

mediocre   6. The singer's voice is only ___, but he's very popular because his personality is so appealing.

      a. notable   b. mediocre   c. vital   d. elite

ritual   7. For an Arab Muslim man, the entire divorce ___ consists of announcing to his wife before two witnesses, "I divorce you."

      a. ritual   b. immunity   c. destiny   d. ridicule

alleged   8. Although the police report mentioned a(n) ___ "break-in," the gold theft may actually have been an "inside" job.

      a. tedious   b. indulgent   c. alleged   d. indifferent

strategy   9. Tokyo, Japan, has a simple ___ for fitting as many people as possible onto rush-hour trains: workers are hired to push people on.

      a. exile   b. stereotype   c. strategy   d. immunity

query   10. My teacher meant to ___, "Why did you miss the history lecture?" Instead he asked, "Why did you hiss the mystery lecture?"

      a. detain   b. recede   c. query   d. allude

(Continues on next page)

___diminish___   11. Why doesn't crabgrass ever ___? The answer is that every time you yank some out, you spread its seeds, causing more to grow.

  a. procrastinate   b. diminish   c. revoke   d. coerce

___transaction___   12. The most important ___ in my parents' lives was the purchase of their house.

  a. stereotype   b. essence   c. query   d. transaction

___refuted___   13. Experts have ___ the idea that giant redwood trees are the oldest living things on Earth. Certain pine trees that are about 4,600 years of age are now known to be older.

  a. refuted   b. coerced   c. emerged   d. provoked

PART B
Write **C** if the italicized word is used **correctly**. Write **I** if the word is used **incorrectly**.

___I___   14. A tornado's winds can *recede* to speeds as high as two hundred miles an hour.

___I___   15. Arthur came down with the flu because he has a built-in *immunity* to it.

___C___   16. *Elite* members of our society include movie stars and athletes.

___I___   17. The *sadistic* herring gull has a special call that invites other gulls to share its food.

___C___   18. As a *gesture* of respect, my boyfriend makes a point of greeting my parents and grandmother whenever he comes to call for me.

___C___   19. Although most *notable* as a scientist, Albert Einstein was also well known as a spokesman for world peace.

___C___   20. The owl can hardly move its eyes. So the ability to turn its head nearly completely around is *vital* to its survival.

___C___   21. Before eyeglasses were invented, some people whose vision was *impaired* looked through clear gemstones shaped like lenses.

___I___   22. The Liberty Bell, so *exotic* to all Americans, was once offered for sale as scrap metal.

___C___   23. If you're entering a movie theater with a crowd, it's *shrewd* to go left. Since most people head right, you'll get a better choice of seats that way.

___I___   24. The old belief that "gentlemen prefer blondes" was *affirmed* by a poll of college students: most males liked brunettes better.

___C___   25. My brother used to *ridicule* me for talking on the phone so much. He would holler, "Get a doctor! A phone is growing out of Stacy's head."

Score   (Number correct) _____ x 4 = _____ %

Enter your score above and in the vocabulary performance chart on the inside back cover of the book.

UNIT FOUR: Test 2

PART A
Complete each item with a word from the box. Use each word once.

a. **adapt**	b. **coerce**	c. **elaborate**	d. **essence**	e. **exile**
f. **indulgent**	g. **procrastinate**	h. **reciprocate**	i. **recur**	j. **retain**
k. **revert**	l. **stereotype**	m. **tactic**		

reciprocate   1. After my brother gave me the measles, I ___(e)d by giving him the mumps.

elaborate   2. The ___ dollhouse included many realistic details, such as tiny lamps, clocks, and flowers in vases.

essence   3. The ___ of a thunderstorm is energy—energy sometimes equal to that of a dozen atomic bombs.

recur   4. To make sure the hamstring injury does not ___, always stretch your leg muscles before working out.

procrastinate   5. There's a club for people who like to ___. They haven't met yet because they keep postponing their first meeting.

stereotype   6. The ___ of the cowboy is that of a rough and romantic fighter, but most cowboys actually spent their days doing routine chores.

exile   7. A well-known Chinese author had to leave his homeland to avoid being imprisoned. He was forced into ___ for attacking the Chinese government in his writings.

revert   8. On New Year's Eve I decided to stop eating chocolate, but by January 4th I ___(e)d to my old ways—stocking up on on Mars bars and M&M's.

adapt   9. Trained dogs help deaf people ___ to a silent world by alerting them to the sounds of such things as doorbells and smoke alarms.

tactic   10. Many students have used the ___ of blaming the computer for their missed deadlines. They say, for example, "It erased my whole paper."

indulgent   11. In ancient Rome, some of the wealthiest and most self-___ people powdered their hair every day with pure gold dust.

retain   12. Built of white marble and decorated with gems, the famous Taj Mahal of India has ___(e)d its beauty for more than three hundred years.

coerce   13. Because a thief might ___ you into handing over a wallet, carry an extra one with little money, an old ID card, and out-of-date credit cards.

(Continues on next page)

PART B

Write **C** if the italicized word is used **correctly**. Write **I** if the word is used **incorrectly**.

_I_   14. Judging by the smile of relief on his face, the x-ray *dismayed* Dr. Ali.

_I_   15. Iris is so *impulsive* that she won't even take a step outside without first listening to a weather report.

_C_   16. I was *skeptical* when the salesman said I could get a month's worth of frozen food for under fifty dollars a person.

_C_   17. Because so many rain forests are being destroyed, the *destiny* of many animals and insects may be to die out.

_I_   18. Anyone who needs a wheelchair is bound to be *indifferent* to a new one that is able to follow spoken instructions.

_I_   19. According to a study, most working couples spend a *liberal* amount of time talking with their children—on average, less than a minute a day.

_C_   20. The poem *alludes* to so many eighteenth-century events that it is difficult for today's readers to get its full meaning.

_C_   21. The construction company had its license *revoked* when its materials were found to be dangerously weak.

_I_   22. Early Latin American Indians had a *tedious* way of making the world's first sneakers. They simply dipped their feet into liquid rubber straight from the tree.

_C_   23. A camel's hump stores fat that breaks down into water. As a *consequence,* a camel can survive for as long as two weeks without drinking.

_C_   24. Today, those who walk or drive in the city are *detained* by stoplights and traffic. In the future, however, moving sidewalks may make city travel faster by doing away with the need for vehicles and stoplights.

_C_   25. Every morning, the original Declaration of Independence *emerges* from an underground container, where it is protected from extreme heat or cold, water, fire, and explosions. It is then on display during the day in a glass case.

Score   (Number correct) _____ x 4 = _____%

Enter your score above and in the vocabulary performance chart on the inside back cover of the book.

UNIT FOUR: Test 3

PART A
Complete each sentence in a way that clearly shows you understand the meaning of the **boldfaced** word. Take a minute to plan your answer before you write.

> *Example:* A **mediocre** essay is likely to _____ *receive a grade of C* _____.

1. One activity I find especially **tedious** is _____ *(Answers will vary.)* _____

   _____.

2. A cab driver might respond to a **liberal** tip by _____

   _____.

3. When the heater broke, I **adapted** to the sudden drop in temperature by _____

   _____.

4. A **tactic** for dieting is _____

   _____.

5. After Gina invited Daniel out for coffee, he **reciprocated** by _____

   _____.

6. One **impulsive** thing I once did was _____

   _____.

7. An **indulgent** parent might react to a child screaming for candy by _____

   _____.

8. I sometimes **procrastinate** when _____

   _____.

9. To achieve my career goals, it is **vital** that I _____

   _____.

10. A **skeptical** response to "I love you" is "_____

   _____."

(Continues on next page)

PART B

After each **boldfaced** word are a *synonym* (a word that means the same as the boldfaced word), an *antonym* (a word that means the opposite of the boldfaced word), and a word that is neither. On the answer line, write the letter of the word that is the antonym.

> *Example:* __b__ **plausible**   a. believable   b. doubtful   c. soft

__a__ 11. **retain**   a. lose   b. keep   c. limit

__b__ 12. **frugal**   a. hasty   b. wasteful   c. thrifty

__c__ 13. **consequence**   a. pattern   b. result   c. cause

__c__ 14. **impair**   a. weaken   b. call   c. strengthen

__a__ 15. **ridicule**   a. praise   b. mock   c. disprove

PART C

Use five of the following ten words in sentences. Make it clear that you know the meaning of the word you use. Feel free to use the past tense or plural form of a word.

a. **coerce**	b. **diminish**	c. **emerge**	d. **gesture**	e. **indifferent**
f. **recur**	g. **ritual**	h. **sadistic**	i. **shrewd**	j. **strategy**

16. _____ *(Answers will vary.)* _____

_____

17. _____

_____

18. _____

_____

19. _____

_____

20. _____

_____

> *Score*   (Number correct) _____ x 5 = _____%

Enter your score above and in the vocabulary performance chart on the inside back cover of the book.

UNIT FOUR: Test 4 (Word Parts)

PART A

Listed in the left-hand column below are ten common word parts, along with words in which the parts are used. In each blank, write in the letter of the correct definition on the right.

Word Parts	Examples	Definitions
_c_ 1. **-able**	comfortable, enjoyable	a. Carry
_d_ 2. **cent-, centi-**	century, centipede	b. By hand
_e_ 3. **in-**	invisible, inexperienced	c. Able to, able to be
_g_ 4. **-ology, -logy**	biology, geology	d. Hundred
_i_ 5. **mal-**	maltreatment, malpractice	e. Not, lack of
_b_ 6. **man**	manuscript, manual	f. Heat
_j_ 7. **mem**	memo, memorial	g. Study of, science of
_h_ 8. **mono-, mon-**	monotone, monogamy	h. One
_a_ 9. **port**	porter, support	i. Bad, badly
_f_ 10. **therm-, thermo-**	thermos, thermometer	j. Remember

PART B

Using the answer line provided, complete each *italicized* word in the sentences below with the correct word part from the box. Not every word part will be used.

a. **-able**	b. **cent-**	c. **in-**	d. **-ology**	e. **mal-**
f. **man**	g. **mem**	h. **mono-**	i. **port**	j. **therm-**

erasable   11. Someone who knows we all make mistakes invented an (*eras . . .*) ___ ink.

Sociology   12. (*Soci . . .*) ___ is the study of the origins, development, and institutions of human society.

memory   13. One mental patient has such a damaged (. . . *ory*) ___ that he can't remember what happened only a few minutes before.

portable   14. After working so hard on my flower garden, I wish it were (. . . *able*) ___. Then I could take it with me next month when I move to a new house.

insane   15. The lawyer claimed his client was (. . . *sane*) ___ when she killed her husband with a steam iron.

(Continues on next page)

PART C
Use your knowledge of word parts to determine the meaning of the **boldfaced** words. On the answer line, write the letter of each meaning.

___b___ 16. My grandmother will be a **centenarian** next month, so we're having a huge party.

      a. student   b. hundred-year-old   c. great-great-grandmother

___b___ 17. The first clay pot I ever made was very **malformed**.

      a. formed too small   b. poorly formed   c. formed by hand

___a___ 18. Tarzan's vocabulary included many **monosyllabic** words: "Jane. Come. We find Boy."

      a. one-syllable   b. few-syllable   c. short-syllable

___c___ 19. The sheriff reached for **manacles** to put on the violent drunk driver.

      a. ropes   b. chains   c. handcuffs

___c___ 20. For silly fun, my family used to go on picnics in the winter. Mother would pack steaming thick soup in a **thermos jug**.

      a. a jug made by hand   b. a jug that can be carried   c. a jug that keeps things warm

Score   (Number correct) _____ x 5 = _____%

Enter your score above and in the vocabulary performance chart on the inside back cover of the book.

Unit Five

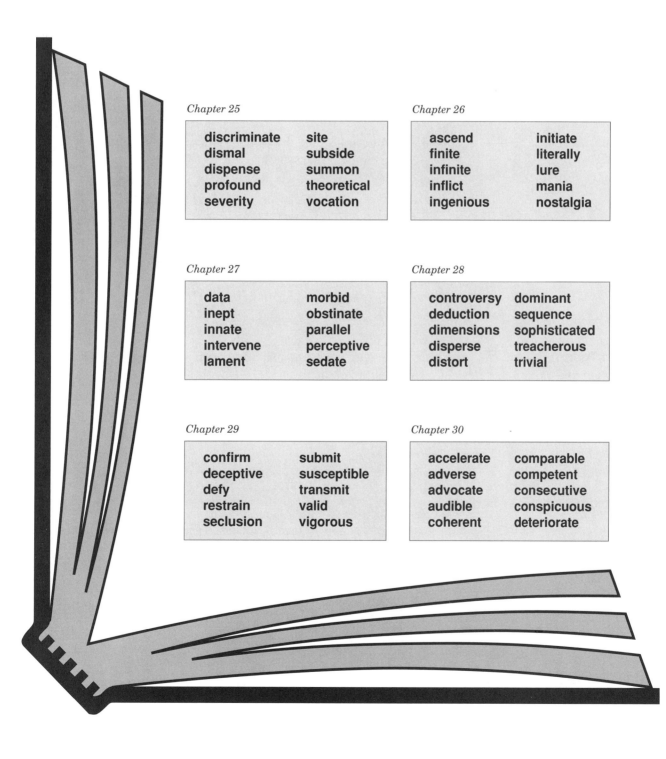

discriminate	site
dismal	subside
dispense	summon
profound	theoretical
severity	vocation

Ten Words in Context

In the space provided, write the letter of the meaning closest to that of each **boldfaced** word. Use the context of the sentences to help you figure out each word's meaning.

1 **discriminate**
(dǐ-skrǐm′ə-nāt′)
-*verb*

- It's easy to **discriminate** between canned and fresh vegetables—fresh vegetables taste much better.
- Tests show that women tend to **discriminate** among colors better than men. Cherry red, cranberry red, and purplish red are all simply dark red to many men.

a *Discriminate* means   a. to tell the difference.   b. to become confused.   c. to make an error.

2 **dismal**
(dǐz′məl)
-*adjective*

- Kyle was disappointed by the **dismal** news that his knee injury would keep him out of college for a whole semester.
- "It is a **dismal** rainy day," Mona told her disappointed children. "But we don't have to cancel the picnic—we can have it on the kitchen floor."

c *Dismal* means   a. welcome.   b. lengthy.   c. gloomy.

3 **dispense**
(dǐ-spěns′)
-*verb*

- The broken soda machine **dispensed** either a cup or soda, but not both together.
- Restroom soap holders that are supposed to **dispense** liquid soap at each push seem to be empty most of the time.

b *Dispense* means   a. to pay.   b. to give out.   c. to do without.

4 **profound**
(prə-found′)
-*adjective*

- The death of a spouse can cause **profound** depression that, in some cases, can even lead to the death of the partner.
- Ever since her stepfather slapped her mother, Stacy has had a **profound** hatred of him.

a *Profound* means   a. deep.   b. mild.   c. accidental.

5 **severity**
(sə-věr′ə-tē)
-*noun*

- The **severity** of the fire could be seen in the burned, smoking ruins of the once beautiful building.
- Mark believes the **severity** of his punishment was too great. A hundred hours of weekend trash cleanup seemed too harsh a penalty for throwing two Coke cans onto the highway.

b *Severity* means   a. gentleness.   b. intensity.   c. cause.

6 **site**
(sīt)
-*noun*

- The oldest private home in the New England town was named a historical **site**.
- Wounded Knee, South Dakota, is the **site** of a conflict between the federal government and the Sioux Indians in 1971.

c *Site* means   a. a state.   b. a fact.   c. a place.

7 **subside**
(səb-sīd′)
-*verb*

• When I'm really furious, a walk around the block makes the anger **subside**.

• Consuela sat in her car until the storm **subsided**. Then she dashed up the sidewalk and into school.

b *Subside* means

    a. to begin.   b. to lessen.   c. to increase.

8 **summon**
(sŭm′ən)
-*verb*

• When the king couldn't sleep, he would **summon** the court clown to come and entertain him.

• The principal liked to **summon** troublesome students to his office by announcing their names over the loudspeaker.

a *Summon* means

    a. to order.   b. to see.   c. to allow.

9 **theoretical**
(thē′ə-rĕt′ĭ-kĕl)
-*adjective*

• At first, Cruz enjoyed simply looking through his telescope. However, when questions occurred to him, he began to read **theoretical** explanations of what he was seeing.

• The teacher explained the **theoretical** basis for the chemistry experiment so the class would understand why it worked as it did.

b *Theoretical* means

    a. about action.   b. about theory.   c. only imagined.

10 **vocation**
(vō-kā′shən)
-*noun*

• Raising collies was just a hobby for Louise. Her **vocation** was library science.

• If you can't decide on a career, you might wish to take a test that reveals which **vocations** you're suited for.

c *Vocation* means

    a. recreation.   b. activity.   c. occupation.

Matching Words with Definitions

Following are definitions of the ten words. Clearly write or print each word next to its definition. The sentences above and on the previous page will help you decide on the meaning of each word.

1. _____*profound*_____ Deeply felt

2. _____*discriminate*_____ To see differences; distinguish

3. _____*site*_____ The past, present, or future location of a building or buildings or an event

4. _____*vocation*_____ A profession or occupation

5. _____*theoretical*_____ About or based on theory (as opposed to practice or practical use)

6. _____*dismal*_____ Gloomy; cheerless; depressing

7. _____*summon*_____ To send for; order to come

8. _____*dispense*_____ To give out in portions or amounts

9. _____*severity*_____ The condition or quality of being severe; harshness; intensity; seriousness

10. _____*subside*_____ To become less active; calm down; decrease

CAUTION: Do not go any further until you are sure the above answers are correct. Then you can use the definitions to help you in the following practices. Your goal is eventually to know the words well enough so that you don't need to check the definitions at all.

➤ *Sentence Check 1*

Using the answer line provided, complete each item below with the correct word from the box. Use each word once.

a. **discriminate**	b. **dismal**	c. **dispense**	d. **profound**	e. **severity**
f. **site**	g. **subside**	h. **summon**	i. **theoretical**	j. **vocation**

discriminate   1. Since the alligator and the crocodile look so much alike, most people cannot ___ between them.

profound   2. Growing up with poverty gave Timika a ___ desire to help others in need.

subside   3. Near the shore, the waves were enormous, but as we rowed out into open water, they began to ___.

summon   4. I thought I was in trouble when my boss ___(e)d me to her office—until she told me I was getting a raise.

vocation   5. Among the most dangerous ___s are deep-sea diving, mining, and construction.

dismal   6. This room is too ___. It needs a party to brighten it up.

dispense   7. Do you think food machines at public schools should ___ only nutritious foods, such as fruit and juices?

severity   8. Medication should match the ___ of a problem. A powerful painkiller isn't needed for a hangnail.

theoretical   9. I can use the geometry formulas, but I don't understand the ___ basis for them.

site   10. Although the ___ where the hiker claimed a spaceship had landed was burned, no one believed him.

NOTE: Now check your answers to these questions by turning to page 177. Going over the answers carefully will help you prepare for the next two practices, for which answers are not given.

➤ *Sentence Check 2*

Using the answer lines provided, complete each item below with **two** words from the box. Use each word once.

profound
vocation   1–2. My visit to the school for retarded children had a ___ effect on me—it altered° my career plans. I was going to be a nurse, but that day I decided my ___ would be in special education.

site
subside   3–4. It is hard to convey° the terror one feels in seeing someone get hit by a car. It was not until I was ten miles away from the ___ of the accident that my shaking began to ___.

_____ *dismal*

_____ *discriminate*

5–6. The movie was meant to be a dark comedy, but I found it to be ___. I often couldn't ___ between lines in the dialog° that were meant to be funny and lines that were just depressing.

_____ *summon*

_____ *theoretical*

7–8. If you have a question about the principles of this music, we will have to ___ Mr. Burns from his office. A notable° author of music textbooks, he has studied music for years. I can play the music, but I have no ___ knowledge.

_____ *severity*

_____ *dispense*

9–10. Some hospitals now allow patients to judge the ___ of their own pain and to ___ small amounts of medication to themselves as necessary.

➤ *Final Check:* A Change in View

Here is a final opportunity for you to strengthen your knowledge of the ten words. First read the following selection carefully. Then fill in each blank with a word from the box at the top of the previous page. (Context clues will help you figure out which word goes in which blank.) Use each word once.

What an education I got yesterday! I am studying to be a nurse. Part of my preparation for this (1)_____ *vocation* _____ is (2)_____ *theoretical* _____ and part is practical experience. Yesterday, after weeks of studying about mental illness in textbooks, I began my training in a mental hospital. Influenced by the movie stereotype° of such hospitals as being full of zombies and wild people, I was scared. I imagined dark, (3)_____ *dismal* _____ rooms where people sat staring and drooling. I pictured screaming, sadistic° patients trying to hurt me so badly that I would have to (4)_____ *summon* _____ the guards. But yesterday my view of mental hospitals and their patients went through a (5)_____ *profound* _____ change. First of all, the (6)_____ *site* _____ of the hospital is at the edge of a lovely small town, and its grounds are green and neat. When I arrived there, I was brought to a big, cheerful room filled with patients whose morale° was high. They were talking, doing craft projects, or playing Ping-Pong or cards.

I spoke to one patient. She seemed like a nice, normal person who happened to have problems. She reminisced° about the time she first came to the hospital, when the (7)_____ *severity* _____ of her illness had been much greater. At that time, she could not always (8)_____ *discriminate* _____ between what was real and what she imagined. Like many patients, she was often upset and confused. But the doctors put her on medicine, which the nurses still (9)_____ *dispense* _____ three times a day. The medicine, as well as talks with the doctors, nurses, and other patients, has helped make her symptoms (10)_____ *subside* _____. Perhaps our conversation was helpful to her; I know it helped me. Now I'm thinking about working in the mental health field after I get my nursing degree.

Scores	Sentence Check 2 _____%	Final Check _____%

Enter your scores above and in the vocabulary performance chart on the inside back cover of the book.

ascend	initiate
finite	literally
infinite	lure
inflict	mania
ingenious	nostalgia

Ten Words in Context

In the space provided, write the letter of the meaning closest to that of each **boldfaced** word. Use the context of the sentences to help you figure out each word's meaning.

1 ascend
(ə-sĕnd′)
-*verb*

- The express elevator **ascends** directly from the lobby to the twentieth floor.
- Edgar is the boss's son, so he expects to **ascend** to the presidency of the company after his father retires.

_c_ *Ascend* means   a. to go slowly.   b. to go down.   c. to move upward.

2 finite
(fī′nīt)
-*adjective*

- The earth's supply of natural resources is **finite** and will be used up if we are not careful.
- Judging by their endless requests for money, my children don't seem to realize our income is **finite**.

_a_ *Finite* means   a. limited.   b. endless.   c. fine.

3 infinite
(ĭn′fə-nĭt)
-*adjective*

- Some scientists do not believe the universe is **infinite**; they think it actually has limits.
- Dealing with my baby brother, who cries a lot, requires almost an **infinite** amount of patience.

_a_ *Infinite* means   a. endless.   b. known.   c. small.

4 inflict
(ĭn-flĭkt′)
-*verb*

- When Marge is angry, she tries to **inflict** pain with a cutting remark—a habit that does not make her popular with her classmates.
- Loud music can eventually **inflict** permanent damage on the ears.

_b_ *Inflict* means   a. to prevent.   b. to cause.   c. to recognize.

5 ingenious
(ĭn-gēn′yəs)
-*adjective*

- Fran thought she had an **ingenious** plan to sneak out of the house, but it wasn't clever enough to fool her grandmother.
- Few people have been as **ingenious** as Thomas Edison, inventor of the electric light, the phonograph, and the movie camera.

_c_ *Ingenious* means   a. average.   b. unimaginative.   c. clever.

6 initiate
(ĭ-nĭsh′ē-āt)
-*verb*

- Eric **initiated** a change in his company's hiring policy by suggesting that all job openings be advertised.
- True leaders **initiate** new practices, rather than simply following other people's programs.

___ *Initiate* means   a. to remember.   b. to begin.   c. to oppose.

7 literally
(lĭt′ər-ə-lē)
-adverb

- As a child, Jan took the term "man in the moon" **literally**. She was sure she saw his eyes, nose, and mouth up there.
- When I told my nephew to "go fly a kite," I was speaking **literally**—I gave him an eagle kite for his birthday.

_a_ *Literally* means   a. exactly.   b. angrily.   c. fearfully.

8 lure
(lo͞or)
-verb

- The bakery **lured** customers by displaying richly decorated cakes and cookies in its windows.
- The loud music and flashing lights **lured** many teens to the carnival.

_c_ *Lure* means   a. to force.   b. to discourage.   c. to tempt.

9 mania
(mā′nē-ə)
-noun

- My sister has such a **mania** for bird watching that she once climbed a tree to get a better view of a woodpecker.
- Because he's so thin, you'd never guess Ken has a **mania** for chocolate, which he eats daily.

_b_ *Mania* means   a. memory.   b. enthusiasm.   c. respect.

10 nostalgia
(nŏ-stăl′jə)
-noun

- Music from the 1940s fills my grandparents with **nostalgia** because it reminds them of their carefree youth.
- When he came across an old photo of his Little League team, Jerry was overcome with **nostalgia**. He wished he could be ten years old again.

_c_ *Nostalgia* means   a. a sense of freedom.   b. thoughts of the future.   c. a longing for the past.

Matching Words with Definitions

Following are definitions of the ten words. Clearly write or print each word next to its definition. The sentences above and on the previous page will help you decide on the meaning of each word.

1. _____initiate_____   To begin something; start

2. _____infinite_____   Without limits; endless

3. _____literally_____   According to the exact meaning of the words

4. _____inflict_____   To give or cause (pain or hardship)

5. _____ascend_____   To go up; rise; climb

6. _____finite_____   Having limits; limited

7. _____ingenious_____   Clever; inventive

8. _____nostalgia_____   Desire for something in the past

9. _____mania_____   Extreme enthusiasm

10. _____lure_____   To attract by tempting

CAUTION: Do not go any further until you are sure the above answers are correct. Then you can use the definitions to help you in the following practices. Your goal is eventually to know the words well enough so that you don't need to check the definitions at all.

➤ *Sentence Check 1*

Using the answer line provided, complete each item below with the correct word from the box. Use each word once.

a. **ascend**	b. **finite**	c. **infinite**	d. **inflict**	e. **ingenious**
f. **initiate**	g. **literally**	h. **lure**	i. **mania**	j. **nostalgia**

_____ initiate _____ 1. We often ___ conversations with routine questions or comments, such as "How are you today?" or "Hello there."

_____ finite _____ 2. Although the English alphabet is ____, the possible combinations of its letters are almost endless.

_____ inflict _____ 3. Many people think of the dentist as someone who actually likes to ___ pain.

_____ nostalgia _____ 4. Sue feels a wave of ___ when she thinks about the happy days of her childhood on the farm.

_____ lure _____ 5. The opportunity to be helpful ___s people to such fields as nursing and teaching.

_____ mania _____ 6. Because of a(n) ___ for Cabbage Patch dolls, stores couldn't keep enough in stock.

_____ ascend _____ 7. By working hard, Lisa quickly ___(e)d the ladder of success, from secretary to office manager.

_____ infinite _____ 8. There are so many stars in the sky that their number seems ___.

_____ ingenious _____ 9. When temperatures are in the nineties, I'm grateful to the ___ person who invented the air conditioner.

_____ literally _____ 10. Fred kicked the bucket—___. In other words, he only stubbed his toe; he didn't die.

NOTE: Now check your answers to these questions by turning to page 177. Going over the answers carefully will help you prepare for the next two practices, for which answers are not given.

➤ *Sentence Check 2*

Using the answer lines provided, complete each item below with **two** words from the box. Use each word once.

_____ finite _____
_____ infinite _____ 1–2. Some say it is good that our lifetimes are ___, that a(n) ___ number of years would make life less meaningful. However, everyone agrees we should still try to find ways to fight illness and prolong° life.

_____ lure _____
_____ nostalgia _____ 3–4. The West continues to ___ my grandfather, who was raised there. Because of his ___ for his youth, he drives from Florida to Colorado every summer.

_____ *mania* _____

_____ *inflict* _____

5–6. Some cult followers develop a(n) ___ for pleasing their leader and defer° to the leader's every command. They will even ___ injury on themselves to show their loyalty. For example, the teenage girlfriends of the murderer Charles Manson cut a symbol into their foreheads as a gesture° of their love.

_____ *ascend* _____

_____ *initiate* _____

7–8. A red-tailed hawk can ___ hundreds of feet into the air by locking its wings open and riding an upward wind. Then it merely folds its wings and aims at the ground to ___ a dive.

_____ *ingenious* _____

_____ *literally* _____

9–10. One of the world's most ___ scientists, Albert Einstein, ___ gave his brain to science. His will directed that his brain be given for study to a laboratory in Wichita, Kansas.

➤ *Final Check:* **Balloon Flight**

Here is a final opportunity for you to strengthen your knowledge of the ten words. First read the following selection carefully. Then fill in each blank with a word from the box at the top of the previous page. (Context clues will help you figure out which word goes in which blank.) Use each word once.

Human flight was (1)_____*initiate*_____(e)d by a rooster, a duck, and a sheep. A(n) (2)_____*ingenious*_____ inventor got them to try out the first flying machine. Of course, skeptical° people ridiculed° the idea that a machine could fly. They were proved wrong when the animals left the (3)_____*finite*_____ world of the ground to fly into the endless sky for eight minutes. The year was 1783, the place was France, and the aircraft was a hot-air balloon. (Because hot air rises, heating the air in the balloon causes it to (4)_____*ascend*_____.)

Since the experience didn't (5)_____*inflict*_____ any serious injury on the animals, three months later the idea of flying (6)_____*lure*_____(e)d a man named de Rozier, who became the first human to look down on the rooftops of Paris from a hot-air balloon.

In the early 1900s, after 125 years had elapsed°, ballooning was at its peak. In 1910, one retail company said of ballooning in its catalogue, "The whole world is before us in the (7)_____*infinite*_____ loveliness of dawn!" (Daybreak, with its calm air, is the best as well as one of the most beautiful times to fly.)

Although flight has certainly evolved° during the twentieth century, balloon rides are still available in some places. For people with (8)_____*nostalgia*_____ for the olden days, before the (9)_____*mania*_____ for faster and faster travel, a balloon flight is a wonderful way to spend some delightful time (10)_____*literally*_____ floating on air.

| *Scores*   Sentence Check 2 _____% | Final Check _____% |

Enter your scores above and in the vocabulary performance chart on the inside back cover of the book.

data	morbid
inept	obstinate
innate	parallel
intervene	perceptive
lament	sedate

Ten Words in Context

In the space provided, write the letter of the meaning closest to that of each **boldfaced** word. Use the context of the sentences to help you figure out each word's meaning.

1 data
(dā′tə)
-noun

- Marva considers the available **data** on a car—including its fuel economy, safety, and repair record—before deciding whether to buy it.
- Jane Goodall collected important **data** on chimpanzees by observing them in the wild.

b Data means   a. dates.   b. information.   c. goals.

2 inept
(ĭn-ĕpt′)
-adjective

- I am so **inept** at carpentry that in my hand, a hammer is a dangerous weapon.
- Since the actress was **inept** at playing comic characters, she decided to try out only for dramatic roles.

b Inept means   a. effective.   b. unskilled.   c. calm.

3 innate
(ĭ-nāt′)
-adjective

- Rick's musical ability must be **innate**. Even as a young child, he could play the piano by ear and make up his own tunes.
- Psychologists try to learn which of our abilities and interests are **innate** and which of them we gain through experience.

a Innate means   a. inherited.   b. worthwhile.   c. learned through experience.

4 intervene
(ĭn′tər-vēn′)
-verb

- The two boxers would have killed each other if the referee hadn't finally **intervened**.
- When my parents argue, I get out of the way rather than trying to **intervene**.

c Intervene means   a. to leave.   b. to pass through.   c. to come between.

5 lament
(lə-mĕnt′)
-verb

- When her mother died, Evelyn **lamented** her passing for weeks, crying every day.
- Blues songs **lament** loneliness, sadness, and the hardships of life, rather than celebrating happy situations.

a Lament means   a. to mourn.   b. to doubt.   c. to disturb.

6 morbid
(môr′bĭd)
-adjective

- Great comedians can turn a topic as **morbid** as murder into a source of laughter.
- On Halloween, sweet little Nickie chose a **morbid** costume—a disgusting-looking monster with a "bloody" hand and hatchet.

a Morbid means   a. horrible.   b. convenient.   c. boring.

7 obstinate
(ŏb′stə-nĭt)
-adjective

- No matter how much I urged him, Andrew remained **obstinate**—he refused to make up with Lamar, who was once his best friend.
- My father is usually very **obstinate**, but not with his sister, who is even more stubborn than he is.

_c_ *Obstinate* means   a. lazy.   b. dishonest.   c. stubborn.

8 parallel
(păr′ə-lĕl′)
-adjective

- To make the stripes he was painting **parallel**, Alexei measured to be sure there were exactly three inches between them at the top, middle, and bottom.
- **Parallel** lines run alongside each other but never meet.

_b_ *Parallel* means   a. clear.   b. apart an equal distance at every point.   c. going up and down.

9 perceptive
(pər-sĕp′tĭv)
-adjective

- Children are more **perceptive** than many people think. They can usually sense their parents' moods and know whether or not it is a good time to ask for something.
- Professor Banks is very **perceptive**. She always seems to know which of her students are under unusual stress.

_b_ *Perceptive* means   a. detached.   b. aware.   c. selfish.

10 sedate
(sĭ-dāt′)
-adjective

- While the officer wrote out the ticket, Beverly remained **sedate**, and then she even wished him a pleasant day. But after he left, she pounded the steering wheel and loudly cursed the police force.
- An experienced surgeon, Dr. Greenbaum remains **sedate** even in an emergency, performing the most complicated operations with complete calm.

_c_ *Sedate* means   a. angry.   b. doubtful.   c. calm.

Matching Words with Definitions

Following are definitions of the ten words. Clearly write or print each word next to its definition. The sentences above and on the previous page will help you decide on the meaning of each word.

1. _____intervene_____   To come between in order to influence an action, an argument, etc.

2. _____sedate_____   Calm and dignified; serious and unemotional

3. _____parallel_____   The same distance apart at every point

4. _____perceptive_____   Understanding and insightful; observant; aware

5. _____data_____   Information gathered for a study or a decision

6. _____innate_____   Possessed at birth; inborn

7. _____lament_____   To express sorrow for or about; mourn for

8. _____morbid_____   Shocking and disgusting; horrible; gruesome

9. _____inept_____   Clumsy; unskillful

10. _____obstinate_____   Stubborn

CAUTION: Do not go any further until you are sure the above answers are correct. Then you can use the definitions to help you in the following practices. Your goal is eventually to know the words well enough so that you don't need to check the definitions at all.

➣ *Sentence Check 1*

Using the answer line provided, complete each item below with the correct word from the box. Use each word once.

a. **data**	b. **inept**	c. **innate**	d. **intervene**	e. **lament**
f. **morbid**	g. **obstinate**	h. **parallel**	i. **perceptive**	j. **sedate**

_____data_____ 1. For his psychology experiment, Rudy is gathering ___ to show which memory aids work best for students.

_____inept_____ 2. I'm so ___ at bowling that I usually roll the ball straight into the gutter.

_____morbid_____ 3. The child had nightmares after he listened to a(n) ___ story about Dracula that was full of attacks by vampires.

_____sedate_____ 4. While my dog gets excited easily, my cat remains ___ even when everyone around her is in a whirl of activity.

_____parallel_____ 5. When you frame a picture, the picture's edges should be ___ to those of the frame, not dipping down or slanting up.

_____perceptive_____ 6. Kwan is so ___ that she often correctly judges a person's character after a brief conversation.

_____intervene_____ 7. When children get into a fight, it is sometimes best not to ___, but to let them work it out themselves.

_____obstinate_____ 8. I tried to persuade my son to join the family for dinner, but he was ___, refusing to leave his room no matter what I said.

_____lament_____ 9. People all over the United States ___(e)d the death of Martin Luther King, who is now honored with a national holiday on his birthday.

_____innate_____ 10. Richard's gift for fixing machines seems ___. Even as a child, he could take one look at a broken machine and know what was wrong with it.

NOTE: Now check your answers to these questions by turning to page 177. Going over the answers carefully will help you prepare for the next two practices, for which answers are not given.

➣ *Sentence Check 2*

Using the answer lines provided, complete each item below with **two** words from the box. Use each word once.

_____sedate_____
_____obstinate_____ 1–2. As a child, Calvin was ___, rarely excited or upset. As a teenager, however, he is often angry and ___—so stubborn that he hates to change his mind. We hope that after adolescence, he'll revert° to being calm again.

_____morbid_____
_____data_____ 3–4. Angie loves shocking films. She has seen every ___ horror movie ever made and even collects ___ about the films—dates, actors, directors, etc.

_____*innate*_____   5–6. Jason's math ability must be ___. By age 2 he could add and subtract,
_____*parallel*_____   and by 7 he understood the concept that two ___ lines can't meet no
matter how long they are.

_____*lament*_____   7–8. "I ___ the passing of the days when employees did their jobs right," the
_____*inept*_____   shop owner complained. "Today, workers not only are ___ but do
nothing to improve their skills."

_____*perceptive*_____   9–10. A good marriage counselor is ___ enough to understand both the
_____*intervene*_____   husband's and the wife's points of view. And rather than ___ in the
couple's arguments, the counselor helps them learn strategies° for
solving their problems themselves.

➤ *Final Check:* **Family Differences**

Here is a final opportunity for you to strengthen your knowledge of the ten words. First read the following
selection carefully. Then fill in each blank with a word from the box at the top of the previous page.
(Context clues will help you figure out which word goes in which blank.) Use each word once.

I am always amazed at how different all of my brothers and sisters are. Sheila, who succeeds
at everything she tries, simply has no patience with the rest of us. She thinks we are
(1)_____*inept*_____ at everything and that it's up to her to (2)_____*intervene*_____ in
what we do so that things will be done the right way—her way. Jack, on the other hand, is very
(3)_____*sedate*_____. He doesn't let anything bother him, and so he rarely loses his temper
and is quite indulgent° of the desires of others. Chris is the one who never gives in. As a baby, he
was already so (4)_____*obstinate*_____ that he would spit food he didn't like right at my
mother. Daisy, the most social, likes people and seems to have a(n) (5)_____*innate*_____
ability to make them feel good. She has always been very (6)_____*perceptive*_____, knowing
just what mood others were in and what they might need. Frank is the weird one. He has always
been attracted by unusual activities. While the rest of us kids would be riding bikes or jumping
ropes, he would be doing something (7)_____*morbid*_____, like holding a funeral for a
dead frog or bird or snake. He got mad at us whenever we failed to (8)_____*lament*_____ a
death as much as he did. Betty has the quickest mind of us all. When she was just 4, she told my
dad, "Those two shelves aren't (9)_____*parallel*_____—they are farther apart on the left
than on the right." By age 6, she was collecting (10)_____*data*_____ for a book she was
writing on insects. Also ingenious°, Betty has devised° various gadgets around our house,
including a doorbell for our dog. Yes, my brothers and sisters are all different. They may be
strange at times, but they're never boring.

Scores	Sentence Check 2 _____%	Final Check _____%

Enter your scores above and in the vocabulary performance chart on the inside back cover of the book.

controversy	dominant
deduction	sequence
dimensions	sophisticated
disperse	treacherous
distort	trivial

Ten Words in Context

In the space provided, write the letter of the meaning closest to that of each **boldfaced** word. Use the context of the sentences to help you figure out each word's meaning.

1 **controversy**
(kŏn′trə-vûr′sē)
-noun

- There was no longer any **controversy**—everyone agreed that the all-male dining club should now accept female members.
- Our class is studying the **controversy** over whether or not we should have the death penalty.

_b_ *Controversy* means
    a. an agreement.
    b. an argument.
    c. an order.

2 **deduction**
(dĭ-dŭk′shən)
-noun

- When the dog barked, I figured he had to go out again. But my **deduction** was incorrect—he was barking at a raccoon in our trash can.
- The great fictional detective Sherlock Holmes was a master at making **deductions**, reasoning out solutions to puzzling crimes.

_b_ *Deduction* means
    a. a mistake.
    b. a conclusion.
    c. a question.

3 **dimensions**
(dĭ-měn′shəns)
-noun

- The pool's **dimensions** were odd—its length and width were huge, yet it wasn't very deep.
- Let's write down the **dimensions** of the kitchen walls so we can buy the right amount of wallpaper.

_a_ *Dimensions* means
    a. measurements.
    b. colors.
    c. wallpaper.

4 **disperse**
(dĭ-spûrs′)
-verb

- The basketball landed in the midst of some pigeons, causing them to **disperse** in all directions.
- The police made the large crowd **disperse** because people are easier to manage in small groups.

_c_ *Disperse* means
    a. to stay.
    b. to call out.
    c. to scatter.

5 **distort**
(dĭ-stôrt′)
-verb

- To sell more papers, some newspapers **distort** the news by reporting rumors as if they were true.
- Don't believe everything you hear—people often **distort** facts when they gossip.

_c_ *Distort* means
    a. to tell accurately.
    b. to blame.
    c. to misrepresent.

6 **dominant**
(dŏm′ə-nənt)
-adjective

- The **dominant** baboons of a troop are the biggest, most aggressive males. Fearful of these males, the other baboons yield to them.
- Mr. Rodriguez may be quiet, but he's the **dominant** person in this office. No one questions his authority.

_c_ *Dominant* means
    a. most helpful.
    b. youngest.
    c. most powerful.

7 sequence
(sē′kwĕns)
-noun

- The code's **sequence** was essential: 342 would turn off the alarm, but 432 or 234 would not.
- The lawyer established the **sequence** of events: The robber first climbed the roof and then entered the house through the attic. Then he went to the bedroom and stole the jewelry.

a *Sequence* means   a. order.   b. purpose.   c. value.

8 sophisticated
(sə-fĭs′tĭ-kā′tĭd)
-adjective

- Having already worked for four years, sixteen-year-old Eddie is more **sophisticated** about the world of work than any of his friends.
- Don't let the professor's simple clothes and manner fool you. When it comes to teaching and science, he's very **sophisticated**.

c *Sophisticated* means   a. honest.   b. lacking in confidence.   c. experienced.

9 treacherous
(trĕch′ər-əs)
-adjective

- During the American Revolution, the **treacherous** American soldier Benedict Arnold tried to aid the British.
- I felt it was **treacherous** of my friend Jack to go out with my old girlfriend the day after she and I broke up.

a *Treacherous* means   a. disloyal.   b. surprising.   c. influential.

10 trivial
(trĭv′ē-əl)
-adjective

- The principal had a bad reputation for suspending students for **trivial** offenses, such as talking too loudly in the hallways.
- When I'm nervous, it helps me to concentrate on some **trivial** activity, such as washing dishes or watching a game show.

c *Trivial* means   a. unusual.   b. serious.   c. unimportant.

Matching Words with Definitions

Following are definitions of the ten words. Clearly write or print each word next to its definition. The sentences above and on the previous page will help you decide on the meaning of each word.

1. _disperse_ — To break up and spread out
2. _treacherous_ — Disloyal; traitorous
3. _deduction_ — A conclusion reached through reasoning
4. _trivial_ — Unimportant; not significant
5. _controversy_ — A debate; an argument; discussion of an important issue with opposing views
6. _dominant_ — Having or using the most control or influence
7. _sophisticated_ — Wise about the ways of the world; knowledgeable
8. _dimensions_ — Measurements in width, length, and sometimes depth
9. _distort_ — To misrepresent; tell in an untrue or misleading way
10. _sequence_ — The order in which one thing follows another

CAUTION: Do not go any further until you are sure the above answers are correct. Then you can use the definitions to help you in the following practices. Your goal is eventually to know the words well enough so that you don't need to check the definitions at all.

➤ *Sentence Check 1*

Using the answer line provided, complete each item below with the correct word from the box. Use each word once.

a. **controversy**	b. **deduction**	c. **dimensions**	d. **disperse**	e. **distort**
f. **dominant**	g. **sequence**	h. **sophisticated**	i. **treacherous**	j. **trivial**

_____disperse_____   1. When I flipped on the kitchen light, roaches quickly ___(e)d in all directions.

_____deduction_____   2. Scientists observe facts and then make ___s based on those facts.

_____controversy_____   3. There's a great ___ in this country over abortion.

_____dominant_____   4. Flora was the ___ person in the business. Her partner, Pat, wasn't the type to take charge of things.

_____distort_____   5. With each retelling of the story, Wes ___(e)d the facts even more. Before long, the fish had become a giant tuna, and the battle had lasted for hours.

_____trivial_____   6. Children often argue about things that seem ___ to adults, such as who gets to sit in the front seat of the car and whose turn it is to feed the cats.

_____dimensions_____   7. In Tokyo, space is so limited that most apartments and homes are very small. The ___ of some bedrooms are barely larger than a closet's.

_____treacherous_____   8. After my family moved and I joined the baseball team at a new school, I felt ___ when I had to pitch against the team from my old school.

_____sophisticated_____   9. If Artie were a more ___ dresser, he might be promoted. But if he continues to wear dirty tennis shoes and sweatbands to work, he'll be in the mailroom forever.

_____sequence_____   10. The ___ of moves for a basketball layup is simple: first leap toward the hoop, and then release the ball with one hand so that it gently hits the backboard and drops into the net.

NOTE: Now check your answers to these questions by turning to page 177. Going over the answers carefully will help you prepare for the next two practices, for which answers are not given.

➤ *Sentence Check 2*

Using the answer lines provided, complete each item below with **two** words from the box. Use each word once.

_____dimensions_____
_____trivial_____   1–2. "Check the ___ of your bookcase very carefully to be sure it is straight and the shelves are parallel°," said the carpentry teacher. "Even a mistake of a quarter of an inch is not ___."

_____treacherous_____
_____disperse_____   3–4. After learning that a ___ member of their unit had told the enemy their location, the sergeant ordered his men to ___ throughout the forest.

_____distort_____
_____dominant_____   5–6. My boss often ___s the truth by suggesting he's the ___ person in the shoe store. In reality, the store owner makes all the important decisions.

_____deduction_____   7–8. On the basis of my experience, I have made this ___: managers are

_____sophisticated_____   often ___ about financial transactions° but not so knowledgable when it comes to handling people.

_____controversy_____   9–10. The ___ on the movie set was about the ___ of scenes. Some actors

_____sequence_____   thought the love scene should come before the chase scene, but the director wanted the opposite.

➤ _Final Check:_ Murder Mystery

Here is a final opportunity for you to strengthen your knowledge of the ten words. First read the following selection carefully. Then fill in each blank with a word from the box at the top of the previous page. (Context clues will help you figure out which word goes in which blank.) Use each word once.

There was a great deal of (1)_____controversy_____ among the London police over who could have killed the city's richest citizen and how to find the killer. They finally agreed to summon° the world-famous detective Ernest G. Mann. Mr. Mann was a shrewd° and (2)_____sophisticated_____ gentleman—he knew the world and understood people. And when it came to murder, he spoke with such authority that no one doubted who was the (3)_____dominant_____ person in the room.

Mr. Mann ordered the crowd of policemen to (4)_____disperse_____ throughout the house so he would have space to work where the murder had occurred, in the dining room. One quick glance told him the room's (5)_____dimensions_____ to the nearest inch. After studying the mess in the room, he also knew the (6)_____sequence_____ of events—the word, the angry toss, the punch, the shot. He circled the room, eyeing every single item in it. "Nothing can be considered (7)_____trivial_____ when murder is concerned," he said. All evidence is important. It is vital° that I see everything! Everything!"

Next he read the police report and questioned the cook. "Ah, Mr. Cook, what you have just told me is different from what you told the police. Are you trying to (8)_____distort_____ the truth?"

At that, the red-faced cook jumped up and headed for the door. "Wait!" called Mr. Mann. "You are only making it worse. But no matter. The mystery is solved." Then he said to the police in the hallway, "That cook is a (9)_____treacherous_____ man. Anyone who would kill his employer over a reprimand° about lumpy gravy is too traitorous to walk the streets. Arrest him, officers."

"But . . . but, how did you know?" cried the cook.

"It was a simple (10)_____deduction_____, sir. The facts were all here. They just needed a logical mind to put them together correctly." And with that, Ernest G. Mann spun around and left.

Scores	Sentence Check 2 _____%	Final Check _____%

Enter your scores above and in the vocabulary performance chart on the inside back cover of the book.

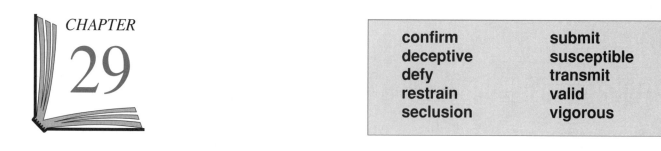

CHAPTER

29

confirm	submit
deceptive	susceptible
defy	transmit
restrain	valid
seclusion	vigorous

Ten Words in Context

In the space provided, write the letter of the meaning closest to that of each **boldfaced** word. Use the context of the sentences to help you figure out each word's meaning.

1 **confirm**
(kən-fûrm′)
-*verb*
- Mr. Smith was released by the police when someone **confirmed** his statement that he had been out of town the day of the murder.
- "Yes, it's true," the union leader said, **confirming** the report that the teachers would refuse to do lunch duty from now on.

_b_ *Confirm* means   a. to deny.   b. to support.   c. to ignore.

2 **deceptive**
(dĭ-sĕp′tĭv)
-*adjective*
- The seeming ease with which Nadia plays the piano is **deceptive**. Actually, she practices four hours each day.
- After stealing the radio, Meg remained silent while another student was wrongly accused. Her silence was as **deceptive** as an outright lie.

_c_ *Deceptive* means   a. modest.   b. flexible.   c. misleading.

3 **defy**
(dĭ-fī′)
-*verb*
- The automotive plant workers voted to **defy** the company and go on strike.
- After being forbidden to go out three evenings in a row, Ted **defied** his parents by walking right out the front door.

_a_ *Defy* means   a. to oppose.   b. to support.   c. to learn from.

4 **restrain**
(rĭ-strān′)
-*verb*
- I **restrained** myself from laughing when my brother made a funny face while Uncle William told us—yet again—the story of his operation. I certainly did not want to hurt Uncle Will's feelings.
- Larry was so angry that we had to **restrain** him by force from punching Neal.

_b_ *Restrain* means   a. to forgive.   b. to prevent.   c. to train.

5 **seclusion**
(sĭ-klōō′zhən)
-*noun*
- The **seclusion** of the mountain cabin started to bother Veronica. She missed the city and being with other people.
- I work best in **seclusion**, where no one can interrupt the flow of my thoughts.

_a_ *Seclusion* means   a. isolation.   b. crowding.   c. relaxation.

6 **submit**
(səb-mĭt′)
-*verb*
- After bucking wildly for several minutes, the horse calmed down and **submitted** to the rider.
- For reasons of safety, travelers must **submit** to having their luggage inspected at airports.

_c_ *Submit* means   a. to object.   b. to admit.   c. to give in.

160

7 susceptible
(sə-sĕp′tə-bəl)
-adjective

• Lina is so **susceptible** to blushing that she turns away whenever she is embarrassed so that no one will see her face change color.
• People who smoke are more **susceptible** to colds than others.

_b_ *Susceptible* means

a. happy about.   b. likely to be affected with.   c. attracted by.

8 transmit
(trăns-mĭt′)
-verb

• Emergency messages were **transmitted** over all the city's radio stations.
• Before the microscope was invented, no one knew that a person could **transmit** a disease to someone else through "invisible" germs.

_a_ *Transmit* means

a. to pass along.   b. to check.   c. to lose.

9 valid
(văl′ĭd)
-adjective

• The research study was not **valid** because much of the "evidence" had been made up by the researcher.
• "Your accusation that I'm not responsible isn't **valid**," Mona told her father. "I've done all my homework already and even cleaned the living room."

_b_ *Valid* means

a. obvious.   b. well-supported.   c. wrong.

10 vigorous
(vĭg′ər-əs)
-adjective

• My eighty-year-old grandmother is still **vigorous** enough to walk five miles every day.
• The best instructors have **vigorous** teaching styles, lively enough to make any lesson interesting.

_c_ *Vigorous* means

a. strict.   b. quiet.   c. energetic.

Matching Words with Definitions

Following are definitions of the ten words. Clearly write or print each word next to its definition. The sentences above and on the previous page will help you decide on the meaning of each word.

1. _____seclusion_____ The condition of being apart or far from others

2. _____susceptible_____ Likely to be affected with or influenced; likely to be infected

3. _____deceptive_____ Misleading; intended or intending to deceive

4. _____defy_____ To boldly oppose; openly resist; stand up

5. _____confirm_____ To support; show the truth of

6. _____valid_____ Firmly based on facts or logic; logical; based on good reasons

7. _____vigorous_____ Lively; energetic

8. _____submit_____ To give in to another's authority or will; yield

9. _____transmit_____ To communicate; pass or spread (information, an illness, etc.)

10. _____restrain_____ To hold back from action

CAUTION: Do not go any further until you are sure the above answers are correct. Then you can use the definitions to help you in the following practices. Your goal is eventually to know the words well enough so that you don't need to check the definitions at all.

➤ *Sentence Check 1*

Using the answer line provided, complete each item below with the correct word from the box. Use each word once.

a. **confirm**	b. **deceptive**	c. **defy**	d. **restrain**	e. **seclusion**
f. **submit**	g. **susceptible**	h. **transmit**	i. **valid**	j. **vigorous**

_____*vigorous*_____ 1. I gave the bottle such a ___ shake that it leaked Russian dressing all over my hands.

_____*valid*_____ 2. The dinosaur theory seemed ___ because all the available evidence supported it.

_____*susceptible*_____ 3. I don't go to the beach because I'm so ___ to sunburn.

_____*confirm*_____ 4. At the party, Nick ___(ed) the rumor that he was engaged when he introduced his date as his fiancée.

_____*submit*_____ 5. In prison, the criminal had to ___ to more rules than he had ever thought possible.

_____*seclusion*_____ 6. The widow stayed in ___ for a period of mourning, not seeing visitors or going to any social events.

_____*restrain*_____ 7. The little boy tried to ___ his big dog from chasing a car, but he could not hold the dog back.

_____*deceptive*_____ 8. "Looks can be ___," Ray's big brother warned. "Wendy may have a cute, childish face, but she's far from sweet."

_____*transmit*_____ 9. Since her parents' phone was out of order, Tia decided to ___ the news about the baby's birth by telegram.

_____*defy*_____ 10. The daring thief liked to openly ___ the police by leaving this note at the scene of the crime: "Love and kisses from 'The Uncatchable One.'"

NOTE: Now check your answers to these questions by turning to page 177. Going over the answers carefully will help you prepare for the next two practices, for which answers are not given.

➤ *Sentence Check 2*

Using the answer lines provided, complete each item below with **two** words from the box. Use each word once.

_____*vigorous*_____
_____*restrain*_____ 1–2. The police made a ___ effort to ___ the angry mob from pushing through the gates. However, the mob prevailed° and pushed the gates open wide.

_____*submit*_____
_____*defy*_____ 3–4. Children who must ___ to overly strict rules often openly ___ their parents when they get older.

_____*susceptible*_____
_____*confirm*_____ 5–6. Buddy is so ___ to ear infections that he is never surprised to hear the doctor ___ his suspicion that he has yet another one.

_____seclusion_____   7–8. The prisoners of war were kept in ___ for three months except for
_____transmit_____   Christmas Day, when they were permitted to see others and to ___
                           messages to their families over a radio.

_____deceptive_____   9–10. The title of the magazine article—"Miracle Weight Loss"—was ___. It
_____valid_____   suggested that there is a magical way to lose weight, but such a claim
                           isn't ___—the facts show otherwise.

➤ *Final Check:* Chicken Pox

Here is a final opportunity for you to strengthen your knowledge of the ten words. First read the following selection carefully. Then fill in each blank with a word from the box at the top of the previous page. (Context clues will help you figure out which word goes in which blank.) Use each word once.

I remember the day my brother Danny dragged himself home from third grade and complained, "Mommy, I don't feel too good." My mother took one look at my usually (1)_____vigorous_____ brother, yelled "Aargh!" and flew up the stairs with him. The other four of us ran after them, demanding to know what deadly disease he had. "Get away!" my mother cried. "It's chicken pox. He has to stay in (2)_____seclusion_____ until all his spots are gone."

Poor Danny had to (3)_____submit_____ to having his spots checked by all the other mothers in the neighborhood. "Spots can be (4)_____deceptive_____," one woman explained. "They might have been measles, but I have to (5)_____confirm_____ your mother's conclusion. These are definitely chicken pox." Another mother brought a photo from a medical book that verified° the diagnosis of chicken pox.

After the women left, my mother said firmly, "None of you is to set foot in Danny's room for at least seven days. I don't want him to (6)_____transmit_____ this disease to you. I don't think I could survive having the other four of you sick all at once."

Then I made an interesting deduction°: if my mother's claim that Danny's spots would last at least a week was (7)_____valid_____, that meant he would get out of school for a week. I was filled with jealousy. Still, I didn't want to openly (8)_____defy_____ my mother, so I didn't go to Danny's room during the daylight hours. However, unable to (9)_____restrain_____ myself, I crawled into bed with him each night, lured° by the promise of a one-week vacation.

Although my mother says I purposely set out to destroy her sanity, the situation wasn't all that drastic°. The four of us didn't get sick simultaneously°. Instead, my sisters got sick two weeks after I did. Today, we are no longer (10)_____susceptible_____ to chicken pox—we all have immunity°. Now, if we want to stay home from school, we'll have to catch something else.

| Scores | Sentence Check 2 _____% | Final Check _____% |

Enter your scores above and in the vocabulary performance chart on the inside back cover of the book.

accelerate	comparable
adverse	competent
advocate	consecutive
audible	conspicuous
coherent	deteriorate

Ten Words in Context

In the space provided, write the letter of the meaning closest to that of each **boldfaced** word. Use the context of the sentences to help you figure out each word's meaning.

1 **accelerate**
(ăk-sĕl′ə-rāt′)
-verb

- The sleds began sliding down the hill slowly and then **accelerated** to flying speed.
- Doug's car **accelerated** rapidly, allowing him to catch up with the slowly moving ice-cream truck.

_b_ *Accelerate* means   a. to go down.   b. to go faster.   c. to hesitate.

2 **adverse**
(ăd-vûrs′)
-adjective

- Mozart created musical masterpieces in spite of his **adverse** circumstances—illness and debt.
- **Adverse** newspaper reviews persuaded many people not to see the violent new movie.

_b_ *Adverse* means   a. unknown.   b. unfavorable.   c. unnecessary.

3 **advocate**
(ăd′və-kĭt)
-noun

- My physician is an **advocate** of using nicotine gum to quit smoking. She says the gum helps one resist cigarettes.
- Our minister is a strong **advocate** of a drug-free America. He often mentions it in his sermons.

_c_ *Advocate* means   a. a critic.   b. an example.   c. a supporter.

4 **audible**
(ô′də-bəl)
-adjective

- Dogs, bats, and other animals can hear high-pitched sounds that are not **audible** to humans.
- The argument next door was barely **audible**. So I put a cup on the wall and put my ear to the cup so I could hear better.

_c_ *Audible* means   a. useful.   b. logical.   c. hearable.

5 **coherent**
(kō-hîr′ənt)
-adjective

- To be sure that your essay has a **coherent** organization, write an outline first.
- The article about the robbery was not **coherent**. The events were not presented in logical order.

_a_ *Coherent* means   a. clear.   b. complicated.   c. long.

6 **comparable**
(kŏm′pər-ə-bəl)
-adjective

- Since the quality of relatively new used cars is often **comparable** to that of to brand-new ones, my parents never buy new cars.
- Because the two jobs were **comparable** in challenge, interest, and salary, Santos had trouble deciding which to take.

_b_ *Comparable* means   a. helpful.   b. close.   c. different.

7 **competent**
(kŏm'pĭ-tənt)
-adjective

- Some secretaries are more **competent** than their bosses. They know more about the business, are better organized, and work much harder.
- To be a **competent** juggler takes a lot of practice.

c *Competent* means   a. honest.   b. friendly.   c. able.

8 **consecutive**
(kən-sĕk'yə-tĭv)
-adjective

- The reporters would work nights for two **consecutive** weeks, and then they'd work days for a month straight.
- First Vera had the flu. That was immediately followed by strep throat, which was followed by pneumonia. These **consecutive** illnesses kept her out of work for two months.

c *Consecutive* means   a. minor.   b. obvious.   c. happening in a row.

9 **conspicuous**
(kən-spĭk'yōo-əs)
-adjective

- Becky's wide-brimmed red hat is so **conspicuous** that it's impossible not to catch sight of her in a crowd.
- The new skyscraper stands fifty stories high, making it the tallest and thus the most **conspicuous** building in the city's skyline.

a *Conspicuous* means   a. noticeable.   b. poor in quality or condition.   c. serious.

10 **deteriorate**
(dĭ-tîr'ē-ə-rāt)
-verb

- Over many years, the abandoned house had **deteriorated** until its walls crumbled and its floorboards rotted.
- Jenny's health continued to **deteriorate** until her classmates started to visit her regularly. Then she began to improve.

c *Deteriorate* means   a. to stay the same.   b. to improve.   c. to decay.

Matching Words with Definitions

Following are definitions of the ten words. Clearly write or print each word next to its definition. The sentences above and on the previous page will help you decide on the meaning of each word.

1. _____audible_____   Able to be heard

2. _____consecutive_____   Following one after another without interruption

3. _____comparable_____   Similar; able to be compared

4. _____adverse_____   Harmful; unfavorable

5. _____accelerate_____   To speed up

6. _____conspicuous_____   Obvious; easily noticed

7. _____coherent_____   Organized in a logical and orderly way

8. _____advocate_____   A supporter; someone who argues for a cause

9. _____deteriorate_____   To become worse; become weaker or damaged

10. _____competent_____   Capable; well qualified

CAUTION: Do not go any further until you are sure the above answers are correct. Then you can use the definitions to help you in the following practices. Your goal is eventually to know the words well enough so that you don't need to check the definitions at all.

➤ *Sentence Check 1*

Using the answer line provided, complete each item below with the correct word from the box. Use each word once.

a. **accelerate**	b. **adverse**	c. **advocate**	d. **audible**	e. **coherent**
f. **comparable**	g. **competent**	h. **consecutive**	i. **conspicuous**	j. **deteriorate**

_____conspicuous_____ 1. Dee doesn't like to be ___, so she sits in the back of the classroom, where few can see her.

_____competent_____ 2. Anyone can become a(n) ___ cook, but few people develop into great chefs.

_____adverse_____ 3. The weather was bad, and two of the astronauts were sick. Because of these ___ conditions, the shuttle flight was canceled.

_____advocate_____ 4. Since I hate pollution, I'm a(n) ___ of passing laws that limit the amount of pollution in the air.

_____accelerate_____ 5. When the comedian sensed his audience was becoming bored, he ___d his pace to more jokes per minute.

_____audible_____ 6. At the movies, Tina put her arm around me and said in a barely ___ whisper, "I love you. Pass the popcorn."

_____deteriorate_____ 7. Our relationship began to ___ after we had a big fight over money.

_____comparable_____ 8. People often bring up their own children in a manner that is ___ to the way they were raised. Thus abused children may become abusing parents.

_____coherent_____ 9. During her high fever, Celia loudly called out broken words and phrases. She seemed unable to speak in full, ___ sentences.

_____consecutive_____ 10. There was no break in the summer's heat. Records were set nationwide for the number of ___ days above ninety degrees.

NOTE: Now check your answers to these questions by turning to page 177. Going over the answers carefully will help you prepare for the next two practices, for which answers are not given.

➤ *Sentence Check 2*

Using the answer lines provided, complete each item below with **two** words from the box. Use each word once.

_____deteriorate_____
_____competent_____
1–2. "Has your marriage started to ___ because of recurring° conflicts?" asked the radio announcer. "If so, you may benefit from the services of Dr. Louis Frank, one of the city's most ___ and perceptive° marriage counselors."

_____consecutive_____
_____audible_____
3–4. Our neighbors have had parties this week on three ___ nights—Friday, Saturday, and Sunday. And they played their stereo so loudly that it was ___ in our bedrooms.

_____adverse_____   5–6. The sun has a(n) ___ effect on the skin. It ___s the aging of the skin,
_____accelerate_____   resulting in more wrinkles at a younger age, and can also cause skin
                            cancer, which can be lethal°.

_____coherent_____   7–8. Since the assembly instructions were not ___, we had to figure out
_____comparable_____   ourselves how to put the bike together. Including such poorly written
                            instructions is ___ to including none at all.

_____advocate_____   9–10. After driving around a neighborhood for twenty minutes before finding
_____conspicuous_____   the address I was looking for, I am an ___ of ___ house numbers—not
                             ones hidden by shrubs.

➤ _Final Check:_ Walking

Here is a final opportunity for you to strengthen your knowledge of the ten words. First read the following selection carefully. Then fill in each blank with a word from the box at the top of the previous page. (Context clues will help you figure out which word goes in which blank.) Use each word once.

I am a strong (1)_____advocate_____ of walking rather than jogging. The two activities

are in no way (2)_____comparable_____. Walking is deceptive°; while it seems very relaxing,

it nevertheless is vigorous° enough exercise to stimulate° the heart and other muscles. Walking can

also be done during all but the most (3)_____adverse_____ conditions, such as icy

sidewalks or a thunderstorm. Walking is also rather easy to learn; most people, in fact, are quite

(4)_____competent_____ at it by their teens (but then they learn to drive, and the ability starts

to (5)_____deteriorate_____). Walking is so harmless that one can walk on as many

(6)_____consecutive_____ days as one wishes. However, jogging jolts the body so much that

one cannot do it even two days in a row without inflicting° damage on one's internal organs. In

addition, the heavy impact° of joggers' steps makes their fronts and rears shake in such a

(7)_____conspicuous_____ manner that passersby can't help staring. Walkers, on the other

hand, keep their pride. Unlike a runner, a walker needs to (8)_____accelerate_____ only if a

growling dog appears nearby. Also, walkers can hold a conversation that is

(9)_____coherent_____ enough to make sense. In contrast, the jogger's brain is too shaken

to produce orderly sentences, and the voice is reduced to a barely (10)_____audible_____

gasp. Certainly, walking is in every way superior to jogging. In walking, you just pass by. In

jogging, you also pass out.

Scores	Sentence Check 2 _____%	Final Check _____%	

Enter your scores above and in the vocabulary performance chart on the inside back cover of the book.

UNIT FIVE: *Review*

The box at the right lists twenty-five words from Unit Five. Using the clues at the bottom of the page, fill in these words to complete the puzzle that follows.

Word box:

adverse
audible
coherent
competent
confirm
data
deduction
defy
deteriorate
discriminate
disperse
dominant
finite
inflict
initiate
innate
lament
lure
obstinate
profound
severity
submit
subside
trivial
vigorous

ACROSS

1. To support; show the truth of
5. Having or using the most control or influence
7. To begin something; start
8. Information gathered for a study or decision
9. To attract by tempting
10. Organized in a logical, orderly way
11. To break up and spread out
12. To give or cause (pain or hardship)
15. To see differences; distinguish
17. Deeply felt
20. To give in to another's power or authority; yield
21. The condition or quality of being severe; harshness; intensity; seriousness
22. Unimportant; not significant

DOWN

2. Stubborn
3. Possessed at birth; inborn
4. To express sorrow or mourn for
5. A conclusion reached through reasoning
6. Harmful; unfavorable
11. To become worse; become weaker or damaged
13. Capable; well qualified
14. Lively; energetic
15. To boldly oppose; openly resist; stand up
16. To become less active; calm down; decrease
18. Able to be heard
19. Having limits; limited

UNIT FIVE: Test 1

PART A
Choose the word that best completes each item and write it in the space provided.

susceptible   1. Bernard is ___ to headaches. Whenever he has to study, his head starts to pound.

     a. perceptive   b. susceptible   c. profound   d. infinite

lure   2. My sister made the mistake of letting a high salary ___ her to a job that bores her.

     a. defy   b. confirm   c. lure   d. disperse

site   3. A huge mall now stands on the ___ where the racetrack had burned down.

     a. site   b. vocation   c. sequence   d. seclusion

inflict   4. As his attacker was about to ___ serious injury, Robert broke free and ran away.

     a. disperse   b. inflict   c. subside   d. restrain

data   5. After doing a great deal of research, Sharon feels she now has enough ___ to begin writing her report on eating disorders.

     a. data   b. severity   c. nostalgia   d. mania

parallel   6. I have trouble parking ___ to the curb. My car is always farther out in back than in front.

     a. audible   b. comparable   c. valid   d. parallel

infinite   7. To devote herself so fully to the poor, Mother Teresa must have a(n) ___ amount of love for them.

     a. morbid   b. susceptible   c. adverse   d. infinite

competent   8. Instead of choosing a ___ typist, my boss hired someone who types with one finger and usually hits the wrong key.

     a. competent   b. theoretical   c. deceptive   d. conspicuous

treacherous   9. Several ___ characters in the soap opera thought nothing of cheating people they supposedly loved.

     a. vigorous   b. treacherous   c. perceptive   d. competent

comparable   10. My English instructor has such high standards that a B from her is ___ to an A from most other teachers.

     a. susceptible   b. adverse   c. comparable   d. finite

(Continues on next page)

_____discriminate_____ 11. Doug bought orange socks instead of red because the store was poorly lit, and he couldn't ___ between the two colors.

      a. deteriorate   b. initiate   c. dispense   d. discriminate

_____sophisticated_____ 12. Because of her world travels, Jessie is more ___ than her cousin Leona, who has never left their small hometown.

      a. sophisticated   b. inept   c. dismal   d. susceptible

_____lament_____ 13. Most of us ___ the end of our first romance. I cried off and on for three whole weeks the first time I ended a relationship.

      a. accelerate   b. lament   c. subside   d. distort

PART B
Write **C** if the italicized word is used **correctly**. Write **I** if the word is used **incorrectly**.

_C_ 14. The boy let go of his balloon, and it quickly *ascended* to the ceiling of the shopping center.

_I_ 15. I felt much worse when my muscle cramp *subsided*.

_C_ 16. My brother had to *restrain* himself to keep from eating the entire cheesecake.

_I_ 17. When the nuclear power plant exploded, its dangers became *theoretical*.

_C_ 18. Gary wore a *conspicuous* red jacket so his blind date could spot him easily.

_C_ 19. The prisoner was put in *seclusion* after causing several fights with other inmates.

_I_ 20. Angela's pregnancy made her so *vigorous* that all she wanted to do was sleep.

_C_ 21. I didn't realize the *severity* of Bill's injuries until I heard he was still in the hospital three months after his accident.

_I_ 22. My apartment is *dismal*. Large windows allow the sun to shine in on the cheerful yellow and white furnishings.

_I_ 23. Paco is *inept* at checkers. He can win most games blindfolded.

_C_ 24. Dad was going to tell the waiter the soup should be hotter but then decided the complaint was too *trivial*.

_I_ 25. When asked to pay for the window he had broken, Larry was *obstinate*. He said "Gladly," and paid for it immediately.

Score   (Number correct) _____ x 4 = _____%

Enter your score above and in the vocabulary performance chart on the inside back cover of the book.

UNIT FIVE: Test 2

PART A
Complete each item with a word from the box. Use each word once.

a. **audible**	b. **deceptive**	c. **deduction**	d. **deteriorate**	e. **dimensions**
f. **dispense**	g. **disperse**	h. **intervene**	i. **mania**	j. **nostalgia**
k. **perceptive**	l. **transmit**	m. **vocation**		

disperse   1. As the sprinkle turned into a downpour, the crowd at the baseball game began to ___.

dispense   2. Certain servers at the school cafeteria ___ larger portions than others.

transmit   3. While Melba was pregnant, one of her students ___(e)d German measles to her.

intervene   4. I rarely ___ in fights between my children. I believe they should work things out for themselves.

vocation   5. On Career Day, professionals came to the high school to tell students about their ___s.

audible   6. No one responded when the speaker asked, "Can you hear me?" because his words were too soft to be ___.

deteriorate   7. I was shocked to see how my old high school has ___(e)d since I moved away. It's in great need of repairs.

deceptive   8. The picture in the magazine ad is ___. It makes the doll look much larger than it really is.

perceptive   9. My counselor is very ___. The other day she knew something was bothering me even though I said, "I'm fine."

nostalgia   10. Looking over his high-school yearbook and remembering all the fun he had made Al feel great ___ for his school days.

dimensions   11. Since I didn't know the exact ___ of my bedroom windows, I had to guess which size curtains to buy.

deduction   12. The inspector concluded that the thief was a woman. His ___ was based on the scent of lilac perfume inside the house and the imprint of high heels outside a window.

mania   13. Henry Ford had a(n) ___ for using soybeans. He once came to a meeting wearing clothing that, except for his shoes, was made of soybean products.

(Continues on next page)

PART B
Write **C** if the italicized word is used **correctly**. Write **I** if the word is used **incorrectly**.

_I_ 14. Of my parents, my father is the *dominant* one. He does almost anything my mother says.

_C_ 15. Jed ran to *summon* the fire department when he saw smoke coming from his neighbor's window.

_I_ 16. We all thought the senator's speech was quite *coherent*. It was too disorganized to follow.

_C_ 17. Before my TV broke down completely, it *distorted* the picture so that everything was stretched sideways.

_I_ 18. Joyce's baby is more *sedate* than most. When he isn't climbing all over the furniture, he's screaming.

_C_ 19. In January the school will *initiate* a stricter dress code. For the first time, cut-off jeans and short skirts will be forbidden.

_I_ 20. Koko is certainly *morbid*. The only movies she ever wants to see are musicals and light comedies.

_C_ 21. As an *advocate* of public transportation, I try to convince more commuters to use buses and trains.

_C_ 22. Eric usually works every other weekend. But when he filled in for Ann on his weekend off, he ended up working three *consecutive* weekends.

_I_ 23. Since words and music can be combined in *finite* ways, there is no end to the number of songs that can be written.

_I_ 24. The words of the song—"Yummy, yummy, yummy, I've got love in my tummy"—were so *profound* that I couldn't help laughing.

_C_ 25. Post-it notes are based on a simple but *ingenious* idea: paper that sticks but can also be removed.

Score (Number correct) _____ x 4 = _____ %

Enter your score above and in the vocabulary performance chart on the inside back cover of the book.

UNIT FIVE: Test 3

PART A
Complete each sentence in a way that clearly shows you understand the meaning of the **boldfaced** word. Take a minute to plan your answer before you write.

Example: A child might **defy** a parent by _____ *refusing to mow the lawn* _____ .

1. A camper might experience such **adverse** conditions as _____ *(Answers will vary.)* _____

   _____ .

2. One **valid** reason for missing class is _____

   _____ .

3. I usually **accelerate** my car when _____

   _____ .

4. Ramon felt **dismal** because _____

   _____ .

5. There is a **controversy** in our country about _____

   _____ .

6. If it were **literally** "raining cats and dogs," then _____

   _____ .

7. Our instructor **confirmed** the rumor that the final exam was being postponed when she _____

   _____ .

8. Babies have an **innate** ability to _____

   _____ .

9. If you were to **submit** to someone's demand for a loan, you would _____

   _____ .

10. One **trivial** annoyance in my life is _____

    _____ .

(Continues on next page)

PART B

After each **boldfaced** word are a *synonym* (a word that means the same as the boldfaced word), an *antonym* (a word that means the opposite of the boldfaced word), and a word that is neither. On the answer line, write the letter of the word that is the antonym.

Example: __b__ **inept**   a. common   b. skilled   c. clumsy

__c__ 11. **initiate**   a. raise   b. begin   c. end

__b__ 12. **conspicuous**   a. obvious   b. hidden   c. greedy

__c__ 13. **subside**   a. examine   b. lessen   c. increase

__a__ 14. **trivial**   a. important   b. gloomy   c. minor

__a__ 15. **defy**   a. obey   b. challenge   c. mislead

PART C

Use five of the following ten words in sentences. Make it clear that you know the meaning of the word you use. Feel free to use the past tense or plural form of a word.

a. **audible**	b. **controversy**	c. **distort**	d. **inflict**	e. **intervene**
f. **mania**	g. **severity**	h. **sophisticated**	i. **vigorous**	j. **vocation**

16. _____ *(Answers will vary.)* _____

_____

17. _____

_____

18. _____

_____

19. _____

_____

20. _____

_____

Score   (Number correct) _____ x 5 = _____%

Enter your score above and in the vocabulary performance chart on the inside back cover of the book.

A. Limited Answer Key

Important Note: Be sure to use this answer key as a learning tool only. You should not turn to this key until you have considered carefully the sentence in which a given word appears.

Used properly, the key will help you to learn words and to prepare for the activities and tests for which answers are not given. For ease of reference, the title of the "Final Check" passage in each chapter appears in parentheses.

Chapter 1 (Taking Exams)

Sentence Check 1

1. candid
2. anecdote
3. drastic
4. avert
5. concise
6. comply
7. compel
8. alternative
9. acknowledge
10. appropriate

Chapter 2 (Nate the Woodsman)

Sentence Check 1

1. erratic
2. refuge
3. fortify
4. forfeit
5. isolate
6. reminisce
7. illuminate
8. dialog
9. extensive
10. urban

Chapter 3 (Who's on Trial?)

Sentence Check 1

1. impartial
2. undermine
3. menace
4. morale
5. legitimate
6. naive
7. delete
8. overt
9. lenient
10. integrity

Chapter 4 (Students and Politics)

Sentence Check 1

1. ruthless
2. bland
3. relevant
4. reinforce
5. prospects
6. antidote
7. agenda
8. radical
9. apathy
10. propaganda

Chapter 5 (Night Nurse)

Sentence Check 1

1. gruesome
2. erode
3. imply
4. novice
5. idealistic
6. hypocrite
7. endorse
8. impact
9. obstacle
10. illusion

Chapter 6 (Theo's Perfect Car)

Sentence Check 1

1. rebuilt
2. visible
3. supermarkets
4. prejudge
5. restful
6. unicorn
7. extract
8. autobiography
9. multipurpose
10. unlucky

Chapter 7 (Relating to Parents)

Sentence Check 1

1. scapegoat
2. sustain
3. denounce
4. concede
5. deter
6. superficial
7. disclose
8. transition
9. contrary
10. conservative

Chapter 8 (Job Choices)

Sentence Check 1

1. derive
2. verify
3. moderate
4. tentative
5. surpass
6. supplement
7. inhibit
8. conceive
9. diversity
10. compensate

Chapter 9 (No Joking)

Sentence Check 1

1. refrain
2. optimist
3. alter
4. prolong
5. ample
6. remorse
7. blunt
8. chronological
9. chronic
10. pretense

Chapter 10 (Museum Pet)

Sentence Check 1

1. phobia
2. anonymous
3. acute
4. arrogant
5. recipient
6. bestow
7. prudent
8. apprehensive
9. donor
10. prominent

Chapter 11 (Unacceptable Boyfriends)

Sentence Check 1

1. assess
2. affluent
3. alienate
4. contempt
5. compile
6. doctrine
7. adhere
8. defect
9. dogmatic
10. absurd

Chapter 12 (Coping with Snow)

Sentence Check 1

1. spectacular
2. phonetics
3. interrupt
4. enclosing
5. autobiography
6. antisocial
7. binoculars
8. cordless
9. Postnatal
10. submerge

Chapter 13 (Our Headstrong Baby)

Sentence Check 1

1. prevail
2. propel
3. retrieve
4. exempt
5. accessible
6. awe
7. compatible
8. cite
9. rational
10. retort

Chapter 14 (Mr. Perfect?)

Sentence Check 1

1. miserly
2. liable
3. fictitious
4. dubious
5. encounter
6. ecstatic
7. pessimist
8. fallacy
9. gullible
10. evolve

Chapter 15 (A Narrow Escape)

Sentence Check 1

1. fluent
2. harass
3. obsession
4. evasive
5. elapse
6. lethal
7. ordeal
8. futile
9. persistent
10. infer

Chapter 16 (The Power of Advertising)

Sentence Check 1

1. devise
2. universal
3. savor
4. subtle
5. vivid
6. stimulate
7. convey
8. delusion
9. unique
10. versatile

Chapter 17 (Waiter)

Sentence Check 1

1. inevitable
2. option
3. equate
4. passive
5. patron
6. malicious
7. impose
8. indignant
9. defer
10. endeavor

Chapter 18 (Black Widow Spiders)

Sentence Check 1

1. predicted
2. pedals
3. tripod
4. transplant
5. partnership
6. conform
7. disagree
8. microfilm
9. Scriptures
10. televised

Chapter 19 (Adjusting to a New Culture)

Sentence Check 1

1. dismay
2. recede
3. refute
4. gesture
5. retain
6. revert
7. adapt
8. exile
9. reciprocate
10. ritual

Chapter 20 (A Dream About Wealth)

Sentence Check 1

1. mediocre
2. indulgent
3. emerge
4. notable
5. liberal
6. elaborate
7. indifferent
8. frugal
9. impulsive
10. exotic

Chapter 21 (Children and Drugs)

Sentence Check 1

1. coerce
2. sadistic
3. impair
4. essence
5. immunity
6. affirm
7. alleged
8. elite
9. query
10. allude

Chapter 22 (Party House)

Sentence Check 1

1. ridicule
2. stereotype
3. plausible
4. shrewd
5. recur
6. tactic
7. skeptical
8. reprimand
9. provoke
10. revoke

Chapter 23 (Procrastinator)

Sentence Check 1

1. transaction
2. diminish
3. procrastinate
4. consequence
5. simultaneous
6. strategy
7. destiny
8. vital
9. detain
10. tedious

Chapter 24 (King of Cats)

Sentence Check 1

1. malnutrition
2. centimeters
3. Criminology
4. monorail
5. memorize
6. manufactured
7. inactivity
8. laughable
9. thermal
10. imported

Chapter 25 (A Change in View)

Sentence Check 1

1. discriminate
2. profound
3. subside
4. summon
5. vocation
6. dismal
7. dispense
8. severity
9. theoretical
10. site

Chapter 26 (Balloon Flight)

Sentence Check 1

1. initiate
2. finite
3. inflict
4. nostalgia
5. lure
6. mania
7. ascend
8. infinite
9. ingenious
10. literally

Chapter 27 (Family Differences)

Sentence Check 1

1. data
2. inept
3. morbid
4. sedate
5. parallel
6. perceptive
7. intervene
8. obstinate
9. lament
10. innate

Chapter 28 (Murder Mystery)

Sentence Check 1

1. disperse
2. deduction
3. controversy
4. dominant
5. distort
6. trivial
7. dimensions
8. treacherous
9. sophisticated
10. sequence

Chapter 29 (Chicken Pox)

Sentence Check 1

1. vigorous
2. valid
3. susceptible
4. confirm
5. submit
6. seclusion
7. restrain
8. deceptive
9. transmit
10. defy

Chapter 30 (Walking)

Sentence Check 1

1. conspicuous
2. competent
3. adverse
4. advocate
5. accelerate
6. audible
7. deteriorate
8. comparable
9. coherent
10. consecutive

B. Dictionary Use

It isn't always possible to figure out the meaning of a word from its context, and that's where a dictionary comes in. Following is some basic information to help you use a dictionary.

HOW TO FIND A WORD

A dictionary contains so many words that it can take a while to find the one you're looking for. But if you know how to use guide words, you can find a word rather quickly. *Guide words* are the two words at the top of each dictionary page. The first guide word tells what the first word is on the page. The second guide word tells what the last word is on that page. The other words on a page fall alphabetically between the two guide words. So when you look up a word, find the two guide words that alphabetically surround the word you're looking for.

- Which of the following pair of guide words would be on a page with the word *skirmish*?

  (**skimp / skyscraper**)   **skyward / slave**   **sixty / skimming**

The answer to this question and the questions that follow are given on the next page.

HOW TO USE A DICTIONARY LISTING

A dictionary listing includes many pieces of information. For example, here is a typical listing. Note that it includes much more than just a definition.

> **driz•zle** (drĭz′əl), *v.*, **-zled, -zling,** *n.* — *v.* To rain gently and steadily in fine drops.
> — *n.* A very light rain. —**driz′zly,** *adj.*

Key parts of a dictionary entry are listed and explained below.

Syllables. Dots separate dictionary entry words into syllables. Note that *drizzle* has one dot, which breaks the word into two syllables.

- To practice seeing the syllable breakdown in a dictionary entry, write the number of syllables in each word below.

  gla•mour ___2___   **mic•ro•wave** ___3___   **in•de•scrib•a•ble** ___5___

Pronunciation guide. The information within parentheses after the entry word shows how to pronounce the entry word. This pronunciation guide includes two types of symbols: pronunciation symbols and accent marks.

Pronunciation symbols represent the consonant and vowel sounds in a word. The consonant sounds are probably very familiar to you, but you may find it helpful to review some of the sounds of the vowels—*a, e, i, o,* and *u.* Every dictionary has a key explaining the sounds of its pronunciation symbols, including the long and short sounds of vowels.

  Long vowels have the sound of their own names. For example, the *a* in *pay* and the *o* in *no* both have long vowel sounds. Long vowel sounds are shown by a straight line above the vowel.

  In many dictionaries, the *short vowels* are shown by a curved line above the vowel. Thus the *i* in the first syllable of *drizzle* is a short *i.* The pronunciation chart on the inside front cover of this book indicates that the short *i* has the sound of *i* in *sit.* It also indicates that the short *a* has the sound of *a* in *hat,* that the short *e* has the sound of *e* in *ten,* and so on.

- Which of the words below have a short vowel sound? Which has a long vowel sound?

  drug __*short*__   **night** __*long*__   **sand** __*short*__

Another pronunciation symbol is the *schwa* (ə), which looks like an upside-down *e*. It stands for certain rapidly spoken, unaccented vowel sounds, such as the *a* in *above*, the *e* in *item*, the *i* in *easily*, the *o* in *gallop*, and the *u* in *circus*. More generally, it has an "uh" sound, like the "uh" a speaker makes when hesitating. Here are three words that include the schwa sound:

in·fant (ĭn′fənt)   **bum·ble** (bŭm′bəl)   **de·liv·er** (dĭ-lĭv′ər)

- Which syllable in *drizzle* contains the schwa sound, the first or the second? _____ *second* _____

Accent marks are small black marks that tell you which syllable to emphasize, or stress, as you say a word. An accent mark follows *driz* in the pronunciation guide for *drizzle,* which tells you to stress the first syllable of *drizzle.* Syllables with no accent mark are not stressed. Some syllables are in between, and they are marked with a lighter accent mark.

- Which syllable has the stronger accent in *sentimental*? _____ *third* _____

sen·ti·men·tal (sĕn′tə-mĕn′tl)

Parts of speech. After the pronunciation key and before each set of definitions, the entry word's parts of speech are given. The parts of speech are abbreviated as follows:

noun—*n.*   pronoun—*pron.*   adjective—*adj.*   adverb—*adv.*   verb—*v.*

- The listing for *drizzle* shows that it can be two parts of speech. Write them below:

_____ *noun* _____   _____ *verb* _____

Definitions. Words often have more than one meaning. When they do, each meaning is usually numbered in the dictionary. You can tell which definition of a word fits a given sentence by the meaning of the sentence. For example, the word *charge* has several definitions, including these two: **1.** To ask as a price. **2.** To accuse or blame.

- Show with a check which definition (1 or 2) applies in each sentence below:

  The store charged me less for the blouse because it was missing a button.   1 ✓   2 ___

  My neighbor has been charged with shoplifting.   1 ___   2 ✓

Other information. After the definitions in a listing in a hardbound dictionary, you may get information about the *origin* of a word. Such information about origins, also known as *etymology,* is usually given in brackets. And you may sometimes be given one or more synonyms or antonyms for the entry word. *Synonyms* are words that are similar in meaning to the entry word; *antonyms* are words that are opposite in meaning.

WHICH DICTIONARIES TO OWN

You will find it useful to own two recent dictionaries: a small paperback dictionary to carry to class and a hardbound dictionary, which contains more information than a small paperback version. Among the good dictionaries strongly recommended are both the paperback and the hardcover editions of the following:

The American Heritage Dictionary
The Random House College Dictionary
Webster's New World Dictionary

ANSWERS TO THE DICTIONARY QUESTIONS
Guide words: *skimp/skyscraper*   Accent: stronger accent on third syllable *(men)*
Number of syllables: 2, 3, 5   Parts of speech: noun and verb
Vowels: *drug, sand* (short); *night* (long)   Definitions: 1; 2
Schwa: second syllable of *drizzle*

C. List of Words and Word Parts